# BETRAYED

AMERICA DIDN'T VOTE FOR THIS

## A DAMAGE ASSESSMENT

COMMON SENSE COALITION

[illegible] SHAPIRO AND ANNE KIM, EDITORS

**Published by Common Sense Coalition.**
**www.CommonSenseCoalition.net**

ISBN: 979-8-9960442-2-1 (paperback)
ISBN: 979-8-9960442-3-8 (ebook)

Cover and book design by Amy Swan.

This book was set in Adobe Caslon.

# DEDICATION

**Eugene Bardach**, one of our contributors,
died on April 24 after a short illness.
Gene was emeritus professor at the
Goldman School of Public Policy
at the University of California, Berkeley.
A brilliant scholar and a wonderful teacher,
Gene brought his characteristic wisdom,
passion, principles, and humor to our work.

***He will be deeply missed.***

# TABLE OF CONTENTS

# EDITORS & CONTRIBUTORS

## COMMON SENSE COALITION

**The Common Sense Coalition** is a bipartisan and nonpartisan group of experts, former government officials, former military officers, academics, and scholars.

## EDITORS

**Ira Shapiro** is a lawyer, longtime senior Senate staffer, and former U.S. trade official. He served as general counsel in the Office of the United States Trade Representative and then as chief U.S. negotiator with Japan and Canada with the rank of ambassador. He is the author of a trilogy of narrative histories about the Senate, starting with *The Last Great Senate: Courage and Statesmanship in Times of Crisis* (2012), which was nominated for a Pulitzer Prize.

**Anne Kim** is a journalist, lawyer, former senior staffer on Capitol Hill, and veteran of several D.C.-based think tanks. She's the author of *Poverty for Profit: How Corporations Get Rich Off America's Poor* (New Press, 2024) and *Abandoned: America's Lost Youth and the Crisis of Disconnection* (New Press, 2020), winner of the 2020 Goddard Riverside Stephan Russo Book Prize for Social Justice. Her writing has appeared in multiple national publications.

## CONTRIBUTORS

**Nicole Dueffert** is a veteran communications strategist.

**Lindsey M. Marcus** is an attorney based in Chicago, Illinois.

**Judy Rainey** is a former staffer to Senators John Rockefeller, Bob Kerrey, Tom Carper, Frank Lautenberg, Doug Jones, and Jon Ossoff.

**Tejas Shah** is an attorney based in Chicago, Illinois.

## NATIONAL SECURITY

**Steve Abbot** is a retired admiral, former commander of the Sixth Fleet, and former deputy commander of the European Command.

**J. Brian Atwood** is a former administrator of the U.S. Agency for International Development and the undersecretary of state; longtime president of the National Democratic Institute; dean of the Humphrey School of Public Affairs at the University of Minnesota; and senior fellow at Brown University.

**John Emerson** is a former U.S. ambassador to Germany.

**David Kanin** is a retired CIA senior analyst and member of the Senior Intelligence Service.

**Kevin Nealer** is a former State Department officer, staffer for the Senate majority leader, and member of the President's Intelligence Advisory Board.

**Joe Reeder** is a former deputy secretary of the Army and chair of the Panama Canal Commission.

**Peter Romero** is a career diplomat, former assistant secretary of state, and former ambassador to Ecuador.

**John Roos** is a former ambassador to Japan.

**David Weiss** is the former CEO of Global Communities, a leading international relief organization; former assistant U.S. trade representative; and former Foreign Service officer.

## GOVERNMENT, CIVIL LIBERTIES, AND THE RULE OF LAW

**Kenneth D. Ackerman** is a former Senate committee counsel, administration official, private attorney, and author of historical biographies.

**Nick Allard** is dean at Jacksonville University College of Law, former dean at Brooklyn Law School, and former senior staffer for Senators Ted Kennedy and Pat Moynihan as well as Al Gore's presidential campaign.

**Alan Bennett** is a retired partner at Ropes and Gray, former Senate committee counsel, pharmaceutical lawyer, and longtime gun control advocate.

**Peter Connolly** is a former Senate staffer and retired communications lawyer.

**Margaret Crenshaw** is a former Senate staff director and longtime senior executive at the U.S. Postal Service.

**Kenneth Feinberg** was special master of the U.S. government's September 11th Victim Compensation Fund and other major mass torts, and chief of staff to Senator Ted Kennedy.

**Bruce Freed** is president of the Center for Political Accountability, former House and Senate staffer, and reporter at *The Wall Street Journal.*

**Jeff Kehne** is a former lawyer at the Department of Justice's Office of Legal Counsel.

**Mamie Kresses** is a former senior attorney at the Federal Trade Commission.

**Jeffrey Lang** is a former deputy U.S. trade representative with the rank of ambassador and a former chief international trade counsel to the Senate Finance Committee.

**Mike Pettit** is a former administrative assistant and chief of staff to Senator Bob Dole.

**Mark L. Shaffer** is a former senior attorney in the Department of Justice and the House of Representatives and a former adjunct professor for trial advocacy at George Washington University.

**David O. Stewart** is a retired lawyer and a historian and author of both nonfiction and fiction, with particular focus on the period of the American Revolution.

**Tom Susman** is a former Senate Judiciary Committee general counsel and longtime Washington lawyer and lobbyist.

**Bruce Wolpe** is an author and former staffer for Representative Henry Waxman and Australian Prime Minister Julia Gillard.

## ECONOMY

**Josh Gotbaum** is a former partner at Lazard, former assistant secretary of treasury and defense, and comptroller in the Office of Management and Budget. He has served on White House economic staffs and in other federal positions and is now a corporate director and consultant.

**Kent Hughes** is a longtime House and Senate staffer, president of the private-sector Council on Competitiveness, former associate deputy secretary of commerce, and scholar at the Woodrow Wilson Center.

**Michael Mitchell** is a former Senate Oversight Committee staffer and vice president of Lockheed Martin.

**Rob Romasco** is a former senior vice president of American Century Investments, former executive vice president of Cigna, former CEO of JCPenney Insurance, and former president and chief national volunteer spokesperson for AARP.

**Paula Stern** is a former chair of the U.S. International Trade Commission, chair of the Advisory Committee of the U.S. Export-Import Bank, cochair of the International Competition Policy Advisory Committee for the attorney general, and senior legislative assistant to Senator Gaylord Nelson.

## HEALTH, SCIENCE, AND EDUCATION

**Larry Atkins** is a former counsel to the Senate Aging Committee and a leading expert on public and private health insurance, long-term care, and other health issues.

**Eugene Bardach** was professor emeritus in public policy at the University of California, Berkeley.

**Richard J. Boxer** is a clinical professor at the UCLA David Geffen School of Medicine and was twice a presidential appointee to the National Cancer Advisory Board.

**William Kirwan** is a former president of the University of Maryland College Park and Ohio State University, and former chancellor of the University System of Maryland.

**Alan Leshner** is a former director of the National Institute on Drug Abuse and the National Institute of Mental Health, and former CEO of the American Association for the Advancement of Science.

**Andy Schneider** is a former health counsel to the House Energy and Commerce Committee, and Research Professor of the Practice at the Center for Children and Families at Georgetown University.

**Susan Shaffer** is a cofounder, chair, and former president of the Mid-Atlantic Equity Consortium, and cofounder and chair of the National Association of Family, School, and Community Engagement.

**Nancy Shapiro** is a former associate vice chancellor of the University System of Maryland and senior adviser to the Civic Learning and Democracy Engagement Coalition.

**Patrick H. Windham** is a lecturer at Stanford University and former senior professional staff member of the Senate Committee on Commerce, Science and Transportation.

**CLIMATE**

**Ken Berlin** is a former head of the environmental practice at Skadden Arps, former president of Al Gore's Climate Reality Project, and cofounder of the Coalition for Green Capital. He is a senior fellow at the Atlantic Council.

**Jennifer Haverkamp** is a former U.S. special representative on climate and environmental issues and former assistant U.S. trade representative for environment and natural resources. She is a professor at the University of Michigan Law School.

**Peter Knight** is a retired founding partner of Generation Investment Management and campaign manager of the 1996 Bill Clinton/Al Gore campaign.

**Jeff Seabright** is a former executive director of the White House Task Force on Climate Change, former executive at Coca-Cola and Unilever, and partner at Starshot Capital.

*The views expressed in this book are solely those of the contributors and do not reflect the views of any organization, institution, or employer with which any individual contributor may be affiliated. Views of contributing signatories to specific topics are theirs alone, and not those of any other person or organization.*

## ACKNOWLEDGMENTS

We also offer gratitude to **Amy Stackhouse** for her eagle-eyed copyediting; **Amy Swan**, for art and graphic design, including the cover design for this book; and **Adam Shapiro**, for marketing and communications.

# INTRODUCTION

As we commemorate America's 250th anniversary, Donald Trump's second presidency represents a fundamental break from those that preceded it. It reflects a sustained effort to expand executive power in ways that strain constitutional limits on checks and balances and concentrate authority in the executive branch to a degree never previously attempted. In his first inaugural address, in 2017, Trump warned of "American carnage."[1] Today, "American carnage" is less a warning than a threat fulfilled.

When he returned to the White House in January 2025, the president vowed to bring a new "golden age" to America, "proud, prosperous, and free." "We will be the envy of every nation," he promised. "The American dream will soon be back and thriving like never before."[2] To date, Trump's "golden age" has fallen far short of those promises. Inflation is untamed, our country is engaged in active military conflict, and many foundational democratic institutions and norms are at risk.

Americans did not vote for this.

The pages that follow assess in some depth the consequences of actions during the first 16 months of this second presidency. Its authors include both bipartisan and nonpartisan experts, former government officials, former military officers, academics, and scholars. Together, we bring centuries of experience to this analysis. And, while care has been taken to ensure that this report is scrupulously fact-based, we are not dispassionate.

This work brought us to a clear conclusion: The course now being pursued by the administration must be stopped. Many Americans, understandably frustrated by a government they viewed as unresponsive, and by their own economic anxieties, no doubt hoped that Trump would deliver the change they sought. The administration, however, has too often substituted retribution for reform, fallen short of the competence its promises required, and produced disorder instead of desperately needed leadership.

So far, the through line of the Trump presidency has been destruction—of the institutions undergirding our democracy, the norms that govern civil discourse and public integrity, and America's standing as a force for global stability and human rights.

★ **America's international stature has been diminished.** Unpredictable actions and provocative rhetoric have disrupted an 80-year period in which America's strength and values were instrumental in contributing to general global peace and rising prosperity. Alliances have been strained, and a major military operation was launched with questionable justification and questionable strategic execution. As the world watched in dismay, the administration dismantled the U.S. Agency for International Development, with grievous humanitarian consequences for millions of the world's poorest people. With a growing number of nations turning to China as a more predictable partner, "America First" risks becoming "America Alone."

★ **Our economy is under pressure.** The global economy has been disrupted by unprecedented tariff policies, strained trade relationships, threats to the independence of the Federal Reserve, and conflict with Iran. The U.S. labor market is showing signs of weakness, and Americans increasingly report difficulty affording basic necessities. Stock market record highs mean little to the majority of Americans who have no investments. Key pledges to voters who contributed to the president's electoral success—bringing down the cost of living and avoiding costly foreign conflicts—have been brushed aside. For many of his core supporters, the American dream Trump promised is receding.

★ **Core civil liberties are threatened.** The administration's battle against "wokeness" has manifested in actions that stifle dissent and free expression, including enforcement actions against peaceful protesters, legally groundless investigations against political foes, and lawsuits against journalists and companies most legal experts view as frivolous. Too often the administration's rhetoric has been harsh and divisive, thereby needlessly heightening the threat of political violence.

★ **The administration's actions are eroding public confidence in the fairness, impartiality, and competence of government.** Serious concerns about corruption and self-dealing have gone unaddressed under a Department of Justice focused more on carrying out administration political priorities. Civil servants have been dismissed in massive waves; sometimes they've been replaced by political loyalists, but often positions have been just left vacant. Serious factual inaccuracies in official government communications are further undermining public trust.

★ **The nation's future prosperity is at risk.** Policies implemented during these first 16 months have jeopardized Americans' long-term health and economic well-being. Administration actions have undermined America's position as the global leader in scientific research and development, thereby hobbling future innovation and ceding our competitive advantage to rival nations. Key medical research has been curtailed, and health care made less affordable and less accessible for many Americans. Investments that could improve our climate outlook, public health, and economic security have been abandoned, while China has seized the opportunity to leap ahead in the global clean energy transition.

Deep concern about this presidency brought the authors of this report together six months ago, prior to the violent ICE enforcement events in Minneapolis and commencement of military operations against Iran. Congress and the American people must ensure this administration adheres to the rule of law. For the sake of the citizens who elected them, senators and representatives must prioritize their constitutional responsibilities above partisan interests and restore Congress as a coequal branch of government. They need to consider the fundamental questions of how this administration can be held accountable.

President Trump won the 2024 election fairly. But that electoral mandate hardly extends to the systematic weakening of foundational institutions, the upending of long-standing alliances, and the destabilization of world commerce through ill-planned military action—much less the deepening of inequality while many in the administration and their families financially benefit. The American electorate did not vote to support the policies and conduct described in this report.

Decades of experience often inclines one to seek compromise and common ground, with confidence that our nation, having weathered serious difficulties before, will do so again. This report seeks to provide factual analysis in a measured manner. But current circumstances are such that niceties sometimes must give way to direct, unvarnished language. This was true when our country confronted the American Revolution, the Civil War, and World War II. Future generations will determine the ultimate fate of the American project. Our purpose here is to report facts we believe require the attention of all voting Americans, now, in order that we, collectively, can help restore and preserve what we each inherited from our Founding Fathers.

# 1

# A RELENTLESS ASSAULT ON THE RULE OF LAW

**Over the past year, the Trump administration has repeatedly violated limits on presidential power and trampled on the protections afforded all people within America's borders. The administration has usurped the powers of Congress, violated judicial orders, and threatened the integrity of the courts. It has hijacked the machinery of government to wage a campaign of retribution against political enemies. Ordinary citizens should take no comfort in having been untouched so far. The rule of law is our nation's safeguard against tyranny. Its erosion jeopardizes every American's freedom and notions of justice.**

★ ★ ★

The American revolutionary Thomas Paine wrote in his pamphlet *Common Sense* "that so far as we approve of monarchy" in America, "the law is king."

President Donald Trump would prefer the inverse—a political order where "the king is law." A single, persistent theme pervades the chaos and institutional demolition characterizing Trump's second term: his contempt for the rule of law.

Trump's claims to limitless executive power are unprecedented—whether on the imposition of massive tariffs, the deployment of federal troops over state governors' objections, or the deportation of immigrants without due process. Even before an extraordinarily friendly Supreme Court, these claims have been too extreme to prevail. For Trump, however, the legal merits are irrelevant. In his view, rulings that limit his power are self-evidently wrong, and the judges who issue them deserve excoriation and impeachment.

Undermining the rule of law does not necessarily require illegality. Indeed, a president who rejects core democratic values can degrade the rule of law without violating a single statute. It's unsavory but not illegal, for example, for a president to pardon supporters who commit crimes on his behalf. No law prohibits a president from directing federal law enforcement officials to target political enemies (though such charges can be susceptible to dismissal for "vindictive prosecution"). Nor is it illegal for a president to level false and inflammatory accusations against judges and legislators to dissuade the exercise of constitutional checks on presidential power.

Nevertheless, abuses like these—a hallmark of the current administration—degrade the health of our democracy, our trust in elected leaders, and our faith in government to act in citizens' best interest.

This chapter does not attempt to provide a comprehensive assessment of the damage done to the rule of law in America since January 2025. That is a project for historians and legal scholars working from a fuller record in the decades ahead. We focus instead on two core aspects of the rule of law that have endured particular abuse under this administration: (1) fidelity to constitutional limits on the scope of presidential power; and (2) the fair and impartial exercise of power within those limits. During his second term, Trump has twisted, bent, and broken legal and normative restraints on his power, and he has weaponized the government to punish opponents, suppress dissent, and achieve his policy agenda.

## USURPING CONGRESS'S CONSTITUTIONAL POWERS

At the heart of our constitutional system are the checks and balances among the three branches of government. The Framers viewed the division of power between the executive and legislative branches as a key feature of this system, and history reveals many examples of how the resulting tension has checked excessive ambition and strengthened our democracy. There is, however, no precedent for the usurpation of congressional power that Trump has attempted.

Article I of the Constitution vests "all legislative power" in the "Congress of the United States." This includes the power to "lay and collect Taxes, Duties, Imposts and Excises," "to regulate Commerce," "to declare War," and "to provide for calling forth the Militia to execute the Laws of the Union, suppress Insurrections and repel Invasions."[1] The Constitution also prohibits the withdrawal of funds from the Treasury "except in Consequence of Appropriations made by Law," thereby bolstering Congress's "power of the purse."

Article II, meanwhile, obligates the president to "take Care that the Laws be faithfully executed."[2] While the president's appointees can issue regulations within the limits set by valid delegations of legislative power (and the president can veto bills), the president cannot legislate by himself. Nor can he violate the "supreme Law of the Land," which includes federal statutes as well as the Constitution and ratified treaties.[3]

This administration's version of "faithful execution," however, encompasses an extraordinary subversion of congressional decisions. Within days of taking office, Trump issued executive orders to upend federal funding and staffing in areas ranging from health care to climate to immigration to foreign policy.[4] The disbursement of billions of dollars in research funding appropriated by Congress was paused, frozen, or rescinded. He also ordered a near-total freeze on foreign aid and the destruction of the U.S. Agency for International Development, established under congressional direction in 1961.[5] Thousands of federal employees were peremptorily fired, without regard to the civil service protections accorded to them by statute.[6]

Trump then continued to trample on congressional authority with his tariffs. In April 2025, he unilaterally levied his "Liberation Day" tariffs on dozens of countries, claiming authority under the International Emergency Economic Powers Act of 1977 that no president had ever asserted.[7] In subsequent months, he invoked the same supposed powers for transparently personal and political purposes. When Brazil refused to withdraw its prosecution of his ally, former President Jair Bolsonaro, Trump levied punitive tariffs of 50 percent.[8] After the Canadian province of Ontario aired ads critical of tariffs during the World Series, Trump raised Canadian tariffs by an additional 10 percent.[9] In February 2026, the Supreme Court ruled that IEEPA does not empower the president to impose tariffs.[10] Trump then immediately announced a fresh round of 10 percent "global tariffs" under the authority of a different statute.[11] These new levies have already drawn legal challenges that are pending as of this writing.[12]

## VIOLATING COURT ORDERS AND ATTACKING JUDGES

The Trump administration has also shown unparalleled disdain for the judiciary's constitutional role in checking executive power—even as appeals courts and the Supreme Court have tended to rule in Trump's favor.[13]

According to one analysis, federal appellate judges appointed by Trump sided with the administration 92 percent of the time in 2025.[14] The Supreme Court also ruled in the administration's favor 21 out of 24 times in 2025 (though 20 of these were interim rulings in cases filed on the Court's so-called emergency docket).[15]

Nevertheless, Trump has been dissatisfied. He has vilified judges who rule against the administration and called for their impeachment. When the Supreme Court struck down his tariffs, Trump attacked the six justices who ruled against him (including two Trump appointees) as "fools and lapdogs" who were "unpatriotic and disloyal" and "a disgrace to our nation."[16] A judge who blocked his deportation plan was labeled "crooked" and "a Radical Left lunatic who "should be IMPEACHED."[17] Other federal judges have been accused of "sedition and treason" for enjoining the implementation of his executive orders.[18]

High-level subordinates have joined the chorus as well. In December 2025, then Attorney General Pam Bondi and Deputy Attorney General Todd Blanche attacked "rogue judges" on social media.[19] Stephen Miller, the White House deputy chief of staff, warned of a left-wing "judicial insurrection."[20] These inflammatory attacks have persisted in the face of extraordinary numbers of threats against judges and their families, and public criticisms of the attacks from Supreme Court Chief Justice John Roberts, retired federal judges, and the New York City Bar Association.[21]

These expressions of contempt for the judiciary by the president and his senior appointees may have helped set the tone for the current administration's unprecedented level of noncompliance with court orders. In at least 35 instances from August 2025 to February 2026, federal judges and magistrates issued "show cause" orders requiring the government to explain why it should not be held in contempt for failing to heed court orders.[22]

The administration has been especially recalcitrant in the face of challenges to its aggressive immigration agenda. In a January 2026 order addressing the Department of Homeland Security's failure to comply with a court order, Chief Judge Patrick Schiltz of the federal district court in Minnesota listed 96 court orders that the Bureau of Immigration and Customs Enforcement had violated.[23] "The Court is not aware of another occasion in the history of the United States in which a federal court has had to threaten contempt—again and again and again—to force the *United States government* to comply with court orders," Schiltz wrote (emphasis in original). (In a supplemental order, issued in late February, Schiltz corrected the initial count to 97 violated orders and identified 113 additional violations of court orders that had occurred in the month that followed compilation of the initial list.)

## UNLAWFULLY COERCING STATES AND INFRINGING ON THEIR AUTHORITY

Donald Trump has, moreover, overstepped constitutional limits on his authority in order to punish and coerce states that oppose his policies.

For example, he has blocked or threatened to withhold federal funds from states that do not comply with his agenda. In January 2026, he froze $10 billion in federal child care funding for five states with Democratic governors, claiming without evidence that the freeze was needed to combat fraud in these programs.[24] He also threatened to withhold wildfire relief funding from California unless the state passed a voter ID law, and he tried to block federal highway funding for New York State unless it abandons congestion pricing in New York City.[25] The Department of Justice has sued the District of Columbia and 30 states because they have refused to provide sensitive voter information protected by state and local law.[26] Following the killing of two anti-ICE protesters in Minneapolis, then Attorney General Bondi requested that Governor Tim Walz provide access to Minnesota's voter rolls to the Department of Justice as a step toward establishing a cooperative relationship with the administration to end the violence.[27]

Most troubling are the administration's deployment of federal troops in states led by Democratic governors, over those governors' objections. This has happened in Oregon, Minnesota, Illinois, and California. (It has also happened in two cities with Democratic leadership, Memphis and New Orleans, where Republican governors have consented, and in the District of Columbia, where Congress has given the president unique power to use federal troops.)

Knowing that the deployment of the military on domestic soil threatens both democracy and civil liberty, Congress passed the Posse Comitatus Act 150 years ago to prohibit the use of federal troops for civilian law enforcement.[28] Trump claimed that his deployments in California, Illinois, and Oregon were authorized under one of the act's few exceptions—an argument rejected by the Supreme Court.[29] In response, Trump has repeatedly threatened to invoke a separate, arguably broader authority—the Insurrection Act of 1807—to suppress protest. He has called it "the strongest power a president has" and claimed "the absolute right to do it," even though the law does not, in fact, give him such unconstrained authority.[30]

## WEAPONIZING THE DEPARTMENT OF JUSTICE

As the nation's chief law enforcement agency, the Department of Justice should be dedicated to fair, independent, and impartial justice. Under the direction of President Trump, however, the department has veered far from its historic mission (still stated on its website) "to uphold the rule of law, to keep our country safe, and to protect civil rights."[31] Instead, it has become an instrument of retribution against Trump's political enemies. Rather than upholding the rule of law, it aggressively undermines it.

During his 2024 presidential campaign, Trump promised to investigate and prosecute political opponents and public officials he believed had wronged him. Once back in office, he insisted that his appointees put a high priority on carrying out this vow. His targets have included former FBI Director James Comey, who oversaw a probe of alleged Russian interference in the 2016 election; New York Attorney General Letitia James, who won a civil judgment against Trump and his family for business fraud; members of the House select committee that investigated the January 6 insurrection, who Trump said should "go to jail"; six lawmakers who taped a video urging members of the armed forces not to follow illegal orders, a message that Trump labeled "SEDITIOUS BEHAVIOR, punishable by DEATH"; and even the chair and a governor of the Federal Reserve.[32]

In each instance, the Justice Department has opened spurious investigations or filed frivolous charges that have failed to withstand serious scrutiny. Trump has also pressured prosecutors in violation of long-standing norms and replaced career prosecutors with inexperienced loyalists. The prosecutions of Comey and James, for instance, were triggered by Trump's repeated, public demands on Bondi, who was told, "We can't delay any longer."[33] After multiple top prosecutors quit or were fired for declining to bring what they regarded as unsupported charges, Trump installed Lindsey Halligan, the president's former personal lawyer with no prosecutorial experience, as the interim U.S. attorney for the Eastern District of Virginia.[34] Her subsequent indictment of James was dismissed by a judge on the grounds that her appointment was unlawful, after which two separate grand juries declined to indict James.[35] Comey's indictment was also dismissed (though as of this writing, he has since been indicted on new, equally dubious charges involving an Instagram post).[36] Likewise, a grand jury refused to indict the members of Congress who appeared in the military orders video, and the Justice Department's efforts to prosecute Federal Reserve Bank Chair Jerome Powell have so far been blocked by judges.[37]

Yet Americans can take, at most, modest comfort from the Justice Department's failures so far in pursuing politically motivated investigations and prosecutions. Targets incur enormous financial and personal costs even when they ultimately prevail. The result is a chilling effect on any officials who might consider opposing Trump. Even more troubling, however, is the reputational damage to the Justice Department itself, as it has become more feared than trusted, and more deserving of contempt than admiration.

## SHIELDING FRIENDS AND ALLIES FROM LEGAL ACCOUNTABILITY

At the same time that Donald Trump has worked to prosecute his political enemies, he has bestowed undeserved clemency on friends and allies convicted or accused of crimes—an appalling violation of the nation's expectations about the impartial administration of justice.

Trump has particularly abused his constitutional power to pardon, which the Framers originally intended as a check on the excesses of the judicial branch. On the day of his second inauguration, Trump granted more than 1,500 pardons and commutations, benefiting nearly everyone accused or convicted of crimes relating to the January 6 insurrection, including the most violent offenders.[38] Other beneficiaries have included the "fake electors" who conspired to overturn the results of the 2020 election, wealthy donors, and individuals convicted of money laundering and facilitating illegal drug transactions involved in the crypto industry (in which Trump and his family are heavily invested).[39]

In the meantime, ordinary citizens hoping for clemency are finding their applications delayed or denied. "If you're just an average citizen, you can't even get in the line," one attorney who represents clemency petitioners told ProPublica. "I told my guy he'd probably be better off if he broke into the Capitol or made a major donation to Trump's inauguration."[40]

Trump has also dropped investigations or chosen not to prosecute friends, allies, and donors accused of illegality. In just the first six months of his presidency, the administration canceled or halted enforcement actions against more than 170 corporations, many of them big donors to Trump's campaign and inauguration, according to the watchdog organization Public Citizen.[41] The Justice Department has also reportedly withdrawn thousands of white-collar criminal prosecutions in favor of cracking down on immigration enforcement and "divisive DEI policies."[42]

There are strong indications that Trump has used his authority over the Justice Department to conceal the extent of his dealings with the late convicted sex trafficker Jeffrey Epstein. The department slow-walked the release of the files for months, until public anger prompted Congress to enact the Epstein Files Transparency Act in December 2025. The department then released a large tranche of documents, more than a month after the statutory deadline. Journalists and congressional investigators are still working to resolve questions concerning improper omissions and redactions. And despite thousands of references to Trump in the files that have been released, including allegations of serious wrongdoing, no federal investigation is ongoing or imminent.[43]

★ ★ ★

*The dangerous effects of this administration's utter disregard for the rule of law will outlive his presidency. His unrestrained actions have deepened the cracks in our democracy and have potentially emboldened others to follow his example. It has taken Trump mere months to shatter norms that have been generations in the making. Their restoration will be a long-term undertaking that could take decades.*

# 2

# A WEAKER AMERICA AND AN UNSTABLE WORLD

**For 80 years, from the end of World War II, American military and economic power, American alliances, and American values provided the foundation for a period of general global stability and rising prosperity. President Donald Trump has shattered that foundation. He has launched costly and impetuous worldwide military adventures with little strategy, foresight, or respect for the rule of law. He has abandoned long-standing alliances and cozied up to authoritarians and dictators. At a time when the United States faces multiple challenges—the wars in Ukraine and Gaza, the rise of China, and the dangers of nuclear proliferation posed by Iran and North Korea—Trump has made the United States and its allies uniquely vulnerable to their enemies.**

★ ★ ★

Presidents of both parties have launched military attacks without seeking authorization from Congress, including Ronald Reagan in Grenada, George H. W. Bush in Panama, Bill Clinton in Kosovo, and Barack Obama in Libya. But while steadily eroded, the War Powers Act, enacted in 1973 as a response to the "imperial presidencies" of Lyndon Johnson and Richard Nixon, remains the law. Prior presidents explained to the American people their reasons for acting, and Presidents George H. W. Bush and George W. Bush sought and received authorization from Congress to wage wars against Iraq in 1991 and 2003. They recognized that this momentous decision should not be made by one person, and they understood the importance of seeking congressional and public support by making the case for military action.

In contrast, Trump has unilaterally plunged our country into multiple conflicts, with little regard for the limits on his authority, and even less apparent regard for the consequences. When asked, shortly after the incursion into Venezuela in January 2026, if there was any check on his power, Trump told the American people, "There is one thing. My own morality. My own mind. It's the only thing that can stop me."[1] Recent polls show that roughly two-thirds of Americans do not share his view.[2]

In February 2026, Trump decided to attack Iran in what appears to be an unlimited military operation. Remarkably, Trump professed surprise about Iran's willingness to spread the war by attacking other countries in the region that host U.S. military facilities and by closing the Strait of Hormuz,[3] although most experienced analysts found Iran's responses to be completely predictable.[4] It will be many months before the results and repercussions of this decision can be assessed reliably. But it is already clear that the decision reflected many of the traits that characterize Trump's foreign policy decision-making: impulsiveness; an obsession with "lethality"; contempt for the rule of law (domestic, international, and constitutional); indifference to the concerns and interests of allies; and an inability to make reasonable decisions based on an informed analysis of possible impacts.

## A STUNNING NATIONAL SECURITY "STRATEGY"

Under federal law, each presidential administration must deliver to Congress a "National Security Strategy," a comprehensive report intended to communicate the executive branch's commitments, objectives, and policies for national security, along with an assessment of potential threats. In December 2025, the Trump administration issued an NSS that Mara Karlin of Brookings called "a full-scale repudiation of America's approach to the international community over the last 80 years or so."[5] According to this document, Russia and China—as well as North Korea and Iran—pose less of a threat to the United States than uncontrolled immigration, narco-terrorism, and the behavior of "U.S. foreign policy elites."[6]

Especially shocking is the NSS's no-holds-barred assault on America's European allies, condemning them for inadequate defense funding and unlimited immigration that was leading to "civilizational" decline. Indeed, the NSS expressed a clear preference for the right-wing nationalistic parties in Europe rather than the more centrist national governments (as evidenced by Vice President J. D. Vance's embarrassing efforts to prop up ousted Hungarian strongman Viktor Orbán).[7]

At the same time, the president's new strategy barely acknowledged the challenges that Russia poses to the United States and its national interests. Since 2022, Russia has launched the largest war that Europe has seen since 1945, conducted hybrid attacks against American allies, violated the New START Treaty, loudly rattled its nuclear saber, and developed exotic new strategic nuclear weapons that can strike America. Yet the administration's NSS called for efforts to "reestablish … strategic stability with Russia," perhaps in keeping with Trump's mystifying affinity for Russia's president, Vladimir Putin, to whom he has gladly subordinated U.S. interests.[8]

But if the administration's NSS has only one virtue, it is honesty. As Caitlin Talmadge, another Brookings scholar, observed, the NSS simply laid bare the "ethno-nationalism, militarism, xenophobia, and transactionalism" that have characterized Trump's dealings with the world.[9]

Unfortunately, we Americans are paying the price. Though Trump may call his strategy "America First," the result is "America Weaker" and, ultimately, "America Alone."

## TRASHING OUR ALLIANCES

During Donald Trump's first term, his "America First" philosophy, his outspoken contempt for our European allies, his scorn for U.S. military leaders, and his distrust of America's intelligence agencies prompted deep concerns in Congress and around the world. Central to Trump's worldview is an inexplicable and abiding admiration of Vladimir Putin; Trump outraged Congress and shocked the world by accepting at face value Putin's assertion that Russia had not interfered in the 2016 election, rather than the contrary conclusion of the U.S. intelligence community.[10]

To our country's lasting disgrace, Trump effectively switched sides in the Ukraine war, for the first time in history aligning U.S. interests with a vicious international aggressor rather than with the lives and territorial integrity of a free people. Trump has treated Moscow and Putin better than the democratic government in Kyiv and Ukraine's president, Volodymyr Zelensky, openly seeking to humiliate Ukraine and its people.[11] He cut off U.S. aid to Ukraine in an effort to force the country to make concessions that Russia could not win on the battlefield. Trump now seems to have lost interest in a war he once promised to end "in a day."[12] It has become the deadliest conflict in Europe since the end of World War II, with thousands of civilian deaths and nearly 2 million military casualties—deaths and injuries—on the two sides.[13]

The central principle of Trump's "America First" foreign policy is that "might makes right." Strength unquestionably matters, but Trump fails to understand how America's network of worldwide alliances enables it to project its strength credibly. Trump shook America's alliances in his first term; returning to office, unconstrained by wise and experienced advisers, he quickly turned on virtually every major U.S. ally.

He shocked Canada, our closest neighbor, strongest ally, and largest single export market, by insisting that it should become America's 51st state.[14] Despite expressing respect for Mexican President Claudia Sheinbaum, Trump mused about sending our military, uninvited, against cartels in Mexico.[15] He threatened Denmark with the annexation of Greenland, and he asserted that America would take back the Panama Canal.[16] Despite Trump's professed bond with India's prime minister, Narendra Modi, his irresponsible rhetoric, unpredictable negotiating style, and punitive tariffs gravely damaged the painstaking diplomatic work of five administrations (including his first) to build a closer relationship with India.[17] After threatening the nations of Latin America by asserting that the hemisphere was our special sphere of influence, Trump acted on that belief by attacking Venezuela to capture its president, Nicolás Maduro.[18]

As Kori Schake, a former senior national security official under George W. Bush, now at the American Enterprise Institute, wrote in *Foreign Affairs* in July 2025:

> *When it comes to burning bridges, nothing matches the speed and destructiveness of Trump's policies in the past few months ... Trump has a deep-seated ideological conviction that allies are a burden ... [His] erratic trade war, which targets rivals and allies alike, has whipsawed markets, spooked investors, and convinced Washington's partners that they can no longer trust the United States.*[19]

Trump fails to recognize that our network of alliances contributed to our position as the world's leading nation and our ability to keep the peace and promote prosperity. He acts as though our allies have no choice but to accept his dictates, ignoring the likely consequences when they no longer see the United States as a trusted, reliable ally, trading partner, or friend.

It became clear early in Trump's second term that our bruised allies would respond to Trump's economic threats by seeking trade agreements with friendly countries, and even accommodation with China. In March 2025, Japan and South Korea, our two most significant allies in the Asia-Pacific region, held a trade summit with

China in which they announced a plan to pursue a new trilateral trade agreement and work for "a predictable trade and investment environment in the region."[20] In January 2026, Canadian Prime Minister Mark Carney led a three-day mission to China, as a centerpiece of his efforts to build Canada's non-U.S. trade by more than 50 percent in the next decade.[21] In the same month, the European Union announced a far-reaching trade agreement with the four Latin American countries of Mercosur (Argentina, Brazil, Uruguay, and Paraguay), seeking new trading partners as an alternative to Trump's tariffs and bullying.[22] At the same time, our allies are now wary of sharing intelligence with the United States as they question whether their sources and methods of collecting sensitive information will be protected.[23]

As Schake soberly predicted:

> *In the years to come, the alliances it took decades to foster will begin to wither, and U.S. rivals will waste no time in leaping to exploit the resulting vacuum . . . Trump and his team are destroying everything that makes the United States an attractive partner because they fail to imagine just how bad an order antagonistic to American interests would be.*[24]

Trump and Vance might claim that their trashing of alliances somehow reflects public weariness of America's entanglement with international affairs. The evidence shows otherwise. In April 2024, the Republican Congress authorized $60 billion in military aid for Ukraine despite the strident opposition of Trump, soon to be the Republican presidential nominee.[25] In October 2025, after 10 months of Trump's attacks on alliances, the Chicago Council on Global Affairs reported on a major survey showing that U.S. public support for alliances was at an all-time high. The survey showed the highest levels of American support yet recorded for U.S. security alliances in Europe (68 percent), Asia (72 percent), and the Middle East (67 percent); the alliances were seen to benefit the United States along with its regional allies. While self-described Democrats were most convinced about the effectiveness of alliances (64 percent), a majority of Republicans agreed (53 percent), along with about half of independents (48 percent).[26]

As the Chicago Council stated, "These data suggest that if alliance relations are undercut by US policy, that shift is not being driven by US public discontent." Rather, we were witnessing Trump and Vance on a disastrous march of folly destructive to America and its interests throughout the world.

## UNDULY FOCUSING ON THE WESTERN HEMISPHERE

The 2025 National Security Strategy and the National Defense Strategy (issued in 2026) seek to "pivot" U.S. policy toward the Western Hemisphere by imposing "American preeminence" in the region.[27] The Monroe Doctrine, proclaimed in 1823, was intended to warn departing European colonial powers not to try to reestablish themselves in the hemisphere. The Trump administration's "might makes right" unilateral actions and the expansive "Trump Corollary" have made the United States the newest colonial power in a region with a historical hatred of colonialism.

Curbing illegal drug importation is the principal stated objective of Trump administration policy in the hemisphere. The administration has undertaken performative naval strikes[28] (Operation Southern Spear) against suspected drug-laden boats headed to the United States, killing dozens,[29] without having produced any credible evidence to support the claim, nor any explanation why the able and experienced U.S. Coast Guard was not used to seize vessels, crews, and contraband. Trump professes to have saved thousands of American lives from imported fentanyl, despite U.S. intelligence having known for decades that fentanyl is neither manufactured in nor shipped from Venezuela.[30] Notwithstanding Trump's avowed "war on cartels," he gave a "full and complete" pardon[31] to former Honduran President Juan Orlando Hernandez, who was convicted by a U.S. federal court of involvement in trafficking more than 400 tons of cocaine during his time in office.[32]

When U.S. Special Forces captured Venezuelan President Maduro to face justice in the United States, Trump declared that he himself would "run" Venezuela and struck a deal with the country's remaining leadership to invite U.S. investment and sell oil together. He did not insist on any transition away from the repression and corruption that has driven Venezuela into poverty and resulted in 8 million Venezuelans fleeing the country.[33]

The Western Hemisphere is certainly our neighborhood, but this administration's unilateral, arbitrary military attacks in the region are decimating our influence to shape events there. The gunboat approach deprives the United States and other democracies in the hemisphere of the ability to collectively address our common challenges in any lasting way: a shrinking middle class, deepening income gaps, climate change, and organized crime—all of which are immigration accelerants. The United States cannot bomb its way to greater security. The administration is pushing neighbors to choose China as a more reliable partner than the United States.

## EVISCERATING OUR SOFT POWER

China's rise as a global power has been fueled in part by its extraordinary worldwide investments, particularly in Latin America and Africa. It has long been clear that the United States will come nowhere near China's level of financial commitment to developing nations. To the extent we have held our own in competing with China, we have done so through what the political scientist Joseph Nye termed our "soft power"—our alliances, of course, but also our leadership in international organizations, our democratic values, the skill of our diplomats, and our commitment to helping developing nations and the poor.

In one year, the Trump administration has shredded every element of our soft power: withdrawing the United States from 66 international organizations;[34] silencing the Voice of America and the Agency for Global Media; reducing our diplomatic corps through layoffs of 1,300 State Department employees;[35] recalling 30 career ambassadors;[36] and allowing Elon Musk and DOGE to end the work of the U.S. Agency for International Development during the first two weeks of the administration.

The destruction of USAID, an agency created by an executive order issued by President John F. Kennedy in 1961 and codified by Congress in 1998, has been reported to have resulted in the death of an estimated 762,000 people due to starvation or disease as of January 2026, more than 500,000 of them children.[37] Bill Gates, whose foundation focuses on global health challenges around the world, decried Musk's actions as indirectly "killing the world's poorest children."[38]

As Brian Atwood and Andrew Natsios, two former USAID administrators, wrote, "The Trump administration has taken many controversial actions, but none may prove more consequential over the long term to the health, safety and prosperity of the American people than the destruction of USAID."[39] The precipitous action took place despite this observation of White House Chief of Staff Susie Wiles: "I think anybody that pays attention to government and has ever paid attention to USAID believed, as I did, that they do very good work."[40]

## POLITICIZING AND MISUSING THE WORLD'S BEST MILITARY

President Trump deployed America's military power forcefully in the first year of his second term, and our service members brilliantly executed the bombing of Iran's nuclear facilities in June 2025 and the capture of Maduro in January 2026. No one doubts the tactical capabilities of our military. What alarms countless defense and intelligence experts is the wholesale politicization of the military—a dangerous and fundamental departure from our 250-year history and tradition of a military subject to civilian control but assiduously removed from politics.

The political science professor Risa Brooks observed that as early as April 2025, the Pentagon's civilian leaders, led by Secretary of Defense Pete Hegseth, were making it clear that "the uniformed military, resolutely non-partisan by tradition, and law, will now be expected to align itself with the administration's partisan priorities and echo its ideological world view."[41] This change was hammered home by the firing of General Charles Q. Brown Jr., the chair of the Joint Chiefs of Staff, who Hegseth asserted had gotten the job only because he was African American, and Chief of Naval Operations Lisa Franchetti, who was fired because of Hegseth's strongly stated views, as an author and Fox News commentator, that women have no place in combat.[42] At the same time, Hegseth fired the top lawyers in the Army, Navy, and Air Force, who were likely to provide independent and apolitical legal advice.[43]

These early actions sent a chilling message that independent judgment and certain types of leaders were unwelcome. Hegseth went on to fire General Timothy D. Haugh, director of the National Security Agency; the acting chair and vice chair of the National Intelligence Council; and the head of the U.S. cyber command. Lieutenant General Jeffrey A. Kruse, a 35-year Air Force intelligence officer who led the Defense Intelligence Agency, was forced from his position after his agency cast doubt on Trump's assertion that the June 2025 U.S. airstrikes had "obliterated" Iran's nuclear program.[44] "These actions, along with reports of pressure on analysts to alter or downplay assessments of foreign threats, reflect a concerted effort to bend intelligence to fit political preferences," noted the National Security Leaders for America.[45]

Hegseth fired or sidelined at least two dozen generals or admirals in his first nine months at the Pentagon. He delayed or canceled the promotions of at least four officers because they had previously worked for General Mark A. Milley, a former chair of the Joint Chiefs of Staff whom President Trump loathes. One was Major General James Patrick Work, who was expected to be the deputy commander of the U.S. Central Command, which oversees troops in the Middle East. One of the Army's most combat-experienced officers, Work played a crucial role in defeating the Islamic State during the first Trump administration. Yet he was viewed skeptically by the administration because he had served as Milley's executive officer.[46]

Other officers fell out of favor after being targeted on social media by right-wing influencers or because they had voiced support years earlier for diversity, equity, and inclusion programs. Rear Admiral Milton Sands, the commander of the Navy SEALs, who pushed to have female instructors in SEALs training, was fired by Secretary Hegseth in August.[47] Still others were ousted for offering candid military assessments. Hegseth soured on Admiral Alvin Holsey, the head of the U.S. Southern Command, after he raised questions about the deadly military strikes on boats in the Caribbean.[48] In April 2026, during the ongoing war with Iran, Hegseth fired Army Chief of Staff Randy George—a decision that Pentagon officials described as "insane."[49]

"Many of Mr. Hegseth's dismissals have left senior military leaders and even Trump administration officials puzzled and speculating about the cause," *The New York Times* reported.[50] Democratic Senator Elissa Slotkin of Michigan, a former CIA officer who analyzed foreign militaries, described Hegseth's moves as a "purge," comparing them to the actions of China and Iraq, who "would do the same thing."[51]

Repeatedly, Trump has blatantly misused the military as a political prop. In a February 2026 visit to Fort Bragg, in North Carolina, one of the world's largest military bases, Trump addressed the troops with praise for the capture of Maduro, but then lashed out at the Democrats for "weakening the country," and attacked Joe Biden as "the worst president in the history of the country." He also charged that years of "political correctness" had undermined America's military readiness, as his soldier audience sat in stone-faced silence.[52]

At the same time Trump and Hegseth have been undermining the nonpartisan nature of our military, they have also removed constraints on the use of the military for domestic law enforcement. Trump has dictated that the National Guard and even regular Army combat troops should be deployed in American cities to carry out his harsh immigration policies, and, where needed, to quell domestic dissent. The president and the defense secretary compounded those changes by relaxing the rules that for generations, dating to the Civil War, had protected civilians from the use of military force.

Hegseth believes that "international law and human rights are a hindrance to U.S. warfighters," as *The Washington Post* described his views.[53] He is unabashed in rejecting traditional American military policies on the protection of civilians, declaring that his goal is "ensuring that the men and women on the frontlines have the opportunity to destroy … the enemy, and that lawyers aren't the ones getting in the way."[54] We have witnessed the results of these policy changes in the eastern Pacific and the Caribbean, where U.S. military strikes on alleged drug traffickers, which experts on the use of military force have condemned as violations of U.S. and international law, have killed a reported 183 people as of April 2026.[55]

Ronald Reagan is often given credit for the axiom that "personnel is policy." Given that commonsense truth, our nation's current insecurity reflects the shameful abdication of the Senate, which confirmed the nominations of Hegseth, former Director of National Intelligence Tulsi Gabbard, FBI Director Kash Patel, and former Director of Homeland Security Kristi Noem with full knowledge that they were placing extreme, unqualified, and incompetent people in the positions most responsible for protecting America.

It is frightening to contemplate this administration's national security team confronting multiple challenges in the world today while cavalierly entering into a contest to resume the testing of nuclear weapons, ending the long period after 1945 in which arms control agreements limited the number of nuclear nations and deterred the use of those devastating weapons. The untold damage the Trump administration has already done is best measured by the urgent responses of the National Security Leaders for America and the Steady State, two organizations of more than 1,700 military, defense, and intelligence veterans who have spoken out in an unprecedented way against a wide range of the president's actions.

★ ★ ★

*America has by far the largest defense budget in the world, spending nearly $1 trillion annually—more than the next nine countries combined.[101] The Pentagon and Congress can debate whether we are building the right weapons in an era of drone warfare. But in turbulent times, every national security issue requires civilian and military leaders who are experienced, capable, and laser focused on our real national interests, rather than slavishly loyal to the dictates of an impulsive, unstable, and highly irrational president.*

# 3

# AN UNAFFORDABLE ECONOMY

**The Trump administration's policies have sabotaged the American economy and jeopardized our nation's future prosperity. His reckless and illegal tariffs have sown chaos around the world. He has shattered long-standing relationships with trusted allies, and decimated American small businesses and farmers. Not only has he failed to solve the nation's affordability crisis, he has also aggravated them with his war on Iran. His "One Big Beautiful Bill Act" (OBBBA) has set the nation on course for crippling deficits and has accelerated the nation's insolvency. He has threatened the independence of the Federal Reserve and undermined global confidence in America's financial stability. He has kneecapped America's capacity for innovation, shunned global talent, and bargained away our competitiveness to benefit himself and his friends. He has betrayed his political base in favor of billionaires and has diminished opportunities for all Americans to succeed.**

★ ★ ★

There is no doubt that public dissatisfaction with the U.S. economy in 2024 helped propel Donald Trump back to power. Inflation was far and away the number one economic concern among American voters, despite the efforts of President Joe Biden to restrain it.

The economy, however, has not improved under President Trump. In fact, many Americans' financial situations have grown more dire. Even before Trump's attack on Iran, which immediately sent markets into turmoil and threatened long-term volatility, Americans were pessimistic about their economic future. A recent *New York Times*/Siena survey found "a widespread belief that a middle-class lifestyle is out of reach for most people." Nearly six in 10 voters said they worried about affording basics like rent and groceries, and more than one in 10 said they couldn't afford these necessities at all.[1] Seven in 10 Americans rated the economy as "fair" or "poor," according to a January 2026 survey by the Pew Research Center, and 38 percent expected conditions to worsen in the following year.[2]

This administration has not only failed to solve the "affordability" crisis, it has also taken a wrecking ball to the nation's economic capacity and global stature. American businesses and consumers are reeling, while our rivals have seized the opportunity to leap ahead. China, for instance, recently announced the world's largest-ever trade surplus—$1 trillion in 2025, achieved despite Trump's double-digit tariffs on Chinese imports.[3] (The United States, meanwhile, recorded a record trade deficit in 2025 of $1.2 trillion—also despite Trump's aggressive tariffs.)[4] China now leads the world in clean energy investment, including electric vehicle production, and is fast catching up on artificial intelligence.[5] Trump's economy added a scant 181,000 jobs in all of 2025, according to the Bureau of Labor Statistics.[6] (By comparison, the economy created nearly 1.5 million jobs in 2024, the final year of Biden's presidency.)[7]

Trump's policies are already weakening our economy. And the deficits he created to cut taxes for the wealthy will do more damage in the decades to come.

## BURDENING AMERICANS WITH ILLEGAL AND ARBITRARY TARIFFS

From the start, tariffs have been President Trump's favored economic tool—and his favorite economic weapon. In practice, they have proved ineffectual and injurious to U.S. interests.

During his first term, Trump used tariffs to launch his first trade war against China, with significant levies on Chinese imports like aluminum and steel.[8] While his initial stated goal was to reduce trade deficits and protest unfair practices, Trump has since used tariffs as an all-purpose cudgel for his political aims. In doing so, he has exceeded his constitutional authority, wreaked havoc on the global economy, destroyed long-standing alliances, and burdened U.S. consumers with unnecessary taxes on basic goods. Even after the Supreme Court's decision ruling many of Trump's tariffs unlawful, Americans paid an average tariff of 10 percent on imports as of April 2026, according to the Tax Policy Center, amounting to an annual estimated tax burden of $1,050 per household.[9] A February 2026 study by the Federal Reserve Bank of New York confirmed that 90 percent of the cost of Trump's tariffs has fallen on U.S. firms and consumers, despite his claims that foreign countries would foot the bill.[10]

This administration's tariff policies have hobbled, not helped, American businesses. For instance, they have generated enormous uncertainty, making planning and investment difficult. In the aftermath of the "Liberation Day" tariffs that were announced on April 2, 2025, when Trump threatened to impose rates as high as 50 percent on adversaries and allies alike,[11] the S&P 500 index lost $5.8 trillion in value, its "steepest four days of losses since the index was created in the 1950s,"[12] according to the University of Michigan's *Journal of Economics.* Trump was forced to backtrack with a 90-day "pause," the first of many such on-again, off-again lurches in policy that have led to significant volatility.[13] In a January 2026 survey by the Conference Board, 43 percent of American CEOs ranked "uncertainty" as the "top threat" to their businesses.[14]

Tariffs have also raised costs for U.S. companies, especially small businesses that do not have the cushion to absorb unexpected expenses. Fully half of all small businesses reported that Trump's tariffs had "a negative impact" on their businesses in 2025, according to a survey by the small-business payroll processor Gusto.[15] And in an August 2025 analysis, the U.S. Chamber of Commerce calculated that the tariffs, as initially proposed, would have exacted a $200 billion burden on small businesses.[16] Trump's tariffs have also invited retaliation from America's trading partners, the impacts of which have landed especially heavily on U.S. farmers. Soybean growers, for example, faced "historic export losses" in 2025, according to the American Soybean Association,[17] the result of a boycott imposed by China in response to the tariffs.[18] The boycott ended in November, but China's increasing reliance on Brazil for soybeans means that U.S. farmers may never fully recover. Overall, rural America is hurting badly. Farm bankruptcies in 2025 rose by 46 percent over 2024,[19] according to industry reports, and the Department of Agriculture reported significant declines in farm income that were only partially offset by government payments aimed at mitigating these losses.[20] After a similar boycott in his first term, Trump spent nearly $30 billion in an attempt to compensate farmers.[21] He has already spent $12 billion in his second term.[22]

At the same time, Trump's tariffs have failed to generate the kind of economic gains that he promised. Manufacturing employment has declined along with output, resulting in a net loss of 70,000 jobs from December 2024 to December 2025, according to the Cato Institute.[23] A January 2026 survey by the Association for Supply Chain Management and CNBC found that 32 percent of supply chain managers reported layoffs, 65 percent experienced increased costs, and 56 percent feared an imminent recession.[24]

Nevertheless, Trump has shown every indication of clinging to his failed policies, even as the Supreme Court has ruled many of his levies unconstitutional.[25] In the wake of his defeat before the Court in February 2026, administration officials sought other statutory authority justifying the continuation of tariffs, including under Sections 301, 122, and 232 of the 1962 Trade Act. American consumers and businesses may see little relief.

## TORPEDOING LONG-STANDING ECONOMIC ALLIANCES

The Trump administration's trade and economic policies have also caused irreparable damage to America's relationships with its closest allies and trading partners, with U.S. businesses suffering the consequences of the president's whims.[26] American industries are now the target of retaliatory tariffs and the subject of global boycotts by consumers angered by Trump's behavior.[27] Boycotts alone cost U.S. companies as much as $90 billion in 2025, according to an analysis by Goldman Sachs.[28]

Perhaps most tragic is the rupture of America's relationship with Canada, which Trump has abused with punitive tariffs and insults to its sovereignty. Both economies have been damaged as a result.[29]

One sector that's been especially hard hit is the U.S. auto industry, which has been integrated across North America for the past 40 years, with vehicles and parts crossing borders multiple times before landing in a dealer's lot. In 2024, the United States, Canada, and Mexico together produced 16 million vehicles, or 17.4 percent of global output, according to the Center for Strategic and International Studies.[30]

Trump's tariffs upended supply chains and raised prices for U.S. automakers and consumers. When Trump announced 25 percent tariffs on Canadian automobiles in March 2025, the Canadian Chamber of Commerce estimated that the levies would raise the purchase price of a pickup truck in the United States by about $8,000.[31] More troubling for American automakers is the potential loss of the Canadian market. The U.S. share of Canadian auto sales fell to a record low in 2025, according to Bloomberg.[32] Moreover, Canada has entered into its first-ever trade agreement with China to import electric vehicles, an arrangement that could shut U.S. electric vehicles out of the market in the future.[33]

## BANKRUPTING AMERICA'S FUTURE

This administration's budget-busting economic policies have set the nation on a path to financial ruin while boosting the fortunes of those least in need of help. The OBBBA, signed into law in the summer of 2025, will add a whopping $3.4 trillion to the federal deficit over the next 10 years, according to the Congressional Budget Office.[34]

America was already living far beyond its means. When Trump first took office in 2017, the national debt exceeded $26 trillion. But by the end of April 2026, the debt was approaching $39 trillion—the fastest increase in U.S. history.[35] If the first rule of holes is to stop digging, Trump is driving a steam shovel.

The primary effect of this administration's spending bills is to deliver massive tax cuts to America's wealthiest citizens, not to invest in future growth or create opportunities for the nation's needy and the working and middle classes. Trump's first tax cut bill, passed in 2017, bore a price tag of $1.9 trillion over 10 years[36] and provided an average tax cut of $61,090 to the top 1 percent of American households, according to the Tax Policy Center.[37] The top 0.1 percent received an average tax break of $252,300, while the bottom 20 percent of households benefited by an average of just $70. The OBBBA will deliver an additional $1 trillion in tax cuts to the top 1 percent while slashing $1.4 trillion in federal spending for essential programs like Medicaid, SNAP (food stamps), and student loans.[38]

The vast sums of borrowing required to finance these tax cuts will beggar the nation's future. By 2054, according to the Yale Budget Lab, the U.S. national debt will be nearly double the size of our GDP (194 percent). One result will be higher interest rates, which will tamp down investment and burden consumers. The Yale Budget Lab predicts that 10-year Treasury rates will be 1.4 percentage points higher than they would have been in the absence of the law.[39] This means higher interest rates for mortgages, car loans, credit cards, and other consumer credit.

Another consequence will be a vast diversion of federal revenues just to pay the interest on our obligations. Already, net interest on the national debt is crowding out funding on other priorities. In 2025, the federal government paid $970 billion in interest, compared to a proposed $82.4 billion for the Department of Education.[40]

Much of this debt is also in the hands of foreign countries, thereby increasing our dependence on their willingness to continue to lend us money. All told, the national debt load created by the Trump administration will be an albatross on growth, the Yale Budget Lab concludes, "such that by 2054 the level of GDP is more than 3 percent smaller than it would have been if the bill were not enacted."[41]

## POLITICIZING MONETARY POLICY

Trump has destabilized America's financial system, the bedrock of the global economy, by jeopardizing the independence of the Federal Reserve. In a desperate bid to mitigate the damaging impacts of his economic policies, he has relentlessly pressured the central bank to reduce interest rates and has attempted to punish it for its refusal to act on his demands. The result has been increased uncertainty in America's financial markets.[42]

Congress has long recognized the importance of insulating the nation's central bank from political pressures and has established guardrails to protect its governors from the whims of an aggressive executive. Each of the seven members of the Federal Reserve's Board of Governors serves a 14-year term,[43] and they are nominated on a rotating basis to ensure that bank officials outlast any given president's tenure and that the partisan makeup of the board remains relatively balanced.

Trump, however, has worked to demolish these foundational safeguards. He has threatened to fire the Fed's chair, Jerome Powell, and even launched a spurious criminal investigation against him (which as of April 2026 had been dropped).[44] He has attempted to oust another Fed governor, Lisa Cook, on dubious claims of "mortgage fraud," with the hopes of also replacing her with one of his loyalists.[45]

The economic risks of politicizing monetary policy are clear. The experience of other nations shows that the loss of central bank independence can bring on episodes of unusually high inflation, increase borrowing costs, and sap investment.[46] Trump's efforts to turn the Federal Reserve into an institution loyal only to him have spooked investors and even alarmed the Supreme Court, which has otherwise deferred to his power as the chief executive.[47] If Trump succeeds, the United States could lose its stature as the world's principal haven of investment, thereby opening the door for economic rivals to assume that role.[48]

## THE ART OF THE RISKY DEAL

Trump has frequently bragged of his prowess as a businessman and has touted the numerous deals he's allegedly struck on the nation's behalf. Unfortunately, his boasts have proved largely hollow. His deals have so far failed to deliver the promised benefits, except perhaps to his billionaire cronies.

Trump claims to have negotiated $17 trillion in new foreign investment that would bring manufacturing back to America.[49] An Associated Press investigation, however, concluded that this figure "appears to be exaggerated, highly speculative, and far higher than the actual sum."[50] Much of this touted investment is also contingent on other nations making good on vague commitments to Trump (often after having been threatened with tariffs). Japan, for instance, purportedly pledged $550 million in new U.S. investments, but the details have yet to be agreed upon.[51] A Goldman Sachs analysis concluded that many of the pledges included transactions that were already in motion, and that the real value to GDP would be between $30 billion and $135 billion—not trillions.[52]

Other deals are of dubious value and may pose greater risk than rewards for the U.S. economy. For instance, the government has acquired equity stakes in at least 10 companies, including Intel and U.S. Steel.[53] Several investments were in companies focused on the development of rare earths. While the investments can serve national security needs, the strategy poses a host of legal and political risks, including the potential for conflicts of interest and the consequences of choosing winners and losers. The Cato Institute's Scott Lincicome has warned of the "misallocation of capital" resulting from these investments, especially if the government sinks money into industries and companies that are uncompetitive.[54] More troubling are transactions where Trump appears to have bargained away U.S. competitiveness in industries like artificial intelligence, where America currently holds the global advantage. In late 2025, the Trump administration agreed to allow sales of Nvidia's powerful H200 AI chip to China, which many experts denounced as the prioritization of short-term gains over long-term economic and security interests.[55] As former National Security Advisor Jake Sullivan told *The New York Times*, "This decision is nuts."[56]

Most worrisome of all are the government's dealings that potentially put the U.S. economy at risk while arguably benefiting Trump and his family's businesses. The most obvious example is cryptocurrency, in which Trump and his family hold billions of dollars in assets through their entity World Liberty Financial.[57] Since taking office, Trump has repeatedly favored the crypto industry with deregulatory policies, the establishment of a crypto "strategic reserve,"[58] and privileged access for crypto industry donors.[59] In a 2025 report, Brookings warned of mounting risks to the American public and the U.S. economy from the lack of adequate safeguards on the crypto industry: "From financial instability to investor fraud to environmental and public safety risks, the potential consequences are real and growing."[60]

## BETRAYING HIS BASE

Trump promised a "manufacturing boom," a revival of coal, and "millions and millions of blue-collar jobs and jobs of every type."[61] He said America would recapture its supremacy as a "manufacturing powerhouse."[62]

This hasn't happened. Since his election in November 2024, America has lost more than 100,000 manufacturing jobs.[63] We have almost 2,000 fewer coal miners.[64] Trump has also failed to arrest the slide in labor force participation by white men, the core of his voter base, whose participation in the labor force peaked in 1956 at 88 percent. In March 2026, the workforce participation rate for this group was 68.8 percent, down from 69.6 percent in March 2025.[65] And despite the Trump administration's claims of a surge in work for "American-born" workers as a result of its deportation campaign,[66] the unemployment rate for native-born men (of all races) in March 2026 was the same as it was in January 2025—4.3 percent.[67] At the same time, Trump has instituted policies actively hostile to the economic security of his voters. The cuts to food assistance (SNAP) included in the OBBBA will fall hardest on rural communities, which suffer from higher rates of poverty and food insecurity than in the country at large. Rather than lift the fortunes of his core supporters, he has worsened their hardships.[68]

Yet another promise Trump has failed to deliver on is his April 2025 pledge "to reach and surpass 1 million new active apprentices" in blue-collar trades and other occupations.[69] Though he vowed to reach this milestone within 120 days of his executive order on apprenticeships, his administration has fallen far short of the mark. By contrast, at the end of Joe Biden's term, there were nearly 680,000 active apprentices in America, nearly double the roughly 359,000 nine years earlier.[70] Under Trump, however, the number of apprentices fell for the first time in 10 years. That's because Trump has systematically dismantled the federal government's Office of Apprenticeship in the Department of Labor and stripped apprenticeship programs of crucial funding. Key leadership staff in the Office of Apprenticeship were purged during Elon Musk's DOGE initiative,[71] and millions of dollars in grants for apprenticeship programs and apprenticeship research have been paused or canceled.[72]

★ ★ ★

*One year in, the Trump economy is a bust. The Trump administration's policies have set the nation on track to be less prosperous, less globally competitive, and less equipped to provide all Americans the opportunities they need to succeed. Americans deserve better: leadership that works in their interests and policies that invest in the nation's potential.*

# 4

# A SICKER, UNHEALTHIER AMERICA

**The COVID-19 pandemic, which began during Donald Trump's first term, had killed more than 1 million Americans by 2022. Trump's mishandling of the crisis, including his attacks on science and his embrace of misinformation, contributed to this grim toll. In his second term, the Trump administration's health care policies are no less dangerous and destructive. His top officials have embraced conspiracy theories over science and have undermined trust in public health. America is woefully unprepared for the next pandemic. Moreover, Trump's attacks on Medicaid and the Affordable Care Act will strip millions of Americans of access to affordable medical care. He has canceled promising research that could lead to future cures and has gutted the federal government of crucial expertise. All of this is cynically promoted under the banner of "Making America Healthy Again."**

★ ★ ★

In January 2026, on the eve of the first anniversary of his return to office, President Trump unveiled his "Great Healthcare Plan"—an agenda that falls far short of its grandiose title. The single-page document offers vague promises, few details, and proposals that many experts consider unworkable. One of Trump's demands is that hospitals and doctors "prominently post their pricing," as if patients in crisis have the leverage or wherewithal to negotiate the cost of their medical care.[1] The "plan" would not undo the damage that the Trump administration has already done to America's leadership in medical research, to its public health infrastructure, and to publicly funded health care programs.

Trump's shambolic, unserious, and destructive "plan" also typifies his administration's careless approach to Americans' health. During the first year of his second term, Trump has appointed loyalists with dubious qualifications to fill the roles most crucial to the guardianship of public health. These officials have undermined public faith in expertise and have discarded accepted scientific consensus, while embracing fringe ideas. The administration has gutted the infrastructure of public health, firing hundreds of inspectors, scientists, and other experts crucial for the safety of our food and medicines, including many who were on watch for emerging diseases.[2] Childhood scourges like measles and whooping cough, which U.S. public health officials have worked for decades to eradicate, are surging, along with a rise in anti-vaccine sentiment. In 2025, the United States reported more than 2,200 cases of measles and three deaths from the disease (compared to 285 cases and no deaths in 2024).[3] America is likely to lose its measles elimination status when international public health experts meet in the fall of 2026.[4]

Trump has also failed to keep his promise of making health care more affordable. Instead, he has put it out of reach for millions of Americans, including many of his supporters. The One Big Beautiful Bill Act (OBBBA), which Congress passed in the summer of 2025, cut federal Medicaid spending by more than $900 billion and imposed work reporting requirements that will burden working-poor Americans with red tape and cut them off from the medical care they need. Trump's refusal to extend premium subsidies for working- and middle-class Americans who get their health insurance under the Affordable Care Act has already raised these citizens' monthly premiums to unaffordable levels, causing many to forgo coverage. All told, the Congressional Budget Office (CBO) estimates that 16 million additional Americans will be uninsured by 2034 as a result of the Trump administration's policies.[5]

Trump has further jeopardized Americans' health through executive actions that will decimate scientific and biomedical research. In 2025, the Trump administration terminated or froze more than 7,800 research grants and slashed staff levels at the various science-related federal agencies by 15 to 25 percent.[6] It proposed draconian cuts to funding for the National Institutes of Health, which luckily Congress blocked. But the general attack on science has left its mark, putting the preeminence of American science at risk. Tomorrow's cures are now as likely to come from Europe or China, leaving U.S. patients to wait for new treatments rather than being at the front of the line.

## MAKING HEALTH CARE COVERAGE LESS AFFORDABLE

In 2009, the year before the enactment of the Affordable Care Act, 50 million Americans—one in six—had no health insurance, leaving them vulnerable to being deprived of care or mired in unmanageable debt. Coverage was particularly difficult and expensive for individuals and small employers to secure. When Americans with preexisting medical conditions applied for insurance coverage as individuals, a third of them were denied coverage.[7] U.S. hospitals charged higher fees to patients without insurance, sent unpaid bills to debt collection, and bore the losses as "uncompensated care"—which then required additional government spending to keep the hospitals running. In the year before the ACA took effect, more than 70 percent of the care to uninsured non-elderly adults ($62.8 billion) was uncompensated.[8]

The ACA created state-run and federal marketplaces in which insurance was priced the same for everyone regardless of health status. Many individuals also qualified for subsidies that made health insurance premiums more affordable and assured that healthy people would participate in the marketplace, thus keeping costs low for everyone.[9] During the COVID-19 pandemic, Congress passed temporary additional ("enhanced") subsidies that further broadened access to coverage. For low- and moderate-income individuals, the ACA provided states the option of expanding their Medicaid programs to cover individuals and families with incomes that were otherwise too high to qualify but too low to afford a health plan through the marketplace.

By 2024, the share of Americans without health insurance had been reduced from 16 percent before the ACA was enacted to 7.6 percent. More than 45 million Americans got their health care coverage through the ACA in 2025—about half through the marketplace and the other half through Medicaid expansion (in the 40 states, plus the District of Columbia, that took advantage of it).[10] The ACA has been effective in decreasing by one-fifth the rate of uninsurance among people with low incomes, chronic conditions, or disabilities.[11] These are people who would otherwise likely be unable to obtain or afford coverage.[12]

Despite the ACA's success, President Trump has waged a long-standing campaign against it, including several failed attempts to repeal it in his first term. He has vowed repeatedly to propose a health insurance coverage alternative to the ACA, but has not done so. Instead, he and the Republican majority in Congress have passed legislation and supported policies that will cause millions of Americans to lose their coverage.

The elimination of the enhanced ACA subsidies as of the start of 2026 is expected to more than double the average premium that many Americans will have to pay, with an average increase of more than $1,000.[13] The consequences will be devastating. In anticipation of an exodus of healthier enrollees from the ACA health plans, health insurers have already been raising their premiums by an average of 26 percent and as much as 59 percent, to account for these higher average costs.[14] The CBO estimates that the expiration of the enhanced subsidies alone, when combined with new rules adopted by the Department of Health and Human Services, will increase the number of uninsured by 5.1 million over the next 10 years.[15]

The intent of Trump's termination of the ACA enhanced subsidies may well be destabilization of the individual health insurance market, as rising premiums contribute to what insurance experts refer to as the "death spiral," leaving only extremely expensive coverage for the sickest patients. Many administration officials have argued for an individual responsibility for health care—providing a combination of health savings accounts, high-deductible plans, and enhanced tax deductions to pay for medical expenses, and encouraging Americans to avoid full-coverage health insurance plans.[16]

The idea that Americans would pay all of their hospital and physician bills and prescription drug expenses with their own cash is delusional. The average total cost of health care per person in the U.S. was $15,474 in 2024 (including government, private, out-of-pocket, research, and infrastructure spending).[17] But the majority of people don't use much health care in a year; for those who need it regularly, the costs would be devastating. The average three-day hospital stay in the United States currently costs $30,000.[18] Before the ACA was implemented, more than half of all personal bankruptcies were linked to medical debt, and one in five Americans was being pursued by collection agencies for medical debt.[19] Trump's health care proposals would Make Americans Greatly in Debt Again.

## DEPRIVING VULNERABLE AMERICANS OF ACCESS TO CARE

The Trump administration has also pushed through drastic cuts in Medicaid, the nation's largest public insurance program—and a vital source of health care coverage for many of Trump's core supporters, particularly in rural America. As of November 2025, 69 million people were enrolled in Medicaid, including 30 million children. Medicaid pays for 40 percent of births and 60 percent of all long-term care.[20]

Beginning in 2027, the OBBBA will require that, in addition to meeting their state's income eligibility standards, most nondisabled adults report at least 80 hours per month of work or community service in order to qualify for Medicaid. (The law does not provide funding for the child care, transportation, or training that would actually support work.) Even though the majority of nondisabled adults on Medicaid already work full- or part-time, this reporting requirement is intended to be burdensome on applicants and enrollees, in the hope that they will give up on filing all the necessary documentation and will thereby lose Medicaid coverage.[21]

Starting in 2028, the same law will limit the revenues that most states can raise from taxing hospitals and other providers in order to pay for their share of Medicaid expenses. Most if not all of these states will not be able to replace those lost revenues and will instead have to reduce payments to medical providers, tighten eligibility standards, and/or cut back on optional benefits.[22]

Because of their delayed effective dates, the impact of these policy changes will not be felt until after the November 2026 midterm elections. The CBO projects that once they do take effect, the eligibility changes alone will cause 5.7 million Americans to lose their Medicaid coverage by 2034, and that 5.3 million of those will become uninsured. Overall, the CBO estimates that the financing and eligibility changes will result in 7.5 million additional uninsured Americans by 2034—more than the current populations of Alaska, Delaware, North Dakota, Rhode Island, South Dakota, Vermont, and Wyoming combined.[23]

These cuts will fall especially heavily on adults and children in rural areas. Many rural Americans may soon find that they cannot get access to care at all. Since 2010, more than 150 rural hospitals have been closed or converted into non-acute care facilities, according to Harvard University's T. H. Chan School of Public Health, and many more are vulnerable to closure because of their dependence on Medicaid for revenues. While the OBBBA included a $50 billion "Rural Health Transformation" fund, Harvard's analysis concludes that it will be far from adequate to ensure access to care for the many Americans who will be left out in the cold.[24]

If these cuts in federal Medicaid spending are not reversed, the consequences will be far-reaching. Not only will the health of millions be jeopardized as they lose access to needed medical care, and not only will they and their families be at real risk of incurring medical debt, but the financial stability of the hospitals, clinics, and other providers that now serve them—as well as the rest of their communities—also will be put under potentially catastrophic strain.

## JEOPARDIZING WOMEN'S HEALTH

Women are particularly vulnerable to the consequences of Trump's policies. In 2022, the Supreme Court overturned *Roe v. Wade*, a longtime goal of the antiabortion movement, ruling that reproductive rights should be left to the states. Not content with that victory, Trump has continued in his second term to jeopardize women's health by further restricting abortion and reproductive care, even in states where abortion remains legal.

In 2025, the federal government withdrew its guidance to hospitals, under which emergency abortion care was protected, even in states with abortion bans. The result of this action was that medical providers in those states became hesitant to perform abortions—even if necessary to protect the life of the mother—for fear of prosecution or other penalties. This situation is especially dangerous for low-income women, who are less likely to have the means or time to travel to a state that protects abortion rights in order to receive health care.[25]

The Trump administration has also made it harder for women in states with abortion rights to access care. The Department of Veterans Affairs banned abortion counseling and care at its facilities, affecting approximately 365,000 women veterans who live in states that protect abortion access. Cuts to Medicaid in the OBBBA defunded community health care providers, leading to the closure of 20 Planned Parenthood health centers, which offer many services unrelated to abortion.[26] The administration also froze millions of dollars in Title X grants, the only federal program solely dedicated to funding birth control and family planning services to low-income and uninsured individuals. As a result, many aspects of women's health that are unrelated to abortion, including pregnancy and primary care, have been harmed.[27]

Finally, as in multiple areas of health care, the administration has relied on unproven assertions to justify restrictions on reproductive health and abortion access. Most notably, the Food and Drug Administration is reevaluating abortion pill safety despite 25 years of research showing that the pill is overwhelmingly safe.[28]

## DISMANTLING THE INFRASTRUCTURE OF PUBLIC HEALTH

Even critics of the U.S. health system agree that America offers some of the most advanced health care in the world and has been a global leader in medical research, innovation, and technology. It has produced great numbers of new drugs, advanced treatments, and state-of-the-art technologies and procedures. However, since January 2025, the Trump administration has dramatically cut programs, budgets, and staff at virtually every federal health agency, including the National Institutes of Health, the Centers for Disease Control and Prevention, the Substance Abuse and Mental Health Services Administration, the health service of the Department of Veterans Affairs, and others.[29] The administration has also forced out many agency leaders, whether political appointees or not, often without any clear justification. As of March 2026, the NIH had 15 acting or temporary directors among its 27 institute and center directors.[30] SAMHSA is operating with no director and acting or temporary staff in 50 percent of its other leadership positions. The consequence is a lack of stable leadership and clear direction for the agencies and their work.[31]

Either through direct elimination or sudden policy changes, many health programs have been significantly diminished. One study found that 383 clinical trials were cut or interrupted due to the proposed cuts, leaving vulnerable patients who had volunteered to be subjects without treatments.[32] *Forbes* reported that because of a sudden policy change in the way grants are made, the NIH supported 22 percent fewer projects in 2025 than in 2024, including a similar decline at the National Cancer Institute.[33] These cuts are not consistent with the administration's pledge to "Make America Healthy Again," considering that 99.4 percent of new drugs approved by the FDA between 2010 and 2019 were the result of discoveries conducted or funded by the NIH.[34]

At the CDC, the administration proposed and has begun implementing substantial budget cuts, including a proposed 50 percent reduction in the agency's overall funding. These cuts have led to the elimination or suspension of key programs, including those for chronic disease prevention, injury prevention, HIV/AIDS prevention, and infectious disease surveillance labs.[35] The administration also abruptly terminated more than $11 billion in COVID relief grants to states and local communities, which were used for testing, vaccination efforts, and addressing health disparities.[36] In addition, thousands of CDC employees were laid off, including hundreds of officers at the Epidemic Intelligence Service, who are key personnel for investigating disease outbreaks.[37]

## SUBSTITUTING IDEOLOGY AND INTUITION FOR SCIENCE

Biomedical science has been the basis for American health and public health policy for almost a century, and it has paid off well in terms of improvements in the prevention and treatment of illnesses and the extension of Americans' life expectancy and promotion of their overall well-being. The Trump administration, primarily through Robert F. Kennedy Jr., the secretary of health and human services, has adopted a set of vastly different, non-science-based policies, with the result that the health of millions of Americans is now at risk.

Vaccines are the most prominent example. For a century and longer, they have been a public health success story, particularly for children, saving billions of lives around the world. In January 2026, Kennedy and then Acting CDC Director Jim O'Neill introduced a new vaccine guidance schedule for newborns and young children that reduced the list of recommended vaccinations from the long-standard 17 vaccines to a shorter list of 11.[38] When asked the reason for these changes, O'Neill responded, without citing any underlying evidence, that the CDC had done a scientific review and had chosen to align U.S. recommendations with "peer developed countries, specifically Denmark."[39]

Several of the nation's leading medical and public health organizations, including the American Academy of Pediatrics and the California Medical Association, sharply criticized the process and the changes to the vaccine schedule. Critics point out that the rigorous, expert-driven review process that was traditionally conducted by the Advisory Committee on Immunization Practices was bypassed,[40] and that the new recommendations seemed to ignore substantial differences between the populations of the United States and Denmark.

These changes reflected Kennedy's widely known and long-held antipathy to vaccines; they were not based on any new scientific studies. Evidence of the foolishness of such anti-vaccine pronouncements include the recent increases in measles cases, more than 90 percent of which involve unvaccinated individuals.[41] The American Academy of Pediatrics, among others, believes that adopting the new vaccine standards will likely put millions of children at increased risk for contracting infectious diseases.[42]

Also in January 2026, the DHHS and the Department of Agriculture introduced a new, inverted food pyramid as part of the 2025–2030 Dietary Guidelines for Americans.[43] This pyramid prioritizes protein, dairy, healthy fats, and vegetables at the top, moving grains to the bottom—supposedly to emphasize "real food" and reduce processed food consumption. The new guidelines were developed under the direction of Kennedy, again departing from the previous reliance on expert advisory committees. Once again, no clear scientific justification was given for the changes.

## ENDING THE MOON SHOT ON CANCER RESEARCH

Since the National Cancer Institute was established in 1937, the U.S. government has invested $184 billion in funding its research.[44] The NCI's value to the nation in reducing the devastation that cancer visits upon American families is indisputable. Its scientists have discovered preventions, treatments, and cures for cancer, saving an estimated 4.5 million lives over the past 30 years. Since 1991, there has been a 71 percent reduction in pediatric cancer deaths and a 34 percent reduction in adult cancer deaths; mortality rates have declined for 12 of the 19 most common cancers in men and for 14 of the 20 most common cancers in women.[45]

Despite these successes, the "war on cancer" has not been won. In 2024, 612,000 Americans died of cancer, nearly as many as all the battlefield deaths in all U.S. wars since 1775. Forty percent of Americans will develop cancer in their lifetime, and more than 2 million Americans were diagnosed with cancer in 2025. It is not only a disease of the elderly: Early-onset cancer rates are rising today among younger adults, and 1,600 children died of cancer in 2024.[46] Researchers are looking for answers.

Yet, as part of its war on science, scientific research, and research institutions, the Trump administration effectively cut funding for cancer research by 31 percent by March 2025,[47] and in his budget proposal for the 2026 fiscal year, the president called for a 44 percent cut for the NIH (which included a similar percentage cut for the NCI)[48] and a 53 percent cut for the CDC.

This attack on cancer research and disease control flies in the face of reason. Cancer knows no political favorites. In fact, eight of the 10 states with the highest cancer mortality are Republican-leaning states, and Trump's constituency of rural Americans has a higher rate of cancer diagnosis and death than urban populations.[49]

This policy to gut research generally, and cancer research in particular, proved to be wildly unpopular. In the next appropriations act, Congress moved quickly—with broad bipartisan support and ignoring Trump's budget proposal—

to increase funding for cancer research. The increase was minimal—2 percent for the NCI and less than 1 percent for the NIH[50]—but it was a rare victory for research in Trump's war against science.

## SABOTAGING THE SEARCH FOR FUTURE CURES

The modest victory for cancer research, however, cannot offset the long-term impact of the Trump administration's broader attacks on science and its disruption of research. The cancellation of existing research grants and termination of funded clinical trials is destroying the morale of scientists within the science and health agencies. At the same time, the website and communication arms of the NCI have been dismantled. Patients with cancer and their families call the NCI thousands of times per month in search of reliable information. Now their questions go unanswered. Further, interruptions due to firings, rehirings, freezing of funds, and other such disruptions are making one of the world's greatest scientific institutions rife with chaos and destroyed morale.

Senior scientists are reluctantly leaving the NCI, but positions at major research universities are limited by the administration's cancellation of grants and further reductions in federal funding to universities. Their younger counterparts see declining opportunities for new research in the United States and are being courted by the European Commission, which has created a $500 million fund to attract American scientists.[51] In addition, scientists from other parts of the world, who would previously come to the United States to conduct their research, are now discouraged not only by the loss of funding but also by the hostile immigration climate.

★ ★ ★

*The Trump administration has demonstrated its disdain for proven science that has improved our lives for decades. By destroying biomedical research, casting doubt and reversing scientific knowledge, and causing people to lose health insurance, they are reversing a hundred years of medical progress that will result in the exact opposite of their professed claims to "Make America Healthy Again."*

*The effects on our nation's health and prosperity will be long-lasting. It is far easier to destroy biomedical research and confidence than to create it. The wholesale disruption of the CDC, the NCI (and the rest of the NIH), SAMHSA, and the National Science Foundation will take years to correct.*

# 5

## AN UNPRECEDENTED ATTACK ON EDUCATION

**Nothing is more critical to our nation's well-being than the health of its educational institutions. Education is the engine of social mobility and economic growth. Yet President Donald Trump's policies have systematically sought to weaken our nation's public schools and universities—the pride of red states and blue states alike. He has undermined neighborhood public schools by threatening their funding and autonomy. He has decimated the system of federal support for research that is the cornerstone of our scientific leadership in the world, sabotaging our long-term economic strength. And he has sought to suppress academic freedom under the cynical guise of ending antisemitism and "woke" ideology. The harm he has caused to our schools, our students, our economic potential, and our public health is incalculable.**

★ ★ ★

American public education is older than America itself.

The nation's first public school, the Boston Latin School,[1] was established in 1635 by the Massachusetts Bay Colony, one year before the founding of Harvard. Its focus was the humanities, and its mission was "dissent with responsibility."[2] In the 1770s, Thomas Jefferson introduced a bill in the Virginia House of Burgesses to establish a system of free public education in the commonwealth, beginning in the elementary grades. The antidote to tyranny, Jefferson wrote, was "to illuminate, as far as practicable, the minds of the people at large" and to do so "without regard to wealth, birth or other accidental condition or circumstance."[3] Today, the nation's public schools educate nearly 50 million students.[4]

America's early leaders also saw the benefits of investments in higher education. In 1862, Congress passed the first Morrill Act,[5] which established the nation's system of land grant universities and launched the federal government's partnership with higher education. In 1950, Congress created the National Science Foundation to support pure and applied research at American universities. Funding for the NSF has been a bipartisan congressional priority ever since.[6]

Building on this foundation, American universities have become the envy of the world. They have dominated global rankings, become leaders in scientific and research output, and served as incubators of technological innovation.[7] The innumerable scientific breakthroughs that have resulted from this partnership are now woven into the fabric of our lives—inventions like the internet, GPS, and the mRNA vaccines that ended the pandemic.[8]

Most Americans recognize the importance of education for themselves and their families, even as some have questioned its value and expense. A majority of parents want their children to attend universities,[9] and large majorities of college students see their education as valuable to their future careers.[10] More than half of all American adults enroll in postsecondary education either directly after high school or later as returning students.[11]

Higher education continues to be the surest path to financial security. The typical college graduate earns $32,000 a year more than the typical high school graduate, according to a 2025 study by the Federal Reserve Bank of New York, which also found that the "college wage premium" is near a historic all-time high.[12] Over a lifetime, the wage advantage conferred by a college degree can mean as much as $1.5 million in additional earnings.[13]

Yet in the eyes of the second Trump administration, education and higher education are "the enemy," as Vice President J. D. Vance declared in a 2021 speech, years before his ascension to the second-highest office in the land.[14] Project 2025, the Trump administration's blueprint for the current term, included a 46-page plan for gutting the nation's educational infrastructure, which U.S. officials have been assiduously working to implement.[15] One year into Trump's second term, public education is under threat, and American higher education is perilously close to losing its high global stature. American students, meanwhile, risk the loss of access to the education they need for success.

## UNDERMINING THE FUNDING AND AUTONOMY OF PUBLIC SCHOOLS

The pandemic inflicted enormous damage on student achievement, and it has yet to recover. Instead, scores have continued to decline. In math, for instance, just 28 percent of eighth-graders were at or above a "proficient" level in 2024—6 percentage points lower than in 2019, according to the National Assessment of Educational Progress (also known as the "Nation's Report Card").[16] The Trump administration has done nothing to reverse these trends. Instead, it has enacted policies that rob schools of precious resources that would otherwise be directed toward student learning.

In the first few months of his administration, Trump issued an executive order to abolish the Department of Education, despite lacking the legal authority to do so.[17] His officials framed the department's proposed demise as an act of bureaucratic efficiency and a return of control to the states.[18] In truth, it's an attempt to weaken the nation's system of public education, with the effect of harming America's most vulnerable students.

At the same time, administration officials froze at least $12 billion in federal school funding already allotted to states and districts by Congress. Educators lost jobs while districts scrambled to raise funds to cover these unexpected deficits. Significant chunks of this money were intended for special education, according to an analysis by *EducationWeek*, while other funds were meant for vital programs in mental health, literacy instruction, nutrition, building modernization, and services for immigrant children.[19]

The administration's cuts and cancellations especially hurt low-income students, minorities, and students with disabilities, who now have fewer resources for the services they need, and less recourse if districts don't comply with existing federal protections.[20] In a perversion of its original mission, the Education Department's Office of Civil Rights has shifted its focus away from the enforcement of U.S. civil rights laws and toward the enforcement of Trump's policy priorities. According to a March 2026 investigation by ProPublica, "Complaints about transgender students playing sports and using girls' bathrooms at school have been fast-tracked,[21] while cases of racial harassment of Black students last year were ignored."[22]

The administration, moreover, has retaliated against Democratic states and cities that have resisted Trump's agenda, forcing schools to spend hundreds of thousands of dollars on legal fees instead of school instruction. For instance, in February 2026, shortly after mass protests in Portland, Oregon, of immigration enforcement activities in the city, the Office for Civil Rights opened an investigation against the public schools there.[23] The Trump administration also threatened to withhold grant funding from five districts in northern Virginia that refused to institute policies discriminating against transgender students.[24] Fairfax and Arlington Counties have sued to release the funds, which amount to $200 million.[25]

## MAKING COLLEGE LESS AFFORDABLE

The Trump administration has called for massive cuts in federal programs that are aimed at making college more affordable, especially for low-income Americans. Congress has so far rebuffed his proposals, but there's little doubt of Trump's hostility toward expanding access to higher education.

Trump's budget request for the 2026 fiscal year proposed slashing the maximum federal Pell Grant for low-income students by about 25 percent, from $7,395 to $5,710.[26] It also proposed to slash the federal work study program and to defund three programs that seek to help disadvantaged students attend college. Among the programs Trump sought to eliminate was TRIO, which the Pell Institute found to be effective in increasing college enrollment and graduation rates. Thankfully, the appropriations bill passed by Congress rejected these proposed cuts.[27]

Congress did, however, pass a series of administration proposals that significantly limit federal student loan programs, as part of the One Big Beautiful Bill Act. The legislation ended the Grad PLUS loan program, capped Parent PLUS loans at $20,000 a year, and, most significantly, limited federal loans for most graduate school programs to $20,500 a year (with a lifetime cap of $100,000). (Before the law was enacted, parents and students could borrow up to the cost of the program with no set limit.)[28] The law also placed a limit of $50,000 per year for federal loans for so-called professional programs like medicine and law, a restriction that the American Medical Association said would worsen physician shortages and limit opportunities for lower-income students.[29] Moreover, the "professional" designation excluded nursing, which the American Nurses Association said would "jeopardize workforce sustainability" and "limit access to care."[30] As a result of these restrictions, many students will be discouraged from pursuing an education in fields important to societal well-being. Others may have to resort to high-interest private loans that lack federal protections and, critically, are ineligible for the Public Service Loan Forgiveness program. In either instance, an affordable education will be further from reach.

## CUTTING OFF THE PIPELINE FOR TECHNOLOGICAL BREAKTHROUGHS

Trump has also disrupted the unique and successful partnership between universities and the federal government that has produced decades of cutting-edge innovations and research. The result has been to jeopardize scientific progress, including important cures and treatments that benefit American patients; to weaken local and regional economies dependent on research-generated economic growth; and to sabotage America's future competitiveness and technological leadership.

Over the past 80 years, the research carried out at U.S. universities, funded in large part by federal grants, has helped lay the foundation for America's prosperity. Universities have developed important innovations and advances in such fields as health and medicine, communications, food science, energy, environmental science, and national security. In the 2023 fiscal year, approximately $108 billion was spent on research at American universities, with the lion's share of this support coming from the federal government.[31] Until Trump's return to the White House, these appropriations were noncontroversial and enjoyed broad bipartisan support.

In his first few months in office, however, the Trump administration froze, paused, or canceled at least $11 billion in funds already appropriated by Congress, much of which had been designated for university research.[32] It also halved the number of students participating in the NSF's prestigious graduate student research program and severely limited the funding for international students, thereby choking off the pipeline for future talent.[33] In the fall of 2025, American universities reported a 17 percent decline in new international student enrollments.[34]

One damaging consequence of these policies has been to halt progress on the search for cures to many diseases, to the detriment of American patients. At Johns Hopkins University, for instance, researchers lost $50 million in funding (in addition to $800 million in losses from canceled grants at the U.S. Agency for International Development).[35] As the nation's largest recipient of funding from the National Institutes of Health, the university could ultimately risk losing as much as $200 million a year in federal funds—a result that could jeopardize hundreds of clinical trials for treatments in cancer, diabetes, and infectious diseases.[36] Johns Hopkins has been at the forefront of developing the mRNA vaccines that have shown immense promise in treating chronic diseases, as well as cancer, but the potential loss of $500 million in funding for mRNA vaccine development[37]—the result of false claims and misinformation about vaccine safety—could set back this research for decades, costing untold numbers of lives.

Cuts to research also have been and will be devastating to local economies, in both Democratic and Republican states. According to researchers at the University of Maryland and the University of Pennsylvania, Trump's proposed cuts to NIH funding alone could result in future annual losses of $17 billion in economic activity and 72,000 lost jobs.[38] The loss of international students could deliver a further blow. The Institute of International Education estimates that international students contributed $55 billion to the U.S. economy in 2024 and supported more than 355,000 jobs.[39] Much of this economic boost flowed to small towns and rural America. Though many Americans may associate international students with elite institutions like the Ivy League, many regional and small private colleges depend on tuition revenues from international students, who typically pay full freight, to subsidize American students. At West Virginia's Wheeling University, for instance, international students made up 20 percent of the student body in 2024, according to *U.S. News & World Report.*[40]

Similarly, universities provide ample benefits to many states' economies. University research launches start-ups and creates jobs. A study by the Andersen Consulting group, for instance, found that public universities in Michigan generate nearly $45 billion in economic activity each year, yielding a 28-to-1 return on taxpayer investment in these institutions.[41] In Durham and Wake Counties in North Carolina, according to the Center for Strategic & International Studies, "universities have launched 756 start-ups since 1998,[42] helping transform Research Triangle Park into a biotech hub that generates $82 billion in economic impact annually while supporting more than 200,000 jobs."[43]

Trump's cuts to research funding will mean forgoing new jobs and innovation. It also means ceding to China the global lead in scientific research. Recent international rankings show that Chinese universities have already seized the global lead in the quantity and quality of scientific papers produced. According to a major ranking in research productivity by Leiden University in the Netherlands, Chinese universities held 16 of the top 20 spots in scientific publications in 2025. Harvard placed third, and only two other American universities—Johns Hopkins and the University of Michigan—ranked in the top 25. Two decades earlier, seven U.S. universities were in the top 10, and Harvard was ranked number one.

## STIFLING FREEDOM OF THOUGHT

The Trump administration has also abused its financial leverage in its attempts to control universities' hiring and admissions practices, to mandate curricula, and to suppress academic freedom. This effort represents nothing less than a dire threat to the freedom of speech and inquiry that has helped our universities lead the world.

Nowhere has this been more apparent than in the administration's all-out assault on Harvard, the nation's oldest and wealthiest university. The federal government has frozen $2.2 billion in research funding; opened an investigation of Harvard's foreign gifts and contracts; begun an investigation by the Equal Employment Opportunity Commission into the university's hiring practices; and commenced a civil rights investigation into alleged antiwhite discrimination by the *Harvard Law Review*. In May 2025, the Department of Homeland Security terminated the certification Harvard needed to admit foreign students,[44] and in August of that year Secretary of Commerce Howard Lutnick threatened to strip Harvard of its patents developed with federal funding.[45] While a federal judge has since held that the administration's freeze of federal research funding was unconstitutional,[46] these claims must now make their way through the appellate courts, with uncertain results.

Other universities, including Columbia, Brown, Cornell, and Northwestern, have been subject to similar targeting and have been forced to make concessions to stay viable. Those settlements have included making policy changes and paying substantial fines to resolve the administration's complaints. Brown, for instance, agreed to pay $50 million in exchange for restoration of federal funding and the resolution of federal investigations.[47] Columbia, meanwhile, agreed to pay $200 million and acceded to the appointment of an "independent monitor" of its operations.[48]

Emboldened by these victories, the administration has since proposed a "compact," offering universities preferential access to federal money if they adopt policies consistent with Trump's agenda. Among its numerous onerous conditions, universities would have to agree to limit foreign students to 15 percent of the undergraduate population; refuse to acknowledge transgender identity; ban any consideration of race; disclose detailed admissions data, including grades and test scores; and protect the expression of conservative ideas.[49] Ted Mitchell, the president of the American Council on Education, called the proposed compact "a naked exercise of power" and "extortion" and argued that it would turn colleges and universities into "instruments of the state, rather than institutions seeking truth."[50] Of the nine universities originally offered the compact, seven had declined as of March 2026. Trump has since extended the offer to all colleges and universities, which some institutions under financial duress may ultimately find difficult to resist. The consequence will be the slow erosion of academic freedom and the stifling of the creativity that has led to American breakthroughs in technology, culture, and innovation.

★ ★ ★

*Whatever one's opinion about reforms that ought to be instituted in American higher education, the fact remains that the Trump administration is using the heavy hand of government in ways never before seen in our nation's history. Lee Bollinger, a First Amendment scholar who served nearly 30 years as the president of the University of Michigan and Columbia University, reminds us that our universities have a special mission.[51] They serve as an extension of government, nurturing vital research and educating the next generation of citizens and leaders, through a vigorous exchange of ideas and constant inquiry. We cannot allow an erratic, uninformed president and the group of fierce ideologues advising him to destroy this vital enterprise so necessary for our nation's well-being and economic vitality.*

# 6

# A GUTTED AND WEAPONIZED GOVERNMENT

**Within days of his return to the White House, Donald Trump began dismantling the federal government—slashing the federal workforce and deciding by fiat which programs to keep and which to discard. Thousands of highly qualified and dedicated civil servants lost their jobs, and the American people lost the benefit of their experience and expertise. The result has been the degradation of basic governmental functions and essential services affecting every facet of American life: disaster relief, weather forecasts, food safety, tax collection. Trump has also undermined the ideals of a civil service based on merit, competence, and neutrality. He has instead politicized it and weaponized it to serve his own ends. Because of Trump's policies and reckless destruction, the infrastructure of government will take decades to rebuild.**

★ ★ ★

The federal government has long been a favored punching bag for presidents of both political parties. Ronald Reagan declared government to be "not the solution" but "the problem,"[1] while Bill Clinton campaigned on "reinventing" government.[2] Harry Truman created the Hoover Commission,[3] headed by one of his predecessors, Herbert Hoover, to recommend improvements to the executive branch.

Clinton's and Truman's initiatives, for the most part, were good-faith efforts to root out inefficiency and promote better stewardship of taxpayer dollars. Not so with Donald Trump, whose goal has been less to fix the federal government than to raze it.

Among Trump's first acts in office was to establish, without congressional sanction, the "Department of Government Efficiency," headed by the billionaire

Elon Musk. With an ostensible mission to eliminate waste, fraud, and abuse, DOGE was given the authority to bulldoze agencies at will.[4] Musk posed for photos wielding a chainsaw at a conference of Trump's supporters, signaling his intent to slash his way through the federal workforce. What followed was DOGE's dismissal or retirement of more than 300,000 career civil servants, along with the termination of approximately 13,000 federal contracts and 1,500 grants.[5]

It is unclear whether DOGE accomplished very much besides destruction. Despite grandiloquent claims of massive savings, independent analyses verify that DOGE pruned only about $1.4 billion from federal expenditures.[6]

The wreckage, however, has been vast. Indiscriminate and illegal purges have hollowed out the U.S. government's capacity to carry out its core functions, and many agencies have had to rehire key employees they discovered they can't do without. The Department of Energy, for example, fired hundreds of workers in February 2025, only to realize that among those dismissed were employees crucial to maintaining the safety of the nation's nuclear stockpile.[7]

Also among the casualties of these mass dismissals were a large number of "probationary" employees—newer, often younger, workers who had not yet earned civil service protections. Trump and DOGE's firing spree wiped out a generation of rising talent[8] and inflicted lasting harm on America's ability to attract talented public servants and leaders.[9]

Trump has also warped the fundamental nature of the civil service through his efforts to politicize and weaponize all aspects of government in pursuit of his political and personal agenda. He has sought to replace career civil servants with loyalists and has run roughshod over traditional civil service protections and collective bargaining rights. He has fired inspectors general who could hold his appointees to account,[10] and he has punished whistleblowers who have protested abuses.[11]

In 1883, Congress passed the Pendleton Civil Service Act to end the "spoils" system of staffing government, which had led to chaos, corruption, and inefficiency.[12] The resulting merit-based system has created a professionalized civil service that is competent and politically neutral, and treats all citizens equally. Trump, however, seems intent on reinstating the spoils system of old and bending the architecture of government to his will.

## HOBBLING CORE FUNCTIONS AND ESSENTIAL SERVICES

The mass firings of thousands of federal workers without cause or rationale and in blatant violation of the law has materially diminished the quality of the government services Americans expect and pay for to protect their health, safety, and well-being.

The abrupt dismissals of scientists, experts, researchers, and other personnel from agencies like the Centers for Disease Control and Prevention have left the United States less prepared for the next pandemic and less equipped to protect itself against bioterrorism or other threats.[13] The loss of safety inspectors at the Food and Drug Administration means less quality control for pharmaceuticals and a greater likelihood of unsafe products reaching consumers.[14]

Massive layoffs at the Internal Revenue Service have hindered the government's ability to process tax returns and refunds as well as audit potential scofflaws.[15] The unit that audits billionaires lost nearly 40 percent of its workers in the spring of 2025,[16] thereby dramatically improving the odds that ultrawealthy fraudsters will get away with their crimes.[17] Dramatic reductions of staffing at the Social Security Administration have meant the closure of several field offices, long wait times, and delayed claims for elderly and disabled beneficiaries in dire need of aid.[18] Many farmers are suffering after cuts to the Department of Agriculture,[19] which oversees critical assistance such as conservation planning and crop insurance.[20]

Among the agencies hardest hit by Trump's purges is the Department of Veterans Affairs, where nearly 30,000 employees were dismissed or induced to retire. (Many of them are veterans themselves.) The result has been critical shortages of doctors, nurses, claims processors, mental health professionals, and social workers[21]—all roles directly impacting veterans' care and benefits.[22] An estimated 1.2 million veterans have lost their VA providers, and wait times have almost doubled in many locations. The VA has slashed its crisis line staff, despite suicide being the second leading cause of death for veterans under the age of 45, and has dismantled protections for homeless veterans. VA cuts also have upended or delayed clinical trials on cancers, dementia, heart disease, and stroke risk.[23]

## INCREASING RISK FROM SERIOUS THREATS

Diminished federal capacity has also made the nation more vulnerable to threats, both man-made and natural.

Cuts to the National Oceanic and Atmospheric Administration have blindsided the agency's ability to fully maintain National Weather Service operations and conduct critical forecasting and modeling for extreme storms and hurricanes.[24] Drastic cuts have also shuttered numerous field offices that provided essential services to state and local governments.[25]

Deep reductions at the Federal Emergency Management Agency have significantly undermined the nation's disaster response capabilities at a time when natural disasters are becoming more frequent and violently destructive.[26] Meanwhile, cuts to the National Park Service have degraded essential services, like medical assistance and search and rescue, and have undermined the service's capacity for maintenance, resulting in profound habitat destruction.[27]

And at the same time that Trump is swelling the ranks of immigration enforcement officials, he has made sweeping cuts to federal offices protecting the United States from foreign threats, including the National Security Agency; the Cybersecurity and Infrastructure Security Agency, which oversees U.S. critical infrastructure;[28] and the FBI's Foreign Influence Task Force, which combats foreign influence campaigns to sow chaos in American elections. As Frank Figliuzzi, a former head of FBI counterintelligence, summed it up, "It's astounding … It's now a free for all for foreign intel services seeking influence."[29]

## POLITICIZING THE CIVIL SERVICE

For more than 140 years, the civil service has upheld political neutrality, unbiased reporting, technical expertise, and an oath to protect the Constitution. In fact, a key purpose of the Pendleton Act was to eliminate cronyism and ensure that government employees were selected based on merit and education, rather than political favoritism. Civil service employees are bound by the restrictions of the Hatch Act on partisan political activity.

The Trump administration, however, has worked to subvert these ideals of professionalism, neutrality, and fairness. Instead, it has hijacked the civil service for political purposes, prioritizing loyalty over competence and weaponizing branches of government to punish the president's perceived enemies.

At the Justice Department and the FBI, the ranks of respected career professionals have been decimated while toadies pursue their plans for retribution against Trump's political opponents. These losses reflect a combination of loyalty purges; the firings of career employees who do not show sufficient fealty to President Trump or have worked previously on investigations touching on him or his associates; high-pressure retirement buyouts, particularly in the Civil Rights Division; and the resignations of senior and mid-career attorneys who cannot in good conscience support the department's political priorities. In a public letter signed by 200 former employees, career attorneys in the Civil Rights Division accused the administration of "largely abandoning its duty to protect civil rights."[30]

Likewise, the FBI, under the leadership of Kash Patel, has suffered from multiple career leaders being forced out or fired, including senior officials who resisted handing over lists of agents tied to politically sensitive cases, such as the January 6 investigation.[31] Many career staffers have resigned to avoid carrying out or being targeted for political retribution.[32]

## POLITICIZING INDEPENDENT FEDERAL AGENCIES

Independent federal agencies have also been forced to buckle under Trump's will, despite federal laws that preserve their independence and lawsuits to enforce these protections. The administration effectively shut down the Consumer Financial Protection Bureau, which enforces consumer financial laws and regulations. Russell Vought, the director of the Office of Management and Budget, who was also serving as the director of the CFPB, had the bureau's office doors locked to prevent employees from returning to work while constitutional challenges to his mass firings were litigated.[33] Vought also shut down enforcement actions and rescinded consent orders that required companies to pay millions of dollars in redress for unlawful financial practices.[34]

The Federal Trade Commission and Consumer Product Safety Commission have also suffered large losses to their civil service workforces. Congress had deliberately structured the independent agencies as bipartisan five-member commissions, where no more than three commissioners can be from the same political party, to shield them from undue political influence and to promote sound decision-making. But in an unprecedented partisan move, Trump fired the Democratic FTC and CPSC commissioners without cause in the spring of 2025, breaking a norm that, in the case of the FTC, had stood for a century.[35]

Yet another agency that has been politicized under Trump was the Federal Communications Commission. The president's appointee as chair, Brendan Carr, had once declared that "the Commission should focus its efforts on creating a market-friendly regulatory environment that fosters innovation and competition,"but in office he has "chosen instead to achieve political goals by increasing the regulatory reach of the agency to intrude into corporate decisions to achieve political goals," in the words of one of his predecessors, Tom Wheeler.[36] Examples include Carr's investigation into Comcast's diversity, equity, and inclusion practices; reopening an FCC review of CBS's *60 Minutes* interview with Kamala Harris and tying that to a review of CBS license transfers; and citing investigations of the public broadcast networks PBS and NPR as potentially "relevant to" legislative debate over public funding.[37]

## WEAPONIZING GOVERNMENT AS AN INSTRUMENT OF IDEOLOGY

President Trump has also commandeered the federal government's vast ability to communicate with the American public in order to enforce his ideological agenda and his vision of what America should be. Trump has made no secret of his hostility to immigrants (whether legal or unauthorized), minorities, and DEI policies, and he has used his power to erase history, police official language, and propagandize his priorities.

Through an executive order, Trump has begun the wholesale whitewashing of history exhibits and educational materials at national parks that conflict with his crusade against DEI and all forms of "wokeness."[38] Censored content includes climate change and rising seas, George Washington's ownership of slaves, and the mistreatment of Native Americans. This assault on the parks' cultural and historical integrity is a national tragedy.[39]

The Trump administration has also tied arts funding and leadership decisions to ideological tests, mandating a focus on narrow "patriotic" themes, as it defines them. Administration officials have accused the Smithsonian Institution of "divisive, race-centered ideology" and used this as a justification for overhauling exhibits that address slavery and racism[40] and for prohibiting funding for projects that "promote gender ideology."[41]

The administration has also terminated about 560 grants by the National Endowment for the Arts as not in line with its "priorities,"[42] and its budget proposal for the 2026 fiscal year called for elimination of the NEA, the National Endowment for the Humanities, and the Institute of Museum and Library Services.[43] Though Congress later rejected defunding the NEA and the NEH, Trump's grant cuts to one-third of U.S. museums and arts programs caused immediate disruption.[44]

Trump has also been intent on taking over flagship artistic and cultural institutions to ensure that their programming aligns with his priorities. At the John F. Kennedy Center in Washington, D.C., he fired longtime staff members and trustees, installed loyalists in key leadership positions, and even added his name to the building's facade, alongside the name of President Kennedy.[45]

When artist boycotts and event cancellations arose in protest to these actions, Trump announced that the Kennedy Center would soon close for renovations.[46] He also sought to fire the director of the National Portrait Gallery and the first female African American librarian of Congress, alleging that she supported DEI and "inappropriate books" for children.[47] In the aftermath of federal funding recissions, the Corporation for Public Broadcasting voted to dissolve, ending nearly 60 years of federal support for PBS and NPR.[48]

★ ★ ★

*Trump's drastic cuts to federal institutions and his politicization of them have caused seismic instability in federal government operations. His dangerous push to eliminate expertise in favor of cronyism jeopardizes the government's ability to attract and retain the high-caliber, competitive workforce needed to meet the current and future challenges facing the United States, and further erodes Americans' trust in their government. Americans deserve a federal government dedicated to their interests and whose mission is to serve the people without prejudice.*

# 7

# A COSTLY ATTACK ON CLIMATE

**President Donald Trump has attacked climate action just as the costs of inaction are accelerating and the economic opportunities for solutions are exploding. His administration has moved aggressively to dismantle long-standing climate policy, hollow out federal capacity, undercut scientific understanding, withdraw from international climate diplomacy, and reward the fossil fuel sector. At the same time, he has reversed the most significant clean energy and industrial momentum the U.S. has ever built.[1]**

**These actions are not merely a change in policy preference. They represent a direct assault on American interests. While the benefits accrue narrowly to incumbents in the fossil fuel economy, the costs—lost jobs, higher health burdens, rising household expenses, mounting disaster losses, increased migration pressures, and eroded national security—will be borne by ordinary Americans and future generations.[2]**

★ ★ ★

Before Donald Trump's return to the presidency, agencies across the federal system—including the Departments of Energy, Agriculture, Housing and Urban Development, Transportation, Treasury, Defense, and State—had all begun integrating climate risk into decisions that shape infrastructure, markets, and public safety.

The Inflation Reduction Act, passed by Congress in 2022, provided long-term certainty for clean energy, manufacturing, and industrial decarbonization, and it sought to unlock private investment at unprecedented scale. Independent analyses showed that the law put the United States on a credible path to cut greenhouse gas emissions to roughly 40 to 45 percent below 2005 levels by 2030,[3] nearly aligning the country with its international commitments and putting reductions in emissions on track to accord with what science tells us is required to avoid the worst effects of climate change.

That approach ended abruptly on January 20, 2025.

On Inauguration Day, Trump issued sweeping executive orders—most notably "Unleashing American Energy"—that directed federal agencies to prioritize fossil fuels and unwind climate policy across government.[4] He again initiated U.S. withdrawal from the Paris Agreement, as he had done during his first term, and signaled hostility to virtually all federal climate action.

By the end of his first year, the administration had gone further still: freezing clean energy deployment, attacking the legal foundations of climate regulation, gutting climate science funding, and withdrawing the United States from all international climate institutions.[5]

The result was not policy recalibration. It was institutional sabotage, designed to destroy federal climate capacity and move decisively to lock in more fossil fuel pollution.

## SUPERCHARGING CLIMATE-DESTROYING FOSSIL FUELS

On day one, Trump declared a "National Energy Emergency" to fast-track the production and infrastructure for fossil fuels, including coal, oil, and liquefied natural gas (LNG).[6]

Coal was being phased out in the United States as a result of economic pressures,[7] but Trump gave it a new lifeline. Thirteen million acres of federal lands were opened to coal leasing with reduced royalty rates payable to the U.S. Treasury. Dozens of coal plants received exemptions from environmental standards for mercury and other toxins, allowing some of the dirtiest generators in the country to operate longer.[8] Other dirty and old power plants that were slated for decommissioning, like the Consumers Energy plant in Michigan, were forced to keep operating, costing both utility owners and ratepayers. As a result, U.S. coal use increased by 13 percent in 2025, even as India and China saw real declines for the first time.[9] At a time when the growth of data centers is requiring tremendous additional power capacity, the Trump administration is virtually guaranteeing increased costs to ratepayers by requiring uneconomic fossil fuel generation while hampering the addition of lower-cost renewable energy.

For oil, Trump's promise of "drill, baby, drill" was realized when he directed agencies to remove barriers to oil and gas drilling across federal lands and waters, including in the Arctic National Wildlife Refuge.[10] More than 1 billion acres of coastal waters were opened to drilling, often over the objections of coastal governors of both political parties.[11]

Trump also lifted the Biden-era pause on new LNG export approvals and directed the Department of Energy to resume permitting—bad news, given that LNG is as potent as coal as a driver of climate change due to its leakage of methane, which is 80 times more damaging than carbon dioxide over a 20-year period. These moves revived the construction of stalled multibillion-dollar export terminals on the Gulf Coast and in Alaska.[12] Locking in LNG infrastructure today commits communities and markets to emissions trajectories that the scientific evidence advises must decline sharply.

The consequence of these actions will be to accelerate the existential problem of climate change. We are no longer debating a future risk; we are already living inside the climate crisis.

Atmospheric carbon dioxide concentrations have now risen above 420 parts per million—higher than at any point in roughly 13 million years—locking in levels of heat that the planet has not experienced since long before human civilization emerged.[13] Global average temperatures have already increased by about 1.2 to 1.3 degrees Celsius above preindustrial levels, pushing Earth dangerously close to thresholds that scientists warn could trigger irreversible "tipping points," from accelerating ice sheet loss and permafrost thaw to forest dieback and disrupted ocean circulation.[14]

These shifts are no longer theoretical: They are beginning to manifest, amplifying one another and increasing the risk of cascading, self-reinforcing damage. The past three years have been the hottest on record, and the rate of change is accelerating. The consequences are showing up in daily life: more intense and prolonged heatwaves; stronger storms and floods; longer wildfire seasons; rising seas; stressed food and water systems; worsening public health impacts; and growing economic and security risks. Each fraction of a degree now matters, because the choices made in this decade will determine whether we stabilize the climate or slide into a far more volatile, dangerous, and unequal world.

## DISMANTLING CLEAN ENERGY AND INDUSTRIAL MOMENTUM

In addition to "unleashing" yesterday's energy system, based on fossil fuels, the Trump administration has moved aggressively to dismantle the policies building tomorrow's plan, based on renewable energy sources. Before 2025, the clean energy sector employed roughly 3.5 million workers, and its growth had outpaced the broader economy.[15] Many of the jobs were in the blue-collar fields Trump had championed as a presidential candidate: electricians, welders, construction crews, manufacturing technicians, engineers, line workers, and small-business contractors across Republican and Democratic states alike. This momentum was abruptly reversed.

Once in office, Trump froze further implementation of the provisions of the IRA. The One Big Beautiful Bill Act, passed in the summer of 2025, further weakened tax credits for renewable energy, grid-scale batteries, electric vehicles and associated charging infrastructure, and energy efficiency measures—triggering a sharp slowdown in project pipelines.[16]

The leadership Trump installed at the Environmental Protection Agency touted "the biggest deregulatory action in U.S. history," with a 31-item "hit list" to dismantle air quality and carbon pollution protections.[17] This was followed in February 2026 by the administration's reversal of the EPA's "endangerment finding" under the Clean Air Act—the legal underpinning for federal climate regulation and the scientific backbone for U.S. climate policy.[18] The administration claimed that the Clean Air Act does not authorize the EPA to regulate greenhouse gases, despite the Supreme Court's clear ruling in the 2007 case *Massachusetts v. EPA* that it does.[19] Trump officials also sought to cast doubt on climate science in general, empowering a panel of "climate deniers" that was later discredited.[20]

Crucially, the administration gutted the economic case for action. It slashed or discarded the social cost of carbon—the government's own metric for quantifying climate damages—and abandoned established methods for valuing mortality risk, effectively removing the cost of human lives from its calculations.

By artificially shrinking the measured benefits of climate regulation, the rollback manufactured uncertainty where the scientific consensus is clear, clearing the way for expanded fossil fuel production while sidelining decades of public health and climate research. Lee Zeldin, the administrator of the EPA, proudly proclaimed that "we are driving a dagger straight into the heart of the climate change religion."[21]

Offshore wind energy production was also targeted, a result of Trump's fixation with its purported dangers (without ever offering any evidence). One of the executive orders issued on January 20 withdrew the entire Outer Continental Shelf from leasing for wind projects.[22] Existing leases and permits were subjected to sweeping reviews. Already-permitted projects and even those under construction faced stop-work orders, litigation risk, and financing uncertainty. The signal to investors was unmistakable: American offshore wind had become politically unsafe.[23]

Trump also undercut U.S. investment in renewable energy onshore. These were not speculative projects; they were factories, grid upgrades, battery plants, and manufacturing hubs planned in communities that had finally begun to see the return of American industrial investment. As a result of the Trump rollback, more than $32 billion in clean energy investments were abandoned and 40,000 jobs were lost.[24]

The competitive context makes this self-inflicted damage even more severe. Globally, the industrial transition to clean energy represents the greatest growth story of the 21st century. In 2025, the International Energy Agency reported $2.2 trillion in clean technology investment globally, compared with $1.1 trillion for oil, gas, and coal combined.[25] More than 90 percent of new power capacity worldwide is now renewable.[26] Since 2010, solar and battery costs have fallen by roughly 90 percent and wind by about 50 percent—structural, permanent reductions.[27] Renewables are now cheaper than fossil fuels, and their costs keep falling. The IEA reported that global clean energy investment last year outpaced fossil fuel investment by a factor of two, and it estimated that the market for clean energy worldwide will grow to $4.5 trillion by 2030—more than double current investment levels.[28]

China understands this. The country already dominates clean energy globally, with 80 percent market share for solar energy projects and 62 percent for EVs in 2025.[29] In 2024, clean technologies accounted for around 10 percent of

China's GDP and more than a quarter of its GDP growth.[30] In the first nine months of 2025, China installed more solar capacity than the United States has built in its entire history. China now dominates EV sales, with two-thirds of global market share. And over the past 12 years, the country has invested more in clean energy in developing nations than the United States spent in total on the Marshall Plan.[31]

Under Trump's policies, China will continue to lead these industries and jobs of the future, as American businesses grow less competitive by relying on increasingly expensive fossil fuels and the stranded assets they represent.

## ATTACKING SCIENCE AND BLINDING THE NATION TO RISK

In 2025, the Trump administration pursued a broad campaign to undermine and muzzle U.S. climate science by cutting capacity, restricting dissemination, and removing sources of trusted public information. These actions made it harder for Americans to access the government's own climate risk information.

The administration has moved to cripple, erase, or bury authoritative federal climate science resources. In late June 2025, legally mandated National Climate Assessments disappeared from official federal websites without replacement links—reducing public access to baseline risk information used by states, insurers, farmers, and emergency managers.[32]

The administration's cuts to the National Science Foundation and to the Department of Energy's climate and clean energy research grants are gutting the university labs and consortia that power U.S. innovation—stalling projects, shedding talent, and eroding America's research leadership. By breaking the funding pipeline that trains the next generation of PhDs, these cuts risk a long-term brain drain as top researchers (and their breakthrough ideas) migrate to better-funded universities abroad.

Trump also defunded the climate research conducted by the National Oceanic and Atmospheric Administration—an explicit attempt to shrink the nation's core climate and weather science pipeline.[33] And in late December 2025, the administration moved to dismantle the National Center for Atmospheric Research, the leading U.S. resource for atmospheric, wildfire, and climate modeling.[34]

In a brazen Orwellian move, the EPA in late 2025 removed all reference to human-caused climate change from its website and emphasized the role of natural phenomena (such as volcanic eruptions)—a discredited trope long employed by climate deniers.[35] But deleting phrases from a website cannot delete the physics of greenhouse gases. Editing a government FAQ section does not lower a family's insurance premiums or make extreme weather events less likely. These acts simply make it harder for science to inform, communities to plan, businesses to price risk honestly, and citizens to hold leaders accountable—exactly when transparency and scientific expertise matter most.

## ABDICATING INTERNATIONAL LEADERSHIP

Climate change is the ultimate collective action problem. If we have any hope of curtailing runaway climate change, nations need to work together. While emissions are local, their impact is global and demands a global response.

By pulling the United States out of the Paris Agreement, Trump showed that for him and his supporters, "America First" means "America Alone."[36] In January 2026, Trump also directed that the United States abrogate the underlying international treaty addressing climate change, the 1992 UN Framework Convention on Climate Change,[37] which had been ratified unanimously by the U.S. Senate and signed into law by President George H. W. Bush, and which every other country in the world has signed. He also directed that the United States withdraw from the Intergovernmental Panel on Climate Change, the preeminent international climate scientific effort, in which the U.S. had played a leading role.[38]

The American retreat from international cooperation and funding—including the bilateral support that the U.S. Agency for International Development (also shuttered by Trump) had provided on climate action[39]—not only hampers the multilateral action needed to address climate change but also emboldens petrostates like Saudi Arabia and Russia to continue their obstruction of climate action.

This damage was compounded by Trump's efforts to use trade and financial pressure to discourage countries from climate action (for example, by blocking the International Maritime Organization's control of shipping emissions), even as the United States was pushing to open more markets for fossil fuel exports.

Trump's withdrawal from international leadership not only damaged the cause but also harmed American soft power and any claim to moral leadership in world affairs. By halting all U.S. funding support for the world's poorest countries to manage climate impacts, Trump further opened the door to China to be the global leader in clean energy and ceded to China the soft power associated with solidarity in the fight against climate change.

## CREATING RISKS TO NATIONAL SECURITY

Trump's insistence on fossil fuel dependence jeopardizes our national security, as does his refusal to acknowledge the geopolitical risks of climate change. His administration's 2025 National Security Strategy explicitly rejects "climate change ideology" as "disastrous."[40]

Yet as Trump's war on Iran has made clear, reliance on fossil fuels increases exposure to volatile regions and supply disruptions, raises the military burden of protecting energy routes, destabilizes energy prices, and weakens the resilience of critical infrastructure—all while strengthening petrostates' geopolitical leverage.

America's defense and intelligence communities have long recognized climate change as a threat multiplier. The instability and displacement fueled by climate change increases the risk that there will be more failed states, driving refugee flows, regional violence, and increased political instability.[41] The migration consequences are already visible. In Central America, climate-fueled drought and crop failure are collapsing livelihoods and driving displacement. Research shows that migration across our southern border rises sharply when agriculture fails.[42] These are not problems that a higher border wall or increased deportations can fix.

Ironically, Trump's war on Iran has triggered further increased global demand for nonfossil energy to reduce economic and geopolitical risk. The Trump administration's policies, however, ensure that America risks falling behind its rivals in meeting these demands and further imperiling itself.

## JEOPARDIZING PUBLIC HEALTH, ESPECIALLY AMONG THE MOST VULNERABLE

Rolling back climate and clean air protections increases exposure to particulates, ozone, and toxic pollutants—driving asthma attacks, cardiovascular disease, hospitalizations, and premature deaths. The EPA's own analyses of Trump's repealed or weakened standards projected additional deaths and illnesses in the United States from higher soot and smog exposure[43]—until January 2026, when the agency removed all consideration of public health from its regulatory analyses.[44] (The EPA's statutory mandate, of course, is to protect public health from environmental damage.)

These harms are not evenly distributed. Those who have done the least to cause this problem bear the greatest impacts. Low-income communities and communities of color, already facing cumulative environmental burdens, absorb the greatest increase in risk when air quality enforcement weakens and safeguards are rolled back. Climate impacts compound the public health damage. Extreme heat, wildfire smoke, floods, and storms drive spikes in emergency room visits, lost workdays, and mental health strain—costs borne most heavily by those with the fewest resources to cope.

## RAISING THE COST OF LIVING: THE CLIMATE TAX

Climate change increasingly functions as a hidden tax on households. Polls show that 65 percent of Americans believe that climate change is already affecting their cost of living.[45]

Household insurance is the clearest signal. Premiums rise, deductibles increase, coverage shrinks, and families have to make last-resort plans—or are forced to move out of high-risk communities altogether. Reinsurance markets are tightening as catastrophic losses mount, accelerating further premium hikes. The Federal Reserve has warned that reduced insurability could threaten the viability of parts of the U.S. housing market, as lenders won't lend without insurance.[46]

Disasters also destroy wealth directly. Families and communities are often trapped in a loop of repair-rebuild-repair that drains savings, erodes local tax bases, and widens inequality. The administration's efforts to defund and dismantle the Federal Emergency Management Agency has only served to exacerbate the cost to American families and communities affected by increasingly frequent climate-driven disasters.

Climate change is already raising the cost of food in the United States—and consumers feel it at the checkout.[47] Extreme weather in 2024 caused an estimated $20 billion in U.S. crop losses alone.[48] Climate impacts abroad also hit American budgets: Warmer, less predictable conditions are squeezing coffee and cocoa production, contributing to price spikes.[49]

★ ★ ★

*The second Trump administration sold its agenda as pro-growth. In reality, it privatizes gains and socializes losses: deregulation and subsidies for fossil fuel companies and cronies; higher disaster and health costs for the public; and a weaker competitive position for the nation.*

*That is not conservatism. It is dereliction.*

*The choice before America is not climate action versus prosperity. That framing is outdated and demonstrably false.*

*The real choice is whether the United States leads the world's largest investment cycle in clean power, grids, storage, buildings, transport, agriculture, and industry—or whether we watch others build that infrastructure and sell it back to us.*[50]

*We can keep paying climate invoices in disasters, displacement, and rising costs. Or we can invest in solutions that are already cheaper, faster, and more secure.*

*This is the defining growth story and moral imperative of the 21st century. The only remaining question is whether the United States insists on being written out of it.*

# 8

# LAWLESS IMMIGRATION ENFORCEMENT

**During his 2024 presidential campaign, Donald Trump pledged to control the influx of migrants at the southern border and to deport criminal immigrants—the "worst of the worst," he called them. While the Trump administration has successfully reduced border crossings to a record low,[1] it has also gone far beyond this limited mandate of border security. Rather, the administration's obsession with reducing legal and illegal immigration has led to the neglect of the country's safety and security, the bulldozing of the rule of law, and damage to the economy.**

★ ★ ★

## JEOPARDIZING AMERICANS' SAFETY

Over the past year, the Trump administration has pursued indiscriminate, race-driven immigration enforcement policies that have led to panic in American communities, violence on American streets, and the arbitrary detention of legal and undocumented immigrants, as well as U.S. citizens.

Since Donald Trump's inauguration in January 2025, detainees and protesters have faced more danger from their own government than at any time in modern history. Indeed, immigration agents have shot or killed 16 people during Trump's second term,[2] including three U.S. citizens.[3] More people died in the custody of Immigration and Customs Enforcement in 2025—a total of 32—than in the preceding 20 years.[4] These numbers are only likely to grow as the Trump administration pursues its extreme and arbitrary goals for detention and deportation.

Millions of people in America, including U.S. citizens, now live in daily fear of detention by masked and armed immigration agents. Trump's arbitrary quotas of 3,000 arrests per day and 1 million deportations per year[5]—figures that far exceed the number of noncitizen criminals in the U.S.[6]—mean that thousands of innocents are getting caught in ICE's dragnet. More than 70 percent[7] of the people who were detained in immigration operations from February through October 2025 had not been convicted of a crime, and of those with convictions, only 7 percent had been convicted of a violent offense.[8] Many of these detainees have faced violence at the hands of ICE agents; they have been beaten, tear-gassed, and shot.

The rise in unnecessary deaths and injuries is a natural outgrowth of the administration's rush to rapidly expand the number of ICE agents and deploy them with inadequate training, coupled with a purging of those in leadership. In January 2026, ICE announced that it had hired 12,000 new officers, agents, and legal staff in about four months—the fastest law enforcement agency expansion ever[9]—while firing or demoting approximately 80 percent of the agency's career field leadership.[10] Despite concerns over the qualifications, aptitude, and physical fitness of these hires (which more than doubled ICE's officer staff), the administration reduced the length of the agency's training course from about five months to just 42 days.[11] The surge in recruits threatened to overwhelm ICE's training centers.

Cutting corners on training exacerbates the growing problems that inevitably arise when undertrained, armed immigration agents face challenging situations where expertise in the use of force and in deescalation techniques are essential. One whistleblower, a former ICE lawyer who conducted training for new recruits, described "widespread concern" among trainers that the new recruits did not have a "solid grasp" on the tactics or the law required for their jobs, even at the end of their training. "ICE is teaching cadets to violate the Constitution," the whistleblower said.[12]

In addition to the risk of brutal treatment at the hands of ICE agents, detainees potentially face further danger at detention facilities that are inadequately staffed and maintained. In what one commentator called the hurried development of the "deportation-industrial complex," the safety and well-being of detainees has seemed to be low on the priority list.[13] At one of the Department of Homeland Security's tent camps in El Paso, Texas, inspectors found 60 different violations in September 2025.[14] ICE facilities are also detaining an average of 175 children a day, according to *The New York Times*, often in subpar conditions. Families of children in detention have described "inadequate medical care, lights kept on all night, scant drinking water and little education."

Despite the promise of rounding up criminals, the Trump administration's immigration policies have made our communities less safe. The actions of ICE and the Customs and Border Patrol have made it harder for local police departments to do their work, as Trump's policies have created a strong disincentive for any immigrant to cooperate with law enforcement. As ICE and the CBP increase the number of people who are being chosen for "expedited removal," they are targeting people who are in the country legally and fulfilling their legal obligations to appear at what used to be routine immigration appointments. As a result, people are avoiding any interaction with law enforcement personnel, including those who can make our communities safer.[15]

Further, the single-minded focus on meeting arbitrary metrics has led to the sacrifice of other national security priorities.[16] Within the CBP and ICE, agents have been diverted from cases involving drugs, child exploitation, and human trafficking. Other agencies have also redirected resources from their core missions to immigration enforcement, such as the Drug Enforcement Administration; the Bureau of Alcohol, Tobacco and Firearms; the FBI; and the U.S. Marshals Service. These agencies are supposed to help keep Americans safe from guns, drugs, terrorism, and violent crime, but their missions have been compromised.[17]

## FLOUTING THE RULE OF LAW

The Trump administration has repeatedly violated court orders, existing law, and the Constitution, prompting one federal judge to threaten ICE with criminal sanctions.[18] In direct violation of a court order, it deported Kilmar Abrego Garcia, a migrant from El Salvador who was in the United States legally. It detained Rumeysa Ozturk, a Turkish student at Tufts University, for 45 days after she published a pro-Palestine op-ed in her university newspaper. It used five-year-old Liam Ramos as bait to lure his father, a legal asylum seeker from Ecuador, out of his house before detaining him a thousand miles from his Minnesota home. In February 2026, Patrick Schiltz, a federal judge in Minnesota (appointed by President George W. Bush), identified approximately 200 court orders from the District of Minnesota alone that ICE had violated just since the start of the year.[19] Schiltz commented that ICE had "likely violated more court orders in January 2026 than some federal agencies have violated in their entire existence."[20]

The administration's disdain for the law has been tacitly approved by Congress, which appropriated an unprecedented $170 billion in the One Big Beautiful Bill Act (OBBBA) for immigration enforcement and detention, including $45 billion for expanding civil immigration detention, without any meaningful oversight.[21] Additionally, the administration has opposed efforts to hold ICE accountable for the way it spends the appropriated funds. The agency has fired inspectors general, dismantled congressionally created watchdog agencies, and blocked efforts to investigate the killing of Renee Good, a U.S. citizen who was fatally shot in her car by ICE agents in Minneapolis in January 2026.

The consequences of this oversight failure have been devastating to the rule of law. One egregious example is ICE's revised stance, expressed in a May 2025 memo from its director, Todd Lyons, that an administrative warrant—signed not by a judge but by an ICE official—is sufficient to forcibly enter a private home. This position contradicts centuries of Supreme Court precedent under the Fourth Amendment, which prohibits the entry into a private home without a warrant signed by a judge and following a demonstration of probable cause. Nevertheless, new ICE hires are being told to follow ICE's memo instead of its own written training materials, which contradict it. The new policy has already been used in Minnesota, where ICE officers have used battering rams and rifles to forcibly enter homes.[22]

The administration has also drastically curtailed the discretion of immigration judges to release immigrants who do not pose public safety or flight risks while they are waiting for their hearings. As a result of this change, discretionary releases fell by 87 percent from January through November 2025. This is a pressure tactic the Trump administration is using to persuade immigrants to self-deport.[23] For those who decide to stay and fight their detention, courts have largely ruled in their favor. Deluged with thousands of habeas corpus petitions from immigrant detainees challenging their detention, courts have ruled in more than 3,000 cases that these detentions were illegal (compared to just over 100 cases in which judges sided with the administration's mass deportation strategy).[24]

The Trump administration's list of legal violations is long and includes expediting deportations without due process by invoking the Alien Enemies Act; seeking to end birthright citizenship, in contradiction of the plain language of the Fourteenth Amendment; canceling student visas over disfavored speech; rushing to deport people to a notorious prison in El Salvador or to third countries where immigrants have no ties and where due process rights may be impossible to enforce; arresting individuals whom immigration agents happen to come across, even if they have no warrant at the time; sending National Guard troops to U.S. cities in violation of the Posse Comitatus Act;[25] and incorrectly instructing ICE agents that they have "absolute immunity" in the performance of their duties.[26] Most of these actions have been struck down by courts or await rulings on their legality.

After ordering the release of Liam Ramos and his father, who were detained despite having pending asylum cases, U.S. District Judge Fred Biery blasted the federal government's disregard of the law in "pursuit of daily deportation quotas." He wrote, "Observing human behavior confirms that for some among us, a perfidious lust for unbridled power and the imposition of cruelty in its quest know no bounds and are bereft of human decency. And the rule of law be damned."[27]

## TARGETING LEGAL IMMIGRANTS

The administration has also pulled the rug out from under hundreds of thousands of immigrants who are in the country legally, throwing due process out the window. For instance, the administration has dramatically expanded the use of "expedited removal," a policy that allows ICE and the CBP to rapidly deport certain noncitizens without a hearing.[28] With no access to courts, those subject to expedited removal have little protection from being permanently removed from the country even if they are entitled to a court hearing. Under this policy, many people have been wrongfully deported, including asylum seekers fleeing persecution and longtime U.S. residents who are integrated in their communities.[29]

The administration has also prohibited new refugee admissions (with the exception of white South Africans) and has begun reviewing thousands of cases of people who have already been admitted.[30] These refugees have typically undergone extensive vetting before being permitted to enter the country. Other measures include revoking or seeking to revoke Temporary Protected Status for more than 1 million immigrants from countries where civil war, natural disasters, or other extraordinary and temporary conditions make living conditions unsafe.[31] The administration's actions suggest that its attempts to terminate TPS status are not based on a review of conditions in the countries impacted, leading several federal judges to block these actions. A judge reviewing TPS status for Haitians found that the administration's termination decision was "arbitrary and capricious" and violated the Administrative Procedures Act by failing to fully consider dangerous conditions in Haiti.[32]

Finally, the administration is seeking to circumvent and neuter the immigration court system. The administration fired or laid off more than 100 immigration judges—many of whom have backgrounds in immigration legal defense—despite a backlog of almost 4 million cases.[33] While the OBBBA increased funding for immigration detention centers by 400 percent, it increased the number of immigration judges by just 14 percent.[34] This disparity in funding strongly suggests that the administration's plan is to detain and deport immigrants regardless of their right to a hearing. The administration is also moving to limit any channels for legal relief; most recently, the administration has taken steps to reduce the period for an immigrant to challenge a deportation order by an immigration judge from 30 days to 10.[35]

## DAMAGING ECONOMIC GROWTH AND WORSENING INFLATION

The Trump administration's immigration policies have shocked the U.S. economy by effectively threatening or terminating work authorization for 1.5 million individuals who are in the country legally.[36] These are individuals with TPS, individuals seeking admission to the United States who lawfully entered during the Biden administration through humanitarian programs, and asylum seekers. Many of these individuals work in essential fields such as agriculture and construction, and their detention has forced farmers and builders to spend more money on labor, reducing productivity. One consequence is that food producer prices are expected to rise 14.5 percent and construction prices 6.1 percent by 2028. Indeed, without factoring in the impact of other economic policies (such as higher tariffs), these actions will force U.S. families to pay an additional $2,150 per year for goods and services by 2028. Since working-class

Americans spend most of their income on food and housing, the impact of these policies will hit them the hardest.[37]

Moreover, Trump's reversal of ICE's policy of targeted immigration arrests in favor of roving patrols and raids at locations where immigrants might congregate has caused panic in Minneapolis, Chicago, and elsewhere, harming small businesses disproportionately. Following the onset of ICE raids in Milwaukee, local companies saw business shrink by more than 50 percent.[38] In Minneapolis, the estimated cost of Operation Metro Surge was $20 million per week; a survey of employers there revealed that 80 percent had experienced canceled, postponed, or reduced sales.[39]

The consequences of this administration's immigration policies will also negatively impact longer-term growth by limiting the available workforce. Like many other advanced economies, the United States faces challenges arising from an aging population and slow natural growth. Robust immigration has allowed the U.S. to continue growing and increase its productivity, unlike many other rich countries. This is critical because there simply are not enough U.S.-born workers to replace the immigrants needed to fuel national economic growth. Yet the administration's policies are expected to result in a drastic contraction of the labor market by reducing the number of worker years by approximately 19 million from 2025 to 2028 and by 102 million from 2025 to 2035.[40] This in turn would lead to a reduction in GDP by $1.9 trillion from 2025 to 2028 and by $12.1 trillion from 2025 to 2035.[41]

Another sector of the economy where many immigrants are losing work authorization and facing deportation is health care. With the proposed termination of TPS status for immigrants from certain countries, such as Haiti, the health care industry could lose more than 50,000 health care workers, many of whom work in hard-to-fill positions.[42] A less recognized problem may also arise from the Trump administration's arbitrary new $100,000 fee for an H-1B visa, which is likely to result in fewer foreign physicians coming to the United States, causing an acute doctor shortage that will leave American patients with fewer, or no, care options.[43] The employment of foreign physicians in medically underserved areas is a critical tool to address chronic physician shortages, particularly when the health care industry is forecast to face a shortfall of more than 124,000 doctors by 2034.[44] The problem will be particularly acute in rural areas and smaller towns.

Finally, another urgent issue is a series of country-specific restrictions that the administration has imposed on individuals legally immigrating to the U.S. As of March 13, 2026, these restrictions affect citizens of 75 countries (more than a third of the world) by preventing the issuance of green cards to individuals abroad. Another series of presidential proclamations have restricted the entry of nationals of 40 countries in full or in part on any type of visa. Arbitrary and racially motivated, these restrictions accelerate economic and public health damage to the country. Citizens of many of the affected countries are doctors and medical professionals willing to work in medically underserved areas in the United States.

## TURNING AWAY GLOBAL TALENT, TO AMERICA'S DETRIMENT

By enacting arbitrary barriers and undermining the rule of law in the immigration system, the Trump administration's actions are deeply harming American competitiveness.

As mentioned in the previous section, in September 2025 President Trump issued a proclamation imposing a $100,000 fee on new H-1B petitions without following normal regulatory channels or authorization by Congress. This new fee provoked immediate panic for hundreds of thousands of existing H-1B workers and their employers, and it will affect decisions by American employers needing to hire highly skilled foreign talent. This proclamation is the subject of three separate lawsuits, including one by the U.S. Chamber of Commerce, challenging the president's authority to impose such a fee. This exorbitant cost undermines the goals of a program that was established by statute three decades ago and has been a key tool for American employers to hire highly skilled workers.[45] It is also an example of the president ignoring Congress and the public, ruling by fiat instead. The new fee is predicted to prompt more U.S. employers to send jobs overseas to Canada or India, resulting in broader job losses in the United States.[46]

Similarly, the Trump administration has implemented significant changes to the selection process for H-1B visas in the annual "lottery,"[47] making it more difficult for international students working in entry-level roles with U.S. companies to be selected and approved for such visas. In the long run, this will reduce the number of international students enrolling at American universities, reducing the innovation pipeline.[48]

Also raising costs for U.S. employers is the administration's new rule ending the practice of automatically extending the validity of employment authorization documents for individuals in certain categories. Individuals eligible for the automatic work authorization extension have legal status, have been vetted, and have often been in the United States for many years or decades.[49] The automatic extension, which had been implemented because of significant bureaucratic processing times, saved U.S. businesses $3.5 billion in labor turnover costs. Revoking the automatic extension process harms U.S. businesses by disrupting business operations and requiring employers to terminate the employment of skilled workers.[50]

The administration has taken many other steps discouraging employers from hiring foreign workers. American businesses in cutting-edge industries, such as quantum computing, are finding that talented foreign workers are apprehensive about coming to the United States on work visas because of political instability and concern about immigration policy. This all redounds to the benefit of America's competitors.[51] In light of the self-inflicted harm these policies are causing to the U.S. economy, the administration's opposition to virtually any form of immigration to the United States smacks of xenophobia as the true driver of these policies.

★ ★ ★

*The Trump administration's immigration policy and the lack of any meaningful accountability have resulted in wide-ranging damage to our economy, our safety, and our democracy. The targeting of Democratic-run cities (where Trump's perceived political enemies are), rather than those with the highest concentrations of unauthorized immigrants, calls into question the administration's true motives in both its brutal tactics and its haste to deport. The visible crackdown on all forms of immigration is rapidly undermining one of America's greatest strengths—the ability to attract the best and brightest to this country. Most immediately, we need immediate checks and balances on this administration's exercise of the authority it possesses under the Constitution to faithfully exercise the law.*

# 9

# THE SUPPRESSION OF FREE SPEECH

**President Donald Trump has undertaken the harshest and most systematic assault on the First Amendment since its words were crafted by James Madison and enshrined in the U.S. Constitution. With his relentless intimidation of the media and his efforts to silence his critics, Trump is attempting to destroy a fundamental pillar of America's democracy: freedom of speech.**

★ ★ ★

The First Amendment stands at the heart of our democracy and provides the foundation of our freedom: the right to speak, to protest, to express ourselves, and, crucially, to criticize our government.

During his presidency, Thomas Jefferson was often enraged by the opposition Federalist newspapers. But as a champion of democracy, he said that if he had to choose, he would prefer to live in a society of "newspapers without a government, rather than a government without newspapers." As he observed in 1787, "Our liberty depends on freedom of the press, and that cannot be limited without being lost."[1]

Historically, clashes between presidents and the press have been an inevitable part of the rough-and-tumble of American politics. John F. Kennedy canceled his subscription to the *New York Herald Tribune* because he was outraged by a story it published. Richard Nixon went much further in trying to put pressure on *The Washington Post* and *The New York Times*, first by attempting to block the publication of the Pentagon Papers and then by threatening the broadcast license of television stations owned by Katharine Graham, the publisher of the *Post*, hoping to curb the paper's coverage of Watergate.[2] During the Civil War, even Abraham Lincoln, generally believed to be our greatest president, imposed draconian restrictions on the press.

Yet no American president has compared to Donald Trump in the scope of efforts to stifle negative press coverage and to silence critics, whether they be U.S. senators or ordinary citizens. He has stonewalled the press in its requests for information, filed frivolous lawsuits, attacked his enemies on social media, and used the machinery of his administration to punish critics.

In many ways, this assault on the press and free expression is unsurprising. No one understands the power of the media better than Trump, who courted the press in order to burnish his reputation as a businessman and, later, to propel himself to the White House. He pioneered the technique of "governing by tweet" and has reveled in his ability to shake global markets with a single post. He is addicted to Fox News and has named some of the network's former hosts to cabinet posts, such as Secretary of Defense Pete Hegseth. This understanding of the press's power is precisely why he seeks to control it and to punish his detractors. He seeks nothing less than to complete his domination of Americans' lives, their thoughts, and their speech.

## SYSTEMATICALLY ATTACKING AND INTIMIDATING THE PRESS

To some degree, Trump's assault on the mainstream press since returning to office in January 2025 is nothing new. Back in 2017, on the first day of his first term, Trump told an audience, "I have a running war with the media."[3] In *The Divider*, their book on Trump's first term, Peter Baker and Susan Glasser described

> *the rapidly expanding war on the media that would become a hallmark of [Trump's] tenure … For a man who needed enemies, the mainstream media proved a convenient foil … The goal was to neutralize one of the major independent power centers in Washington, with Trump in effect telling supporters to trust no one but him and his "alternative facts."*[4]

In an off-camera moment, Lesley Stahl of CBS News asked Trump about his media bashing: "Why are you doing this?"

"You know why I do it," Trump replied. "I do it to discredit you all and demean you all so that when you write negative stories about me, no one will believe you."[5]

Since Trump returned to the White House, after a remarkable political comeback, his assault on the press has been more far-reaching and ominous than in his first term. Within weeks, Trump ordered the Associated Press to be excluded from the pool of journalists who cover the president and all the events and travel he undertakes because the AP refused to use his preferred term "Gulf of America" for the Gulf of Mexico.[6] Instead, Trump's media team has given access to the White House to cable, online, and streaming platforms that are friendly to and supportive of the president, such as Turning Point USA, Newsmax, and RedState.[7]

In October 2025, Secretary Hegseth promulgated unprecedented new rules requiring journalists who cover the Pentagon to sign a 21-page form promising to report only authorized information. Hegseth's objective was to remove mainstream, legacy media from the Pentagon in order to constrain their ability to talk with sources and report the news. More than 40 reporters, including those from the AP, CNN, and *The Washington Post*, refused to sign and lost their credentials. They were replaced by representatives of smaller outlets more supportive of Trump.[8] In March 2026, U.S. District Judge Paul Friedman ruled, in a lawsuit brought by *The New York Times*, that the Hegseth policies violated journalists' First and Fifth Amendment rights to freedom of the press and due process. But in a vindictive act in response, the Pentagon again denied access to reporters who do not comply with new restrictive reporting rules (which have prompted new legal challenges). Hegseth also issued an order barring photographers from press briefings because of his displeasure with "unflattering" photos of himself that had been published in the press.

Trump has consistently singled out for criticism specific journalists he dislikes. He told Jonathan Karl of ABC, "We'll probably go after people like you, because you treat me unfairly."[9] He regularly bullies female journalists. Trump called ABC's Rachel Scott "the most obnoxious reporter" in the White House. He attacked Kaitlin Collins of CNN of being "always stupid and nasty" and "not smiling."[10] He has admonished several Black female journalists. Trump continues to attack *The New York Times.* A typical Truth Social post of his reads: "Their Radical Left, Unhinged Behavior, writing FAKE Articles and Opinions, in a never-ending way must be dealt with and stopped. They are a true ENEMY OF THE PEOPLE."[11] Speaking about CNN, Trump said, "The people that are running that company right now and running CNN, which is a very dishonest group of people, I don't think that should be allowed to continue."[12]

In March, Trump initiated a new round of intimidation of the media, posting a graphic titled "President Trump Is Reshaping the Media," which highlighted the ouster of several named journalists from their networks, the defunding of public broadcasting, "reforms" skewed to favor Trump and coverage of the president, and claims about how he is "winning."[13]

Unmistakably, Trump is determined to silence journalists and media companies that are not aligned with his presidency.

## BULLYING OUTLETS WITH LITIGATION

In his business career, Trump used relentless litigation as a tool to batter and wear down his opponents to accomplish his objectives. As president, Trump continues to rely on litigation as a tool of choice. He has launched the most intensive legal assault ever waged in American history against the press and media, simply because he dislikes some of the coverage he gets.

Trump sued ABC News for defamation in its characterization of a sexual assault for which Trump had been found liable by a court in New York.[14] He sued CBS News for "deceitful" editing of a *60 Minutes* interview with his 2024 opponent, Kamala Harris. Both networks settled, even though they had extraordinarily strong cases under the First Amendment and defamation law. ABC agreed to pay $15 million to Trump's presidential library; CBS paid $16 million.[15] CBS's parent company, Paramount, was seeking regulatory approval to complete its multibillion-dollar merger with Skydance, approval that came swiftly once the settlement was reached. Months later, CBS News, whose proud journalistic history goes back to Edward R. Murrow, bowed to Trump's demands for ideologically supportive coverage by hiring the conservative blogger Bari Weiss as its editor in chief.[16]

Trump has also sued *The New York Times* for $15 billion, claiming that the *Times* defamed him repeatedly, unfairly thrashed his record as a businessman, and published "with malice" articles that were intended to inflict "maximal electoral damage" to bring about his defeat for the presidency.[17] Trump even sued *The Wall Street Journal*—owned by Rupert Murdoch, whose support of Trump played a crucial role in his political success—for $10 billion for its reporting of Trump's contribution to a volume of birthday greetings for the notorious financier and sex offender Jeffrey Epstein.[18] More predictably, Trump is also suing CNN and *The Washington Post*.[19] His goal, as always, is that these major media companies will determine that submitting to Trump's demands is preferable to resisting them.

## COMMANDEERING REGULATORY AGENCIES

Not satisfied with having the largest platform in the world and the ability to use government lawyers to bring frivolous litigation on his behalf, Trump has channeled the enormous regulatory powers of the federal government to favor his supporters and punish his opponents. Over the course of his presidencies, Trump has threatened on dozens of occasions to have broadcast licenses revoked because of reporting and coverage he finds unfavorable.[20]

In the wake of the assassination of Charlie Kirk in September 2025, the ABC late-night host Jimmy Kimmel was taken off the air by his network for his comments. Brendan Carr, the chair of the Federal Communications Commission, threatened ABC affiliate stations with the prospect that their licenses could be revoked. "We can do this the easy way or the hard way," he threatened.[21] Carr is poised to execute Trump's will toward hostile media and take further regulatory action against broadcasters that air strong anti-Trump views.

Trump is quite open about inserting himself into the work of federal regulatory agencies. After the FCC approved the acquisition of Paramount, which owns CBS, by Skydance, a company controlled by the Ellison family (staunch supporters of Donald Trump), the merged company, Paramount Skydance, then sought to acquire Warner Brothers Discovery, which owns CNN.[22] The politics emanating from the White House made clear that Trump wanted CNN in friendly hands and was opposed to a competing bid by Netflix. With the future of CNN in play, Trump said, "I'll be involved in that decision."[23] No previous president has sought to be so directly entangled in determining who gets to own the most prominent media companies in the country.

In the spring of 2026, the FCC appeared to be on the verge of final approval of the consolidation of two of the largest owners of local television stations, Nexstar Media Group and TEGNA, Inc. The merged company would own somewhere between 60 percent and 80 percent of the local television stations in the country, clearly violating federal law, which prohibits any company from owning more than 39 percent of stations nationally.[24] The law, enacted in 2004, was intended to preserve the vitality of local television stations reporting on their communities. The merger would, in the words of Senator Michael Bennet and Representative Joe Neguse from Colorado, "replace diverse community-based reporting with centralized produced content."[25] This prospect apparently pleases Trump, who declared on social media, "We need more competition against THE ENEMY, the Fake News National TV networks ... GET THAT DEAL DONE." At the FCC, Carr dutifully expressed his support for the merger. He is reportedly preparing to issue waivers that would avoid the clear requirements of federal law.

In March 2026, at the end of the second week of Trump's war with Iran, Carr threatened to revoke the licenses of certain television stations because of their coverage of the conflict. Carr accused them of "running hoaxes and news distortions" and said "the fake news ... have a chance now to correct course." He added, "Broadcasters must operate in the public interest, and they will lose their licenses if they do not."[26] Such a threat is unprecedented since the regulation of the airwaves was established by Congress in 1934.

Reflecting on these pro-Trump political and commercial forces that have been unleashed, Norman Ornstein, scholar emeritus at the American Enterprise Institute warned:

> *We are dangerously close to having the vast majority of audiences out there getting information solely or largely from sources either directly manipulating the content or making sure to downplay or ignore anything Trump does not like or want. If we continue to devolve in this way, we will look more like the countries of Russia, Hungary, and China than our own constitutional democracy. Any hope of having the pillar of a free press to provide a meaningful guardrail against incipient authoritarianism will disappear before our very eyes.*[27]

## DEFUNDING PUBLIC MEDIA

In 1967, Congress established and funded the Corporation for Public Broadcasting, to bring to life public television and radio across America. Money from the CPB supports the stations. The stations contract with PBS and NPR to help produce the programming they air, from *PBS NewsHour*, *Frontline*, and *Sesame Street* on PBS to *Morning Edition* and *All Things Considered* on NPR—and much more.

For nearly 60 years, public television and radio have made a profound contribution to American life. Public broadcasting has been an essential service, reaching 99 percent of the households in the United States and bringing important quality programming to every family regardless of their economic status, at the cost of $1.60 per taxpayer annually.[28] The children's programming on PBS is rightfully legendary for its quality and its positive impact. And public broadcasting, reflecting the interests of different communities, has made possible a diversity of programming and views that would not be aired by commercial television and radio.

President Trump has targeted the funding of public broadcasting since returning to office. His purpose, stated clearly in a May 2025 executive order, was to end government funding for public media because of alleged bias. "At the very least, Americans have the right to expect that if their tax dollars fund public broadcasting at all, they fund only fair, accurate, unbiased, and nonpartisan news coverage … The CPB fails to abide by these principles to the extent it subsidizes NPR and PBS," Trump wrote on Truth Social. "Republicans must defund and totally disassociate themselves from NPR and PBS, the radical left monsters that so badly hurt our country."[29]

President Ronald Reagan, in his first budget, attempted to slash funding for public broadcasting. He failed, thanks to support for public TV and radio from Republicans in the House and Senate, especially from rural states that value public broadcasting. This year, Trump succeeded where Reagan failed. The CPB has been shuttered, and dozens of public TV and radio stations are in danger of closing down.

## HARASSING AND INTIMIDATING PROTESTERS AND POLITICAL OPPONENTS

Trump's assault on the First Amendment goes beyond his concerted attacks on the press and media figures. Increasingly, Trump and his senior officials have resorted to a range of actions to curb the free speech and political activities of those who oppose their policies. Trump has ordered the investigation and prosecution of several of his most prominent political opponents, including Senator Adam Schiff, former FBI Director James Comey, and New York Attorney General Letitia James.[30] Shockingly, he called for the execution of Senators Mark Kelly and Elissa Slotkin, and several House members, because of a video they made in which they addressed military personnel, stating, correctly, that they did not have to follow illegal orders.[31]

The most explosive flashpoint has been the Trump administration's brutal tactics to find, detain, arrest, and deport immigrants across the country. Clashes between Immigration and Customs Enforcement and demonstrators have been severe, particularly in Minneapolis, a city rocked by weeks of occupation by ICE agents, which included the killing of two American citizens who were protesting immigration raids in their city.[32] Press reports show that ICE used intensive surveillance tactics, including facial recognition technology, to follow and intimidate protesters in the streets and telling them that ICE is tracking their activities and knows where they live. The administration has also pressured social media companies to identify anti-ICE organizations and protesters and to provide data on individuals whose protests come to their attention.[33] A March 2026 investigation by *The Wall Street Journal* found that 181 American citizens have been accused online of "assaulting" federal officers and ICE agents—even when this is contradicted by video evidence. Though none of these citizens have been convicted, according to the *Journal*, and many of them were not even charged, the purpose of this strategy is clear: to harass and intimidate Americans who dare to speak out.

★ ★ ★

*Periodically, particularly in stressful times, our government has gone overboard in trying to curb dissent. We experienced such government actions during World War I, when the Woodrow Wilson administration orchestrated raids led by Attorney General A. Mitchell Palmer against antiwar protestors, labor unionists, and African Americans. We experienced it again in the 1950s, when the rhetoric and actions of Senator Joseph McCarthy created a climate of fear in Washington and around the country, by targeting the people he believed to be subversive communist elements. And we know of the shameful record of FBI Director J. Edgar Hoover in his pursuit of Reverend Martin Luther King and the compilation of files on thousands of people protesting the Vietnam War. America has come through other difficult periods, but we have never faced a concerted assault on our freedoms led by a president and his administration, using a new generation of technology surveillance capabilities.*

*Most Americans cherish their First Amendment right to speak, assemble, and protest. They also have an instinctive sense of when the government is overreaching. As Justice Louis Brandeis memorably wrote in his 1928 dissent in* Olmstead v. United States,

> The makers of the Constitution undertook to secure conditions favorable to the pursuit of happiness. They sought to protect Americans in their beliefs, their thoughts, their emotions, and their sensations. They conferred, as against the government, the right to be left alone—the most comprehensive of rights and the right most valued by civilized men (and women).[34]

*Donald Trump's unprecedented attempt to dominate every sphere of American life is fundamentally inconsistent with our desire for a government that confines itself to the functions that the Constitution specifies for it.*

# 10

## FREE AND FAIR ELECTIONS IN JEOPARDY

**Donald Trump has worked relentlessly to undermine public confidence in our elections. He has clung to false claims of fraud and attacked the integrity of state election processes. He has advanced legislation and issued executive orders that could disenfranchise millions; he has attempted to limit mail-in voting, which all evidence says is reliable and secure; and he has promoted other voter suppression efforts. He has demanded the gerrymandering of congressional districts to preserve his party's majority. Especially troubling are his efforts to seize control of elections from the states, in direct contravention of the Constitution. Trump has waged a frontal attack on the foundation of American democracy: the right to vote. His success would mark the collapse of the first line of defense in a march toward authoritarianism.**

★ ★ ★

Nothing is more fundamental to our democracy than the right to vote. The expansion and protection of that right has been an essential part of the American experiment. Under the Fifteenth, Nineteenth, and Twenty-sixth Amendments to the U.S. Constitution, all citizens over the age of 18 enjoy the right to suffrage, regardless of race or sex. The Voting Rights Act of 1965 bans discriminatory practices, like literacy tests, that were designed to deny U.S. citizens their vote.[1]

U.S. elections are not only free and fair but also secure. Government watchdogs called the 2020 presidential election "the most secure in American history," and even Donald Trump's staunchest allies have been unable to document widespread fraud.[2] The Heritage Foundation's "Election Fraud Map" notes just 138 cases nationwide between 2017 and 2025—many of them involving Republicans.[3] In one such instance from 2024, a top Republican Party official in Georgia, who had promoted Trump's claims of fraud, was himself fined $5,000 for voting illegally nine times.[4] Of the roughly 60 lawsuits challenging the 2020 results, not one was found to have merit, according to the Campaign Legal Center.[5]

Nevertheless, Trump has done his best to destroy both public trust in the U.S. election system and its integrity. Americans' most cherished right—the right to vote—is now at risk.

## ERODING PUBLIC FAITH IN ELECTIONS

Donald Trump's lies about election fraud and a "stolen" 2020 election were central to his 2024 presidential campaign and continue to animate his presidency. One analysis catalogued more than 500 instances of such false claims in just the first half of 2024.[6] Trump's rallies, social media posts, and interviews with the press featured a constant barrage of untruths about his political opponents "rigging," "cheating," or "stealing" votes. In recent months, his election lies have focused on noncitizen voting—a phenomenon that the conservative Cato Institute calls "virtually nonexistent."[7]

The relentlessness of these accusations, false as they are, has had a corrosive effect on the American public. Just 60 percent of voters "are confident votes will be counted accurately" in the 2026 midterm elections, according to a January 2026 survey by the University of California San Diego's Center for Transparent and Trusted Elections. That figure had stood at 77 percent in 2024. Nearly 40 percent of voters expect to see agents from Immigration and Customs Enforcement at the polls, and significant shares of voters say they worry about being questioned when they show up to vote, despite their U.S. citizenship. Hispanic voters are especially concerned; 31 percent say they're worried about Election Day confrontations with ICE.[8]

Worse yet, a significant number of U.S. voters are persuaded by Trump's false claims. A March 2026 poll by NPR/Marist found that 57 percent of Republicans believe that the number one threat to elections is fraud.[9] An astonishing 82 percent of Republicans are "not confident" that Joe Biden was the legitimate winner of the 2020 election, according to a November 2025 survey by Public Agenda and the SNF Agora Institute at Johns Hopkins University.[10] Overall, just 62 percent of Americans believe that the 2020 election was fair, according to polling by *The Washington Post* and the University of Maryland.[11]

It's hard to overstate the pernicious impact of a loss of public faith in the vote. At best, it generates apathy, if Americans don't believe their votes matter. This creates an opportunity for a minority of motivated partisans to impose their will on the broader citizenry. Declining trust in elections also leads to declining trust in leaders who the voters don't believe to have been fairly elected. That distrust can be harnessed into insurrection, as Trump well knows. On January 6, 2021, pro-Trump rioters invaded the U.S. Capitol to stop the certification of Joe Biden's victory. It "was the first time one American President refused his Constitutional duty to transfer power peacefully to the next," as Representative Liz Cheney wrote in the House select committee's January 6 report.[12]

## INSTALLING ELECTION DENIERS IN KEY GOVERNMENT ROLES

To reinforce his election lies and legitimize his role in the January 6 insurrection, Trump has made election denialism a litmus test for service in his administration. These officials, in turn, have facilitated Trump's efforts to rewrite the history of the insurrection and to punish those who tried to hold him accountable. They have undermined the rule of law and weaponized the tools of government in the service of Trump's false claims. And by collaborating with Trump's effort to reward the January 6 insurrectionists, they legitimize the notion that political violence is an acceptable response to an unfavorable election outcome.

Among the most prominent election deniers elevated to high office was Trump's first attorney general, Pam Bondi, who abused her status as the nation's chief law enforcement officer to enforce Trump's spurious election claims. As one of Trump's earliest and most vigorous election deniers, she spread the lie that Trump had "won" Pennsylvania in 2020. She alleged mass "evidence of cheating," "fake ballots," and votes cast by dead people, despite a complete lack of evidence. In a previous role as the litigation chair of the Trump-aligned America First Policy Institute, she was also involved in multiple lawsuits that "served to amplify baseless conspiracy theories about noncitizen voting," according to the Brennan Center for Justice.[13]

As attorney general, Bondi transformed the historically independent Department of Justice into an instrument of retribution for Trump. On her first day in office, she sent a memo to the department's staff, threatening "discipline and possibly termination" for any attorney who refused to advance the president's agenda—including his revisionism of January 6.[14]

Bondi also established the "Weaponization Working Group" at Trump's direction, with the goal of exacting revenge on the prosecutors and other officials who had investigated the insurrection during Biden's presidency.[15] Its initial director, Ed Martin, was another prominent election denier who had marched outside the Capitol on January 6[16] and later compared the riots to "Mardi Gras."[17] More than 20 Justice Department staffers involved with the investigation have been fired or forced to resign,[18] while a spurious ethics probe was launched against Jack Smith, the special counsel who investigated Trump's involvement.[19]

In the meantime, Trump has hailed the Capitol rioters as "great people"[20] and "warriors"[21] and has lamented their prosecution. On his first day in office, he pardoned more than 1,500 insurrectionists, including members of the Oath Keepers, the Proud Boys, and other groups associated with white supremacism.[22] With the help of Ed Martin, now his pardon attorney,[23] Trump has also pardoned dozens of individuals involved in his "fake electors" scheme to overturn the 2020 results.[24]

## INTERFERING WITH STATE ELECTION INTEGRITY

Donald Trump has also used false claims of election fraud as a pretext for interfering with state election systems and results. These efforts not only threaten election integrity but also violate states' constitutional rights.

The U.S. Constitution's elections clause (Article 1, Section 4, Clause 1) provides that the rules for holding federal elections "shall be prescribed in each State by the Legislature thereof." Congress may "at any time by Law make or alter such Regulations," but the president has no direct role in this constitutional scheme.

Nevertheless, Trump has made multiple unlawful efforts to assert control over state elections, presumably to bend future outcomes in his or the GOP's favor.

In fact, Trump has baldly stated that Republicans should "take over" elections and "nationalize" voting.[25]

In March 2025, Trump issued a far-reaching executive order that aimed to establish federal standards for voter registration and eligibility, in clear contravention of the elections clause. In particular, he directed the Election Assistance Commission—an independent bipartisan agency that assists states with election administration—to mandate that voters show a passport or another similar document to prove their citizenship when they register to vote.[26] He also empowered the Department of Homeland Security and the U.S. attorney general to monitor states for compliance and withhold funds if they fail to fall in line. Nineteen states have sued to challenge the order's legality.[27]

In March 2026, Trump issued a second, even more expansive executive order to seize control of voting by mail and to establish a database of "State Citizenship Lists" approved by the federal government.[28] (This order has also been challenged by states and voting rights groups.)[29] This order follows other efforts by the administration to gain access to state voting equipment, voter files, and other records kept by election officials. As of February 2026, the administration has sued 29 states and the District of Columbia to compel the release of voter registration files to the federal government.[30]

In perhaps the most significant escalation, in February 2026 the FBI seized truckloads of ballots from the 2020 election in Fulton County, Georgia, despite the utter lack of evidence of wrongdoing. Most remarkable was the involvement of Tulsi Gabbard, the then director of national intelligence, who was both present at the raid and also reportedly arranged a phone call between Trump and frontline agents on the scene.[31] Not only was this an unprecedented attempt by a president to influence an ongoing investigation, but Gabbard's involvement was a stunning breach of the clear line between intelligence work and domestic politics established by the National Security Act of 1947. It is also an ominous harbinger of the actions the administration may take if future political losses are certain. In a January 2026 interview with *The New York Times*, Trump said he regretted not having ordered the National Guard to seize voting machines in the aftermath of the 2020 election, despite his clear lack of legal authority to do so and the absence of any evidence of tampering.[32] (In 2023, Dominion Voting Systems, the company that manufactured many of these machines, reached a $787 million settlement with Fox News over the network's amplification of false election claims.)[33]

Any attempt to access voting machines by the administration creates the risk of errors and incentivizes challenges to election results. Some states may also opt for hand-counting ballots, a process that can create errors and delays. None of Trump's actions are serving to make elections more secure. Rather, their effect is the opposite.

## PROMOTING POLICIES THAT WOULD HINDER BALLOT ACCESS

Donald Trump has championed multiple changes to election laws that would have the effect of impeding voter access, suppressing turnout, or disenfranchising citizens outright. These actions were one reason Freedom House lowered the "Global Freedom" score for the United States by three points—a decline matched only by Bulgaria—in its 2026 "Freedom in the World" report.[34]

One of Trump's principal targets is voting by mail, which has been successfully used in the United States for more than 150 years.[35] In 2024, roughly 30 percent of American voters cast their ballots by mail. (In 2020, at the height of the COVID-19 pandemic, the number was 43 percent.)[36] Plentiful research shows that mail-in voting is reliable and secure. States have developed multiple layers of security to protect against malfeasance, and fraud is extremely rare. The Brennan Center notes that it is "more likely for an American to be struck by lightning than to commit mail voting fraud."[37]

Nevertheless, Trump has condemned vote by mail as a mechanism for mass fraud and has moved to restrict it severely. In addition to the "State Citizenship Lists" mentioned above, Trump's March 2026 executive order gives the U.S. Postal Service unprecedented power over voting by mail. Under Trump's decree, states must submit their voter lists to the postal service, which alone will have the authority to issue mail-in ballots. Election experts have called the plan unconstitutional and impractical. It is also likely to limit ballot access while conferring no partisan advantage to Trump. While Trump has claimed that voting by mail is especially a boon for Democrats, research finds that the practice does not in fact benefit one party over another.[38] It is, however, an important option for voters who may otherwise be unable to go in person on Election Day because of work obligations, disability, lack of transportation, or other hurdles. Restricting the ability to vote by mail is therefore likely to limit some citizens' ability to vote.

Trump has also championed a bill in Congress called the Safeguard American Voter Eligibility Act (SAVE Act), which would require documentary proof of citizenship for voter registration. Trump has argued that this requirement is necessary to safeguard against voting by noncitizens, but as noted earlier, this phenomenon is vanishingly rare. Noncitizen voting, moreover, is already illegal under state and federal law, punishable by up to five years in federal prison as well as deportation.[39] The true intent of the SAVE Act is to reinforce public animus against undocumented immigrants, while at the same time casting doubt on election integrity. Its effect, if passed, would be to disenfranchise millions of U.S. citizens, including many of Trump's supporters.

According to the Brennan Center, more than 21 million Americans lack paper proof of their citizenship, and roughly half of Americans have no passport.[40] The SAVE Act would also pose additional burdens on the 80 percent of married women who have changed their names at marriage and who now use names that do not match their birth certificates.[41] A *Washington Post* analysis found that Republican districts were more likely to have significant shares of "inactive" voters who would be required to reregister under the SAVE Act's provisions, were it to pass. This analysis also found that young men—one of Trump's core constituencies—are less likely than other voters to have documentary proof of citizenship readily available, while rural voters may face greater burdens in traveling in person to election offices.[42] As of this writing, the bill has yet to pass Congress, and its passage is uncertain. Some states, however, have begun to consider similar legislation, and Florida passed its version of the SAVE Act in March 2026.[43]

## DEMANDING EXTREME PARTISAN GERRYMANDERING

Faced with declining popularity and the prospect of steep losses in the 2026 midterm elections, Donald Trump has demanded that lawmakers in multiple states redraw their congressional maps to create additional Republican districts and thereby favor a Republican majority in Congress. In July 2025, he ordered lawmakers in Texas to begin redistricting: "Just a simple redrawing we pick up five seats," as Trump told reporters would be the result.[44]

The usual timetable for redistricting is that it occurs immediately after the decennial census; redistricting a state in the middle of a decade is rare.[45] But in the aftermath of Trump's demands, as many as 15 states (as of April 2026) have considered, authorized, or implemented new maps, according to the National Conference of State Legislatures.[46] While many of these states have acted in compliance with Trump's demands, others—like California—have acted in retaliation. The overall effects of this redistricting war will be harmful to democracy: more gerrymandering, more polarization, and diminished public trust.

Perhaps most damaging will be the effective disenfranchisement of millions of Americans gerrymandered into highly partisan districts where their vote will have no impact. According to *The Cook Political Report*, only 17 of 435 House districts are classified as true toss-ups as of the spring of 2026, while 374 are "solid" Republican or Democratic.[47] This means that the overwhelming majority of House contests are decided by party primaries, which tend to draw the most partisan voters. The Unite America Institute calculated that in 2024, "87% of House races were decided in primary elections—meaning the 7% of voters who participated in these elections effectively chose the vast majority of the U.S. House."[48]

★ ★ ★

*The rapid erosion of voting rights and representation under the Trump administration risks propelling the United States into what the political scientists Steven Levitsky and Lucan A. Way call "competitive authoritarianism"—a system "in which the coexistence of meaningful democratic institutions and serious incumbent abuse yields electoral competition that is real but unfair."[49] Americans must exercise their voice—while they still can.*

# 11

## RAMPANT CORRUPTION AND SELF-DEALING

**Donald Trump has launched an effort unparalleled in history to monetize the presidency for personal gain. In 2025 alone, the profits enjoyed by Trump and his family totaled as much as $4 billion, according to one estimate.[1] Trump has violated the constitutional prohibition against emoluments and has openly trashed the norms that limit the use of public office for self-enrichment. His unchecked self-dealing disserves not only American taxpayers but also U.S. interests and national security.**

★ ★ ★

Shortly before the 2024 election, Donald Trump announced the sale of four memberships to his private club at Mar-a-Lago for $1 million each—a significant increase from the $200,000 fee that was charged during his first administration.[2] A 2019 investigation by *USA Today* revealed that at least eight Mar-a-Lago members won ambassadorships or other plum appointments during Trump's first term, and this move was widely seen as another ploy to sell access to a future administration.[3]

Trump has continued these pay-to-play practices in his second term, and he has used his office to extract expensive gifts and payments from foreign leaders, foreign business interests, and wealthy individuals seeking access or favorable treatment from the federal government. Multiple members of his family have likewise benefited, especially Trump's two eldest sons, as have members of his cabinet and other officials. After Donald Trump Jr. and Eric Trump launched the cryptocurrency venture World Liberty Financial,[4] Trump made crypto deregulation a cornerstone of his financial regulatory agenda.[5] The company was worth $5 billion on paper by September 2025.[6]

Trump himself has shown no concern about the conflicts of interest posed by his family's profiteering. "I found out that nobody cared, and I'm allowed to," he told *The New York Times* in January 2026.[7] Yet significant policy decisions have often hinged on these transactions, to the detriment of U.S. taxpayers and interests. Trump's acceptance of the gift of a $400 million presidential jet from the Qatari government in May 2025, for example, raised not only legal and ethical concerns but worries about national security as well. Among those raising the alarm was Republican Senator Ted Cruz, who said that the gift "poses significant espionage" concerns.[8]

Some Americans may shrug their shoulders at Trump's behavior. Trump has, after all, conducted all of this activity in full view—a strategic choice to normalize what should be shocking and to dull the public's sensitivities to serious ethical, legal, and moral violations.

Americans should remember, however, that a corrupt government is also an inefficient one. The experience of other nations with corrupt regimes offers ample evidence of how public corruption can suppress economic growth and contribute to inflation.[9] Policy choices made on the basis of favors, gifts, and other considerations unrelated to merit lead to the misallocation of public and private resources and the stifling of innovation.

Corruption also deepens public distrust in government, if it can't be counted on to act impartially in the best interests of its citizens. The Trump administration's ethical morass is more than a colossal waste of taxpayer money. It is an attack on the very purpose of democratic government: to serve all people, not just those who can write the checks.

## ACCEPTING GIFTS FROM FOREIGN POWERS

The prevention of foreign corruption and influence is a founding principle of our nation. America's first governing document, the Articles of Confederation, included a prohibition on foreign gifts of any kind, which the U.S. Constitution also adopted.[10] Under the Constitution's foreign emoluments clause (Article I, Section 9, Clause 8),[11] no person "holding any Office of Profit or Trust" may accept "any present, Emolument, Office, or Title, of any kind whatever, from any King, Prince, or foreign State" without the consent of Congress. This provision not only reflected the Framers' anti-corruption commitment—a radical notion at the time—it also ensured the independence that America had so recently declared and the loyalty of its leaders to put the new country's interests first.[12]

President Trump, however, has repeatedly violated both the spirit and the letter of this prohibition. He has accepted tens of millions of dollars in gifts from foreign leaders seeking to do business with his administration or his family. In addition to the Qatari jet (technically accepted by the Department of Defense),[13] foreign and business leaders have made major investments in Trump's sprawling network of family businesses, most notably in his crypto platform, World Liberty Financial, and his social media company, Trump Media. Around the time of Trump's 2024 election victory, Switzerland's publicly owned central bank bought $1.8 million in Trump Media shares.[14]

On a smaller scale (but no less troubling), Trump's gifts from foreign leaders in the past year have included a golden pager from Israeli Prime Minister Benjamin Netanyahu, a championship boxing belt from Ukrainian President Volodymyr Zelensky, two portraits from Russian President Vladimir Putin, a gold crown from South Korean President Lee Jae Myung,[15] and the Nobel Peace Prize medal from the Venezuelan opposition leader María Corina Machado.[16] All of these gifts technically belong to the American people, and federal law requires their disclosure to the State Department. However, an investigation by House Democrats after Trump's first term alleged that he had failed to disclose more than $250,000 worth of foreign gifts, which he presumably kept for personal use.[17] So far, there's little evidence that this lack of transparency has changed.

Favorable policy decisions have frequently followed the receipt of large foreign gifts or investments, often to the detriment of U.S. interests and taxpayers. One of many such examples is a $500 million investment in World Liberty Financial by Sheik Tahnoon bin Zayed Al Nahyan, the head of the United Arab Emirates' largest sovereign wealth fund and the nation's national security adviser. (He is known as the "Spy Sheikh" because of this role.)[18] Shortly after this purchase, made in secret before the company's launch, Trump agreed to provide the UAE hundreds of thousands of advanced AI chips not previously available outside the United States.[19] Experts condemned the deal as a threat to national security[20] because of the risk that these chips could end up being transferred to China.[21]

## MONETIZING THE PRESIDENCY

Donald Trump has also had no compunction soliciting donations and gifts from U.S. companies and wealthy individuals, many of whom have business before his administration. (The Constitution forbids domestic emoluments, too.)[22]

Trump's 2025 inauguration festivities raised more than $161 million from corporations, including 104 businesses that donated $1 million or more, according to OpenSecrets.[23] Photos from the ceremony show him flanked by billionaires, including Meta CEO Mark Zuckerberg, Amazon CEO Jeff Bezos, and the world's richest man, Elon Musk.[24] Both Bezos and Musk[25] benefit from billions of dollars in government contracts,[26] while Zuckerberg has sought regulatory relief for his companies.[27] The Trump administration has reportedly paused or dropped federal investigations into or lawsuits against 17 of the companies that donated to his inauguration.[28]

Official events have also served as opportunities for monetization. In 2025, the White House Easter Egg Roll sold corporate sponsorships, with donors like Amazon and YouTube vying for advertising space on the South Lawn.[29] Donors have also lined up for the nation's 250th birthday celebration in 2026, organized by the Trump-aligned group Freedom 250. Those who give $1 million or more "will get invitations to a 'private Freedom 250 thank you reception' hosted by Mr. Trump, with a 'historic photo opportunity,'" according to news reports, while donors who fork over $2.5 million will get speaking roles at a public event.[30] Over the past year, Trump has also visited his own properties 198 times, raking in millions of dollars in lodging, dining, and event fees from visitors coming to kiss the ring, as well as from U.S. taxpayers, who pay for Secret Service protection.[31]

Trump has also used the demolition of the East Wing of the White House and the construction of his new ballroom to raise at least $400 million from private sources.[32] Many of the donors to this project are companies or billionaires looking to curry favor with the administration.[33] In addition, Trump has offered personal tours of the White House to special donors, like the top 25 purchasers of $TRUMP,[34] the cryptocurrency meme coin he launched before his inauguration.[35] Among these invitees was Justin Sun, a Chinese crypto billionaire then being sued by the Securities and Exchange Commission, who had reportedly spent $75 million on investments in the World Liberty Financial crypto coin to get himself invited to the White House.[36] *The New York Times* reported that the SEC asked a judge to put Sun's case on hold shortly after Trump took office[37] and later settled the case for $10 million.[38]

## GRANTING PARDONS TO DONORS AND ALLIES

Donald Trump has made profligate use of his presidential pardon power, especially for donors, political allies, and figures tied to the Trump family's financial interests.

Few of the individuals receiving pardons have been vetted through the Department of Justice's standard processes,[39] which require an official application to the Office of the Pardon Attorney and evidence of an individual's "demonstrated ability to lead a responsible and productive life," according to an investigation by ProPublica.[40] Rather, the primary criterion for a pardon has been access to the president or his inner circle. Moreover, many of these pardon recipients are literally getting out of jail free. A 2025 report by House Judiciary Committee Democrats found that Trump's pardons have wiped out at least $1.3 billion in fines and restitution that would otherwise be owed to victims.[41]

As Margaret Love, who served as pardon attorney under President George H. W. Bush and Bill Clinton, told ProPublica, "It's unfair to the little guy."

Among the recipients of Trump's largesse:

☆ The Chinese billionaire Changpeng Zhao, the founder of Binance, who had pleaded guilty to money laundering and fined $50 million.[42] Binance, the world's leading crypto exchange, has been a strong promoter of World Liberty Financial's crypto coins.[43]

☆ The financier Trevor Milton, who had been convicted of securities fraud and ordered to pay $661 million in restitution to his victims. Milton contributed $920,000 to the Trump 47 committee in 2024 and received a pardon that erased his restitution obligations.[44]

☆ Julio Herrera Velutini, a Venezuelan billionaire facing criminal bribery charges. His pardon was issued shortly after a $3.5 million contribution by his daughter to MAGA Inc.[45]

☆ The reality TV stars Todd and Julie Chrisley, who were convicted of bank fraud and tax evasion. Their daughter Savannah, an ardent Trump supporter, spoke at the 2024 Republican National Convention.[46]

☆ Paul Walczak, a nursing home executive who had pleaded guilty to tax crimes. He received a pardon after his mother attended a fundraising dinner at Mar-a-Lago that cost $1 million a person; he was spared both prison time and $4.4 million in restitution.[47]

☆ These pay-to-play pardons have also launched a lucrative cottage industry for lobbyists who claim they can fast-track a pardon from President Trump. In 2025, clients seeking clemency paid at least $5.2 million in lobbying fees, according to an analysis by *The New York Times*, with some applicants forking over close to $1 million.

## WEAPONIZING GOVERNMENT AND EXTORTING ENEMIES

At the same time that Donald Trump has used the tools of government to shower favors on his donors and allies, he has abused the powers at his disposal to extort financial advantages for himself.

Some countries, for instance, have plied Trump with gifts in an effort to soften the punitive tariffs he levied in the first year of his administration. After Trump arbitrarily slapped a 39 percent tariff on Switzerland in August 2025, a group of Swiss billionaires gave Trump a gold Rolex clock and an engraved gold bar worth $130,000.[48] Trump later reduced the tariffs to 15 percent. The gold crown presented by South Korea, along with an accompanying medal, was also intended to butter up Trump before trade talks.[49]

In March 2025, Trump signed multiple executive orders targeting major law firms that had represented or employed his political enemies.[50] The orders stripped attorneys from these firms of their security clearances or barred their companies from doing business related to government contracts. While several firms challenged these orders as unconstitutional (and won),[51] others entered into settlements involving tens of millions of dollars of free legal work on behalf of causes to be specified by Trump. The law firm Paul, Weiss, for instance, agreed to provide $40 million in pro bono legal work toward causes supported by Trump, while another firm, Skadden, Arps, agreed to provide $100 million in free assistance.[52] All told, these law firms have agreed to provide nearly $1 billion in pro bono aid. While the exact nature of this aid hasn't been specified, Trump indicated to the press that "the pro bono work could be used toward his administration's trade deals and even representing him in a personal capacity."[53]

Trump has also made extortionate demands through litigation, resulting in tens of millions of dollars in settlements for himself. In December 2024, ABC News settled for $15 million after Trump brought a defamation suit against the network.[54] In July 2025, Paramount agreed to give Trump $16 million[55] to settle a

$10 billion suit he filed against CBS News for its editing of a *60 Minutes* interview with Kamala Harris.[56] YouTube (which is owned by Google) paid Trump $24.5 million to settle a suit over the suspension of Trump's account after the January 6 insurrection,[57] while Meta agreed to pay $25 million over Trump's suspensions from Facebook and Instagram.[58] As of March 2026, Trump had six ongoing lawsuits against media outlets,[59] including a $10 billion claim against the BBC and another against *The Wall Street Journal*, as well as suits against *The New York Times*, *The Des Moines Register*, and the Pulitzer Prize board.[60]

Even more egregiously, Trump is suing his own administration in an effort to extract settlements from U.S. taxpayers. In October 2025, Trump filed suit against the Department of Justice, demanding $230 million in compensation for investigations against him during the Biden administration.[61] In January 2026, Trump sued the Internal Revenue Service and the U.S. Treasury for $10 billion over the leak of his tax documents by an IRS contractor. (Under current law, Section 7431 of the Internal Revenue Code, even if his suit succeeds Trump is entitled only to the greater of $1,000 for "each act of unauthorized … disclosure" or actual damages suffered.)[62]

## ENABLING PROFITEERING BY TOP OFFICIALS

Public service has been profitable for many of Trump's top officials and family members as well as for Trump himself. Some officials have used their positions to arrange lucrative business deals for themselves, while others have steered business to preferred contractors.

Among those who appear to have profited handsomely are Trump's principal envoys to the Middle East, his son-in-law Jared Kushner and the real estate developer Steve Witkoff. According to *Forbes*, Witkoff's fortune grew by 15 percent during the first year of Trump's second term, to $2.3 billion.[63] Among his investments are a stake in World Liberty Financial, which his two sons co-founded with Don Jr. and Eric. Witkoff also holds a roughly $210 million stake in SpaceX, which is owned by the on-again, off-again Trump ally Elon Musk. Kushner, meanwhile, has been attempting to raise $5 billion from investors in the Middle East for his fledgling private equity fund, Affinity Partners.[64] That's in addition to the $2 billion stake he received from an investment fund led by Saudi Crown Prince Mohammed bin Salman in 2021.[65] Forbes estimates that Kushner, like his father-in-law, is now a billionaire.[66]

Trump's first year in office has spawned a plethora of similar instances involving cabinet members and other high-ranking officials (for which a full accounting would require a separate volume). For example:

☆ Kash Patel, the director of the FBI, received an $800,000 stake in Trump Media[67] days before his Senate confirmation hearing. He also received stocks worth between $1 million and $5 million from a Cayman Islands holding company linked to the controversial e-commerce giant Shein in exchange for "consulting" services.[68]
☆ Before her abrupt firing in March 2026, Secretary of Homeland Security Kristi Noem reportedly steered $220 million in advertising contracts to a firm to which she had business and personal connections.[69]
☆ Secretary of Commerce Howard Lutnick's family firm, Cantor Fitzgerald, saw a $2.5 billion revenue increase in 2025[70]—a large enough sum that even Trump reportedly "confronted Lutnick directly about it during an episode at Mar-a-Lago," according to *Politico.*[71]
☆ Secretary of Defense Pete Hegseth's broker reportedly tried to make a multimillion-dollar investment[72] in defense stocks shortly before the outbreak of the war in Iran, according to the *Financial Times.*[73]
☆ Vice President J. D. Vance sold his house for $172,000 over the asking price to a former Trump official who is now a government contractor.[74]

★ ★ ★

*Over the past year, Trump has also systematically removed the safeguards that could keep his behavior in check. He has fired inspectors general, the government watchdogs that monitor waste, fraud, and abuse.[75] He has gutted the Department of Justice's ability to prosecute public corruption; in March 2025, he forced out most of the lawyers in the Public Integrity Section.[76] No doubt the Supreme Court's 2023 decision granting him immunity for "official" acts has also emboldened him.[77]*

*In 2025, the United States slid to 29th—its lowest ranking ever[78]—on Transparency International's Corruption Perceptions Index. It is an ignominious decline for a nation founded on the ideals of fair and impartial governance.*

# 12

## A COLLAPSE IN CIVIL DISCOURSE

**Donald Trump has shattered every norm of acceptable political discourse and fostered division and disunity. He has demonized political opponents and scapegoated vulnerable communities. He has glorified political violence and encouraged mobs to help suppress dissent. He has denigrated expertise, mocked the service of men and women in the military, and engaged in open racism and misogyny. Americans are more polarized than they have ever been.**

★ ★ ★

Since the beginning of his political career, Donald Trump has made shock and transgression hallmarks of his political persona. "I tell it like it is, and people have to hear it," he told the Christian Broadcasting Network at the start of his first presidential campaign.[1]

Trump has reveled in his coarseness throughout his presidencies, knowing that bluntness is catnip for his base. In one 2016 exit poll, 78 percent of Republican primary voters said "tells it like it is" was Trump's top quality as a candidate.[2] A 2018 survey found that among his supporters, more than 60 percent thought him "highly authentic."[3]

Claims of "telling it like it is," however, can neither disguise nor excuse the hatefulness, misogyny, racism, and violence that characterize Trump's daily speech. In Trump's twisted version of "telling it like it is," "grabbing women by the pussy"[4] is just "locker room talk,"[5] the January 6 insurrection was a "day of love,"[6] and migrants are "poisoning"[7] the country. Protesters need to be "punch[ed] in the face,"[8] or condemned as "domestic terrorists."[9] Immigrants are "vermin,"[10] and Africa has "shithole countries."[11] Soldiers who have died in war are "suckers and losers." The death of opponents is cause to gloat: "I'm glad he's dead," Trump said of Robert Mueller, the former FBI director who investigated Trump's ties to Russia.[12] Trump even delivered a disrespectful broadside against Pope Leo XIV, whom he derided as "terrible."[13]

Trump's veneer of "authenticity" rings hollow when his statements are peppered with lies. *The Washington Post*'s "Fact Checker" tallied 30,573 "false or misleading claims" in Trump's first term alone,[14] including more than 50 that earned a "Bottomless Pinocchio" rating for the frequency of their repetition.[15] The "Gish Gallop" is Trump's favored rhetorical strategy—a torrent of lies so overwhelming in volume that it's impossible to rebut them all.[16] Some claims are mathematically impossible, such as his promises to cut prescription drug prices by as much as "1,000 percent."[17] Some are simply bizarre, like his claim that windmills cause cancer.[18] Yet mainstream outlets, in his view, are purveyors of "fake news,"[19] and unfavorable coverage is "biased."[20]

The gusher of hate and misinformation spewing from this administration has been deeply destructive to civil society. Political polarization has worsened. Divisions have widened into chasms. Skepticism of institutions has calcified into mistrust. Especially troubling, threats of political violence have escalated. According to a September 2025 survey by Dartmouth's Polarization Research Lab, 63 percent of Americans see political violence as a "very big problem."[21]

## AGGRAVATING POLARIZATION

Trump habitually hurls invectives at his political opponents, calling Democrats "crazy,"[22] "radical,"[23] "dangerous," and even the "enemy from within,"[24] in an echo of fascist regimes. Perhaps taking cues from this divisive language, Americans' partisanship is increasing and risks hardening into extremism.

A November 2025 survey by Public Agenda and the SNF Agora Institute at Johns Hopkins University found that only about a third of Americans "have gotten to know someone whose political views are different from their own," while negative feelings about opposing political parties have intensified. Among the most ardent Trump supporters identified in this survey, as many as 61 percent "strongly agreed" or "agreed" that "members of the opposing party lack the traits to be considered fully human, they behave like animals." Thirty-nine percent of Democrats felt the same. Seventy-three percent of Trump supporters also said they believed the Democratic Party to be "downright evil," while 57 percent of Democrats thought the same of the GOP.[25]

Gallup finds that the share of Americans who self-identify as "moderate" dropped to 34 percent in 2024, down from 42 percent in 1992, while both parties' ideology was the "most extreme in 30 years." Twenty-four percent of Republicans called themselves "very conservative"—an all-time high—while 19 percent of Democrats said they were "very liberal."[26]

Granted, political polarization has been a long-term trend, the result of broader cultural, societal, and technological shifts like the rise of social media and partisan news outlets. Rising viewership of Fox News, for instance, has helped increase the share of Republican votes in federal and state elections by at least 0.5 percentage points since 2000, according to a 2024 study in the *Journal of Public Economics.*[27] Americans have also physically isolated themselves in like-minded communities, a phenomenon that the author Bill Bishop called the "Big Sort" in his 2009 book of that title.[28]

Nevertheless, social science researchers have also discovered a sharp uptick in "partisan animosity" since the start of Trump's first term. In 2022, the Pew Research Center found that 72 percent of Republicans believe that members of the opposing party are "more immoral than other Americans," compared to 47 percent who thought the same in 2016.[29] (The comparable numbers among Democrats are 63 percent and 35 percent.) The share of people in either party who believe that opposing party members are "dishonest," "close-minded," or "unintelligent" also shot up by about 20 percentage points. Given these attitudes, it's no surprise that 80 percent of Americans told Gallup in 2024 that "Americans are greatly divided on the most important values."[30]

As the occupant of the world's most powerful bully pulpit, Trump could have been striving to heal these divisions. Instead, he has worked assiduously to drive deeper wedges between Americans for his own political gain.

## DESTROYING TRUST

Donald Trump's loose relationship with the truth has also made honest debate impossible. If policymakers and the public can't agree on what's true, they can't agree on what the country's problems are—let alone the solutions to those problems. Trump's disinformation campaigns have eroded the public consensus on what were once unassailable truths: that the planet is experiencing climate change;[31] that vaccines can prevent disease;[32] that he lost the 2020 election to Joe Biden.[33] Fully 80 percent of Americans say that "Republican and Democratic voters cannot agree on basic facts," according to a July 2025 survey by the Pew Research Center.[34]

Trump's attacks on the mainstream press, his penchant for misinformation, and his administration's denigration of expertise have left many Americans unsure of where to turn for reliable information. Only 56 percent of Americans say "they have a lot of or some trust in the information they get from national news organizations," according to another survey by the Pew Research Center from September 2025.[35] That's an 11 percentage point decline since March 2025—just seven months earlier—and a 20 percentage point drop since 2016. Democrats are more likely to trust national news outlets than Republicans (69 percent versus 44 percent), but members of both parties have seen steep declines in their trust of news.

Pew also found that trust in government has fallen to historic lows. In September 2025, just 17 percent of Americans said they trust the government to do the right thing "just about always" or "most of the time"—down from nearly 80 percent in 1964 and 60 percent in 2001.[36]

Trust in the federal agencies that have been reshaped by Trump's appointments and policies has especially plummeted in the past year. After the appointment of anti-vaccine advocate Robert F. Kennedy Jr. as the secretary of health and human services, for instance, Americans' trust in vaccine advice from the Centers for Disease Control and Prevention dropped by 16 percentage points, from 63 percent in 2023 to 47 percent in January 2026, according to KFF.[37] Only 38 percent of Americans trust Kennedy to provide reliable public health advice, according to a February 2026 survey by the Annenberg Public Policy Center at the University of Pennsylvania.[38] (Dr. Anthony Fauci, in contrast, enjoyed a 54 percent trust rating at the height of the COVID-19 pandemic,[39] despite Trump's efforts to discredit him.)[40]

Similarly, trust in the government's economic data dropped by 8 percentage points between March and August 2025,[41] when Trump fired Erika McEntarfer, the commissioner of the Bureau of Labor Statistics, over jobs numbers he didn't like.[42] The same survey found that 45 percent of Americans "somewhat distrust" or "completely distrust" government data on the economy, and only 21 percent believe that government unemployment numbers are accurate.

This decline in public trust is not only corrosive, but dangerous as well. Citizens who do not believe the government on matters of public health might ignore lifesaving advice. The next pandemic could be catastrophic. Disputes over data could lead to bad policies that might jeopardize the U.S. economy. Without a common foundation of agreed-upon truth, crises will inevitably lead to chaos.

## NORMALIZING POLITICAL VIOLENCE

After the horrific murder of the conservative activist Charlie Kirk in September 2025, Donald Trump did not issue a statement typical of politicians after such an act of violence. Instead of calling for unity and calm, Trump told reporters that "we just have to beat the hell" out of "radical left lunatics."[43] What followed was an immediate spike in threats to local officeholders, according to data from Princeton University's Bridging Divides Initiative.[44] Dozens of ordinary citizens who had criticized Kirk's views were doxxed or threatened, or faced other online harassment.[45]

Perhaps the most troubling trend coincident with Trump's presidencies is the rise in threats of political violence. In 2025, the U.S. Capitol Police investigated 14,938 "concerning statements, behaviors, and communications directed against Members of Congress, their families, staff, and the Capitol Complex," nearly double the number reported in 2022.[46] After Trump suggested the possible execution of six members of Congress for a video they posted urging service members to refuse to follow illegal orders, Arizona Senator Mark Kelly reported a surge in death threats directed at him and his family for his participation in the video.[47]

Judges have been threatened as well. In 2025, the U.S. Marshals Service reported 564 threat incidents, involving 396 judges, a figure that will likely be surpassed in 2026.[48] As of the end of March, the Marshals Service had already investigated 335 threats involving 210 judges. The situation was so dire that Chief Justice John Roberts issued a statement in March warning that "personally directed hostility is dangerous and has got to stop."[49]

Trump has repeatedly disputed accusations of incitement. He disclaimed responsibility for January 6[50] (although at least a dozen rioters facing prosecution blamed Trump for provoking their crimes).[51] Yet violence and violent speech has been a consistent feature of Trump's public statements. "Maybe he should have been roughed up," Trump said of a protester at one of his rallies.[52] "Stand back and stand by," he told the white nationalist group Proud Boys,[53] who later showed up in force on January 6.[54] And in the week after Roberts's statement on the attacks against judges, Trump did nothing to bring down the temperature. Instead, he escalated his rhetoric and called for a crime bill that "cracks down on rogue judges." "They are criminals, what they do to our country," he said.[55]

★ ★ ★

*Presidents like Ronald Reagan, Franklin D. Roosevelt, Harry Truman, and John F. Kennedy showed that it's possible to confront America's enemies successfully, with strength but without vitriol. Reagan spoke of America as a "shining city upon a hill" whose example to the world was the strongest argument against communism.*[56] *Kennedy navigated the Cuban Missile Crisis, when our nation came the closest it's ever been to nuclear war. "Our goal is not the victory of might, but the vindication of right," he declared in an address to the nation in 1962. But Trump is no Kennedy. Trump is no Reagan.*[57]

*At a time when the United States confronts multiple pressing challenges, deliberation, debate, and compromise are more necessary than ever. Yet the destruction of civil discourse, egged on by Trump, has put the likelihood of consensus further from reach. The loss of common ground risks the loss of a shared future and the bonds that have held our nation together.*

# EPILOGUE: FACING THE CRISIS OF OUR TIMES

The work of our Common Sense Coalition began in the autumn of 2025. We came together because of a shared awareness that the Trump administration was making an unprecedented assault on American institutions, alliances, and values. Our original goal was to produce a comprehensive assessment of Trump's first year back in office, to be released in March.

But the damage continued to metastasize: ICE agents went to the streets of Minneapolis and Trump launched the war on Iran, forcing us to extend our research and writing. Having looked closely at the full range of issues, we came away somewhat humbled. Even our in-depth report can only begin to convey all the damage that has been done by this president and his administration in the past year and a half.

Of course, America has endured difficult times before. But those periods resulted from attacks by external enemies (Pearl Harbor and 9/11); unprecedented economic and financial challenges (the stock market crash and the Depression); and the conflict over slavery written into the Constitution that brought about the Civil War. What we are living through now is quite different: a self-inflicted wound caused by a rampaging president abusing his powers in a concerted effort to remake our country.

Thomas B. Edsall, the eminent journalist and political analyst, offered a succinct summary on April 20: "The damage President Trump has inflicted on the United States, and the world, is so enormous and wide-ranging that it is hard to grasp." We hope that our report will make it more comprehensible. The midterm elections, less than six months away, provide a crucial opportunity for the American people to pass judgment on the Trump administration. Our report provides information that can help voters make their decision. We believe that our report is in the best American tradition of vigorous political debate. Our goal is an informed electorate that better understands how this administration has taken America down a dark and damaging road.

We call on the American people to elect a Congress that will hold this administration accountable for its abuses of power and its betrayal of the interests and hopes of the public. As of this writing, Trump has completed one-third of his term. Ultimately, the new Congress will have to assess whether this destructive presidency can be allowed to run its full course.

We have great confidence in the talents, energies, and potential of the American people. But the rebuilding of the United States can occur only after recognizing the full scope of the damage that is being done and taking the necessary actions to stop it in its tracks. Fortunately, there is a growing recognition among a broad range of Americans that this isn't what they voted for. We should draw inspiration from the recent election in Hungary, where the people revolted against a corrupt, authoritarian regime whose leaders had enriched themselves while neglecting the needs of their citizens. And we should be gratified by the quick decision by the European Union, no longer blocked by Viktor Orbán's veto, to provide $106 billion in aid to Ukraine. Other nations are shaking off the pernicious Trump effect; we hope that America will join them.

Let us be unmistakably clear: America's problems did not begin with Donald Trump. We are a quarter of the way through a century in which our country's steep decline can be charted in striking contrast to China's extraordinary rise. No one can deny that significant reforms will be needed to reduce inequality, broaden opportunities for our people, and rebuild our credibility and competitiveness in the world. But there is a vast difference between the reform and revitalization that our country needs and the destruction and division that this administration has wreaked. Instead of following the dictates of a would-be king, we should rely on the talents, creative energy, and common sense of the American people and the strength of our democratic institutions and values to meet the challenges of this singular moment, as well as those we will face in the coming years.

# APPENDIX: A CITIZEN'S PLAYBOOK

The goal of this report is not to stun the reader into paralysis. Rather, its goal is to galvanize citizens into action.

The scope of the destruction this administration has wreaked may be vast, but so is America's resilience and its capacity for renewal. Nevertheless, the nation can't afford to wait until 2029 to undo the damage. The project to reclaim and rebuild our democracy must begin immediately. Moreover, that work can't just be left to someone else to do: Ordinary citizens must be the basic drivers in the recovery of our democracy.

What can citizens do?

**★ BE INFORMED.**

Many Americans are overwhelmed by the onslaught of negative news and choosing to tune it out. This administration, however, is counting on its ability to numb the public into apathy and submission. By flooding the zone with unlawful acts and outrageous behavior, it seeks to overrun the opposition and bludgeon the public into acquiescence. Americans must stay informed about what's at stake and what they risk losing. This book can serve as a resource and a reminder.

**★ SPREAD THE WORD.**

Share what you learn, both from this book and from other resources through conversations, emails, and social media postings, and encourage those with whom you communicate to do the same. Visit our website—commonsense-coalition.net—and recommend it to others. None of us needs to be afraid to speak if we all speak together.

**★ DEMAND ACCOUNTABILITY.**

Congress has been shockingly supine in the face of the Trump administration's campaign of destruction. It has failed to uphold its constitutional duties as a coequal branch of government, and it has ceded its power to the administration. Members of Congress will not act unless they hear from their constituencies. Demand action. Demand accountability. Demand investigation. Demand change.

**★ VOTE.**

It's no exaggeration to say that the 2026 midterms will be among the most consequential elections in U.S. history. They will determine whether this administration continues its rampage unchecked or faces meaningful opposition. All citizens should exercise their right of franchise and urge others to do so as well. Volunteer to register voters and participate in voter education and "get out the vote" efforts in your community. Citizens can also work to ensure that candidates represent America's best interests; voters shouldn't be left choosing "none of the above." Inaction will be interpreted as consent for the abuse to continue.

# ENDNOTES

### INTRODUCTION

**1.** Donald J. Trump, "The Inaugural Address," January 20, 2017, Trump White House Archives, accessed April 24, 2026, trumpwhitehouse.archives.gov/briefings-statements/the-inaugural-address/.
**2.** Donald J. Trump, "The Inaugural Address," White House, January 20, 2025, whitehouse.gov/remarks/2025/01/the-inaugural-address/.

### 1: A RELENTLESS ASSAULT ON THE RULE OF LAW

**1.** U.S. Constitution, Article I.
**2.** U.S. Constitution, Article II.
**3.** U.S. Constitution, Article VI.
**4.** Matthew J. Vaeth, *Memorandum for Heads of Executive Departments and Agencies: Temporary Pause of Agency Grant, Loan, and Other Financial Assistance Programs*, Office of Management and Budget, January 27, 2025, whitehouse.gov/wp-content/uploads/2025/03/M-25-13-Temporary-Pause-to-Review-Agency-Grant-Loan-and-Other-Financial-Assistance-Programs.pdf.
**5.** Executive Order of January 20, 2025, "Reevaluating and Realigning United States Foreign Aid," White House, whitehouse.gov/presidential-actions/2025/01/reevaluating-and-realigning-united-states-foreign-aid/. The Supreme Court rejected the administration's request for relief from an order requiring payment for past performance under valid foreign aid contracts. Claims that the administration's refusal to expend appropriated funds on additional aid remain in litigation as of April 2026.
**6.** See, e.g., *National Treasury Employees Union v. Vought*, No. 25-5091 (D.C. Cir. 2025), law.justia.com/cases/federal/appellate-courts/cadc/25-5091/25-5091-2025-08-15, in which the district court found that the administration had unlawfully attempted to shut down the CFPB. As of April 2026, this case was pending on appeal before the D.C. Circuit Court of Appeals, which heard the case *en banc* in February. U.S. Court of Appeals for the District of Columbia Circuit, "Oral Argument Recordings (February 2026)," accessed April 24, 2026, media.cadc.uscourts.gov/recordings/bydate/2026/2.
**7.** Executive Order of April 2, 2025, "Regulating Imports with a Reciprocal Tariff to Rectify Trade Practices That Contribute to Large and Persistent Annual United States Goods Trade Deficits," White House, whitehouse.gov/presidential-actions/2025/04/regulating-imports-with-a-reciprocal-tariff-to-rectify-trade-practices-that-contribute-to-large-and-persistent-annual-united-states-goods-trade-deficits/.

**8.** Executive Order of July 30, 2025, "Addressing Threats to the United States by the Government of Brazil," White House, whitehouse.gov/presidential-actions/2025/07/addressing-threats-to-the-us/.
**9.** Lalee Ibssa and Ivan Pereira, "Trump Raises Tariffs on Canada 10% After Reagan Ad Airs During World Series," ABC News, October 26, 2025, abcnews.go.com/Politics/trump-raises-tariffs-canada-10-after-reagan-ad/story?id=126866712.
**10.** *Learning Resources, Inc. v. Trump*, 607 U.S. ___ (2026).
**11.** Daniel Desrorchers et al., "Trump Signs Order Imposing 'Temporary' 10 Percent Global Tariff After Supreme Court Ruling," *Politico*, February 20, 2026, politico.com/news/2026/02/20/donald-trump-10-percent-global-tariff-00791317.
**12.** Josh Gerstein, "Trump's Latest Tariffs Face a Fresh Set of Legal Hurdles," *Politico*, March 15, 2026, politico.com/news/2026/03/15/trump-tariffs-legal-challenges-00828854. These levies were struck down by the Court of International Trade on May 7, 2026, a decision that will certainly be appealed.
**13.** Mathathias Schwartz, "What We Learned After Tracking Every Lawsuit Challenging Trump's Policies," *New York Times*, January 29, 2026, nytimes.com/2026/01/29/us/politics/trump-lawsuits-tracker-takeaways.html.
**14.** Mattathias Schwartz and Emma Schartz, "Trump's 'Superstar' Appellate Judges Have Voted 133 to 12 in His Favor," *New York Times*, January 11, 2026, nytimes.com/2026/01/11/us/politics/trumps-appeals-court-judges.html.
**15.** Ibid.
**16.** Josh Boak and Steve Peoples, "What Happens Next After the Supreme Court Slapped Down Trump's Tariffs," Associated Press, February 20, 2026, apnews.com/article/trump-tariffs-supreme-court-whats-next-b8b6d5d44ebb3640a88f7202754cb361.
**17.** Chris Megerian, "Trump Says Federal Judge Who Ruled Against Deportation Orders Should Be Impeached," Associated Press, March 18, 2025, pbs.org/newshour/politics/trump-says-federal-judge-who-ruled-against-deportation-orders-should-be-impeached.
**18.** Dan Maurer, "On Treason and Traitors," *Lawfare*, June 9, 2025, lawfaremedia.org/article/on-treason-and-traitors.
**19.** New York City Bar Association, "Attacking Judges Is Antithetical to Constitutional Democracy," December 9, 2025, nycbar.org/press-releases/attacking-judges-is-antithetical-to-constitutional-democracy/.
**20.** Aaron Blake, "The White House Claims a Left-Wing Judicial 'Insurrection.' But Many GOP and Trump Nominees Are Rebuking the President, Too," CNN, October 6, 2025, cnn.com/2025/10/06/politics/republican-federal-judges-trump.
**21.** "Protective Investigations—Threat Statistics," U.S. Marshals Service, last modified April 15, 2026, usmarshals.gov/what-we-do/judicial-security/protective-investigations-threat-statistics; John Kruyzel, "U.S. Supreme Court's Roberts Says Personal Hostility Aimed at Judges Has 'Got to Stop,'" Reuters, March 17, 2026, reuters.com/legal/government/us-supreme-courts-roberts-says-personal-hostility-aimed-

judges-has-got-stop-2026-03-17/; Brianna Tucker, "Retired Judges Warn That the Rule of Law Is Unraveling," *Washington Post*, November 28, 2025, washingtonpost.com/politics/2025/11/28/judges-trump-administration-rule-of-law.

**22.** Mattathias Schwartz, Zach Montague, and Ernesto Londono, "Judges Grow Angry over Trump Administration Violating Their Orders," *New York Times*, February 23, 2026, nytimes.com/2026/02/23/us/politics/judges-contempt-immigration-trump.html.

**23.** *Toby Robles v. Noem*, 0:26-cv-0107 (D. Minn. 2026).

**24.** Nick Gwyn, "Trump Administration's Five-State Funding Freeze Is Unlawful, Harmful, and a Major Threat to People in Every State," Center on Budget and Policy Priorities, January 23, 2026, cbpp.org/research/federal-budget/trump-administrations-five-state-funding-freeze-is-unlawful-harmful-and-a.

**25.** Meryl Justin Chertoff, "Trump's Threats to Withhold Disaster Relief Undermine Federalism Principles," *State Court Report*, March 11, 2025, statecourtreport.org/our-work/analysis-opinion/trumps-threats-withhold-disaster-relief-undermine-federalism-principles; Stefanos Chen and Winnie Hu, "Congestion Pricing Wins in Court After Lengthy Battle with Trump," *New York Times*, March 3, 2026, nytimes.com/2026/03/03/nyregion/nyc-congestion-pricing-ruling.html.

**26.** Kaylie Martinez-Ochoa, Eileen O'Connor, and Patrick Berry, "Tracker of Justice Department Requests for Voter Information," Brennan Center, April 17, 2026, brennancenter.org/our-work/research-reports/tracker-justice-department-requests-voter-information.

**27.** Press release, "Statement from Secretary Simon," Office of the Minnesota Secretary of State Steve Simon, January 25, 2026, sos.mn.gov/about-the-office/news-room/statement-from-secretary-simon/.

**28.** *Use of Army, Navy, Marine Corps, Air Force, and Space Force as posse comitatus, U.S. Code 18,* § 1385.

**29.** *Trump v. Illinois*, 607 U.S. ____ (2025).

**30.** Tara Suter, "Trump: Insurrection Act 'the Strongest Power a President Has,'" *The Hill*, thehill.com/homenews/administration/5563329-trump-insurrection-act-the-strongest-power-a-president-has/.

**31.** "About DOJ," U.S. Department of Justice, justice.gov/about.

**32.** Devlin Barrett and Philip Rucker, "Trump Said He Was Thinking of Russia Controversy When He Decided to Fire Comey," *Washington Post*, May 11, 2017, washingtonpost.com/world/national-security/trump-says-fbi-director-comey-told-him-three-times-he-wasnt-under-investigation-once-in-a-phone-call-initiated-by-the-president/2017/05/11/2b384c9a-3669-11e7-b4ee-434b6d506b37_story.html; Mariana Alfaro, "Trump Says Members of Jan. 6 Committee Should Be Jailed," *Washington Post*, December 9, 2024, washingtonpost.com/politics/2024/12/08/trump-january-6-biden-jack-smith/; Joe Walsh, "Trump Administration Investigates 5 Democratic Lawmakers over Their Video Message to Troops. Here's What We Know," CBS News, January 14, 2026, cbsnews.com/news/trump-administration-investigates-5-democratic-lawmakers-over-their-video-message-to-troops/.

**33.** Kyle Cheney, "'We Can't Delay Any Longer': Trump Urges Bondi to Prosecute His Rivals," *Politico*, September 20, 2025, politico.com/news/2025/09/20/trump-bondi-truth-social-00574380.

**34.** Devlin Barrett and Jonah E. Bromwich, "Prosecutors Said to Pursue New Investigation of Letitia James," *New York Times*, January 8, 2026, nytimes.com/2026/01/08/us/politics/letitia-james-trump-justice-department.html.

**35.** Julianna Bragg, "Second Grand Jury Refuses to Indict NY Attorney General Letitia James," *Axios*, December 11, 2025, axios.com/2025/12/11/letitia-james-trump-grand-jury-indictment.

**36.** Jacob Rosen et al., "Comey Indicted Again on Charges Stemming from Instagram Post," CBS News, April 28, 2026, cbsnews.com/news/james-comey-indicted-again-by-justice-dept/.

**37.** Alanna Durkin Richer and Eric Tucker, "Grand Jury Refuses to Indict Democratic Lawmakers in Connection with Illegal Military Orders Video," Associated Press, February 10, 2026, apnews.com/article/trump-military-orders-democrats-video-e1435655587ad9715c4d1cc776edd545; Sam Sutton, Josh Gerstein, and Jasper Goodman, "Court Blocks Probe of Fed Chair Jerome Powell, DOJ to Appeal," *Politico*, March 13, 2026, politico.com/news/2026/03/13/court-blocks-dojs-probe-of-fed-chair-jerome-powell-00828448.

**38.** "Granting Pardons and Commutation of Sentences for Certain Offenses Relating to the Event at or Near the United States Capitol on January 6, 2021," White House, January 20, 2025, whitehouse.gov/presidential-actions/2025/01/granting-pardons-and-commutation-of-sentences-for-certain-offenses-relating-to-the-events-at-or-near-the-united-states-capitol-on-january-6-2021/.

**39.** Carter Walker, "Trump Pardons Alleged 'Fake Electors' and Other Allies Who Tried to Undo His 2020 Election Loss," Votebeat, November 10, 2025, votebeat.org/2025/11/10/trump-pardon-fake-elector-2020-election/; Scott Pelly and Maria Gavrilovic, "Trump Pardon of Crypto Billionaire Sparks Concerns over His Use of the Pardon Power," *60 Minutes*, November 16, 2025, cbsnews.com/news/trump-pardon-of-crypto-billionaire-sparks-concerns-over-use-of-pardon-power-60-minutes-transcript/.

**40.** Jeremy Kohler, "How Trump Has Exploited Pardons and Clemency to Reward Allies and Supporters," ProPublica, November 12, 2025, propublica.org/article/trump-pardons-clemency-george-santos-ed-martin.

**41.** "Tracker: Corporate Enforcement at Risk," Public Citizen, citizen.org/article/corporate-enforcement-trump-tracker/; Rick Claypool, "Deleting Tech Enforcement," Public Citizen, August 13, 2025, citizen.org/article/deleting-enforcement-trump-big-tech-billion-report/.

**42.** Ken B. Morales and David Armstrong, "Trump's Justice Department Dropped 23,000 Criminal Investigation in Shift to Immigration," ProPublica, March 31, 2026, propublica.org/article/trump-doj-immigration-bondi-declinations

-criminal-investigations.
**43.** Steve Eder, Michael C. Bender, and David Enrich, "How Trump Appears in the Epstein Files," *New York Times*, February 1, 2026, nytimes.com/2026/02/01/us/trump-epstein-files.html.

## 2: A WEAKER AMERICA AND AN UNSTABLE WORLD

**1.** David E. Sanger, Tyler Pager, Katie Rogers, and Zolan Kanno-Youngs, "Trump Lays Out a Vision of Power Restrained Only by 'My Own Morality,'" *New York Times*, January 8, 2026, nytimes.com/2026/01/08/us/politics/trump-interview-power-morality.html.
**2.** Alexander Rossell Hayes, "Americans Think the War with Iran Will Last Months or More," YouGov, March 10, 2026, yougov.com/en-us/articles/54284-americans-think-war-with-iran-will-last-months-or-more-march-6-9-2026-economist-yougov-poll; "U.S. Foreign Policy, January 2026," Marist Poll, January 16, 2026, maristpoll.marist.edu/polls/u-s-foreign-policy-january-2026/.
**3.** Andrew Restuccia, "Trump Confirms He Was Surprised by Iran's Strikes on Gulf Countries," *Wall Street Journal*, March 16, 2026, wsj.com/livecoverage/iran-war-us-israel-latest-news-2026/card/trump-confirms-he-was-surprised-by-iran-s-strikes-on-gulf-countries-FulWMVtLwtlfCdk8mQiY.
**4.** Benjamin Jensen, "How Would Iran Respond to a U.S. Attack?," Center for Strategic and International Studies, February 26, 2026, csis.org/analysis/how-would-iran-respond-us-attack.
**5.** Scott R. Anderson et al., "Breaking Down Trump's 2025 National Security Strategy," Brookings, December 8, 2025, brookings.edu/articles/breaking-down-trumps-2025-national-security-strategy/.
**6.** *National Security Strategy of the United States of America*, White House, November 2025, whitehouse.gov/wp-content/uploads/2025/12/2025-National-Security-Strategy.pdf.
**7.** Justin Spike and Sam McNeil, "Hungarian Prime Minister Viktor Orbán Ousted After 'Painful' Election Result, Ending 16 Years in Power," Associated Press, April 12, 2026, pbs.org/newshour/world/hungarian-prime-minister-viktor-orban-ousted-after-painful-election-result-ending-16-years-in-power.
**8.** *National Security Strategy of the United States of America.*
**9.** Anderson et al., "Breaking Down Trump's 2025 National Security Strategy."
**10.** "Trump Sides with Russia Against FBI at Helsinki Summit," BBC News, July 16, 2018, bbc.com/news/world-europe-44852812.
**11.** Mariam Khan, "Trump Administration's 28-Point Ukraine-Russia Peace Plan Presented to Zelenskyy," ABC News, November 20, 2025, abcnews.com/International/trump-administrations-28-point-ukraine-russia-peace-plan/story?id=127735249.
**12.** Daniel Dale, "Fact Check: It Wasn't 'in Jest.' Here Are 53 Times Trump Said He'd End Ukraine War Within 24 Hours or Before Taking Office," CNN, April 25, 2025, cnn.com/2025/04/25/politics/fact-check-trump-ukraine-war.
**13.** "Four Years Since the Full-Scale Invasion of Ukraine: Key Facts and Findings,

February 2026," ReliefWeb, United Nations Office for the Coordination of Humanitarian Affairs, February 16, 2026, reliefweb.int/report/ukraine/four-years-full-scale-invasion-ukraine-key-facts-and-findings-february-2026. Seth G. Jones and Riley McCabe, "Russia's Grinding War in Ukraine," Center for Strategic and International Studies, January 27, 2026, https://www.csis.org/analysis/russias-grinding-war-ukraine.

**14.** Ivan Pereira, "Trump Keeps Talking About Making Canada the 51st State. Is He Serious?," ABC News, March 13, 2025, abcnews.go.com/Politics/trump-talking-making-canada-51st-state/story?id=119767909.

**15.** Maggie Haberman, "Trump Says He Asked Mexico to Let U.S. Military In to Fight Cartels," *New York Times*, May 4, 2025, nytimes.com/2025/05/04/us/politics/trump-mexico-sheinbaum-cartels.html.

**16.** Alys Davies, "Trump Ramps Up Threats to Gain Control of Greenland and Panama Canal," BBC News, January 8, 2025, bbc.com/news/articles/c4gzn48jwz2o.

**17.** Damian Murphy, "Shattered Trust: How the Trump Administration's Actions Threaten the U.S..-India Partnership," Center for American Progress, October 15, 2025, americanprogress.org/article/shattered-trust-how-the-trump-administrations-actions-threaten-the-u-s-india-partnership/.

**18.** Eli Stokols and Daniella Cheslow, "After Venezuela Operation, Trump Says the Whole Hemisphere Is in Play," *Politico*, January 3, 2026, politico.com/news/2026/01/03/trump-venezela-mexico-00710063.

**19.** Kori Schake, "Dispensable Nation: America in a Post-American World," *Foreign Affairs* (July/August 2025), foreignaffairs.com/united-states/dispensable-nation-schake.

**20.** Francis Tang, "Japan, South Korea and China Vow to Strengthen Trade Ties amid Looming U.S. Tariffs," *Japan Times*, March 30, 2025, japantimes.co.jp/business/2025/03/30/japan-china-south-korea-trade-ministers/.

**21.** Rob Gillies, "Prime Minister Mark Carney Says Canada Will Double Its Non-US Exports as Canadians Can't Rely on Us," Associated Press, October 23, 2025, apnews.com/article/canada-carney-trump-budget-exports-c78a41c00167bc1d8177d5d74e34d09f.

**22.** Nayara Batschke and Isabel DeBre, "European Union and Mercosur Bloc Sign Landmark Free Trade Agreement," PBS News, January 17, 2026, pbs.org/newshour/world/european-union-and-mercosur-bloc-sign-landmark-free-trade-agreement.

**23.** Julian E. Barnes, "Democrats Raise Concerns over Allied Curbs on Intelligence Sharing," *New York Times*, November 20, 2025, nytimes.com/2025/11/20/us/politics/democrats-allies-intelligence-sharing.html.

**24.** Schake, "Dispensable Nation."

**25.** Jonathan Weisman and Michael Gold, "Ukraine Aid Divides Republicans, After Trump Tones Down His Resistance," *New York Times*, April 20, 2024, nytimes.com/2024/04/20/us/politics/trump-ukraine-house-vote.html.

**26.** Dina Smeltz and Lama El Baz, "US Public Support for Alliances at All-Time High," Chicago Council on Global Affairs, October 14, 2025, globalaffairs.org/research/

public-opinion-survey/us-public-support-alliances-all-time-high.
**27.** *National Security Strategy of the United States of America.*
**28.** Diana Roy, "The U.S. Military Campaign Targeting Venezuela and Nicolás Maduro: What to Know," Council on Foreign Relations, January 3, 2026, cfr.org/articles/operation-southern-spear-us-military-campaign-targeting-venezuela.
**29.** "U.S. Military Kills 6 in Another Strike on Alleged Drug Boat in the Eastern Pacific," PBS News, March 9, 2026, pbs.org/newshour/world/u-s-military-kills-6-in-another-strike-on-alleged-drug-boat-in-the-eastern-pacific.
**30.** Julian E. Barnes, "Venezuela Doesn't Produce Fentanyl. Trump Is Targeting It Anyway," *New York Times*, November 19, 2025, nytimes.com/2025/11/19/us/politics/trump-venezuela-fentanyl.html.
**31.** Press release, "Juan Orlando Hernández, Former President of Honduras, Sentenced to 45 Years in Prison for Conspiring to Distribute More than 400 Tons of Cocaine and Related Firearms Offenses," Office of Public Affairs, U.S. Department of Justice, June 26, 2024, justice.gov/archives/opa/pr/juan-orlando-hernandez-former-president-honduras-sentenced-45-years-prison-conspiring.
**32.** Annie Correal, Jeff Ernst, Shawn McCreesh, and David C. Adams, "Trump Announces Pardon for Honduran Ex-President Convicted in Drug Case," *New York Times*, November 28, 2025, nytimes.com/2025/11/28/world/americas/trump-pardon-honduras-hernandez.html.
**33.** Roy, "The U.S. Military Campaign Targeting Venezuela and Nicolás Maduro."
**34.** "Fact Sheet: President Donald J. Trump Withdraws the United States from International Organizations That Are Contrary to the Interests of the United States," White House, January 7, 2026, whitehouse.gov/fact-sheets/2026/01/fact-sheet-president-donald-j-trump-withdraws-the-united-states-from-international-organizations-that-are-contrary-to-the-interests-of-the-united-states/.
**35.** Matthew Lee, Farnoush Amiri, and Manuel Balce Ceneta, "State Department Lays Off over 1,300 Employees Under Trump Administration Plan," Associated Press, July 12, 2025, apnews.com/article/layoffs-diplomats-state-department-trump-rubio-bfdb86767b7bd5b6570819d404a7782e.
**36.** Matthew Lee, "Trump Recalls Nearly 30 Career Diplomats from Ambassadorial and Embassy Posts," PBS News, December 22, 2025, pbs.org/newshour/nation/trump-recalls-nearly-30-career-diplomats-from-ambassadorial-and-embassy-posts.
**37.** Atul Gawande, Thomas Jennings, and Annie Wong, "The Shutdown of U.S.A.I.D. Has Already Killed Hundreds of Thousands," *New Yorker*, November 5, 2025, newyorker.com/culture/the-new-yorker-documentary/the-shutdown-of-usaid-has-already-killed-hundreds-of-thousands.
**38.** Neil Vigdor, "Bill Gates Accuses Elon Musk of 'Killing Children' by Cutting Foreign Aid," *New York Times*, May 8, 2025, nytimes.com/2025/05/08/us/bill-gates-elon-musk-killing-children.html.
**39.** J. Brian Atwood and Andrew S. Natsios, "What Americans Lost in the Dismantling

of USAID," *The Hill*, January 8, 2026, thehill.com/opinion/international/5677205-consequences-usaid-dismantlement.
**40.** Chris Whipple, "Susie Wiles, JD Vance, and the 'Junkyard Dogs': The White House Chief of Staff on Trump's Second Term (Part 1 of 2)," *Vanity Fair*, December 16, 2025, vanityfair.com/news/story/trump-susie-wiles-interview-exclusive-part-1.
**41.** Risa Brooks, "The Dangerous New Civil-Military Bargain," *Foreign Affairs*, April 8, 2025, foreignaffairs.com/united-states/dangerous-new-civil-military-bargain.
**42.** Lauren Floyd, "Trump Ousts Top U.S. Gen. Charles 'CQ' Brown and Other Leaders," *Axios*, February 22, 2025, axios.com/2025/02/22/trump-fires-general-charles-cq-brown.
**43.** Lolita C. Baldor, "Hegseth Says He Fired the Top Military Lawyers Because They Weren't Well Suited for the Jobs," Associated Press, February 24, 2025, apnews.com/article/pentagon-hegseth-firing-chairman-lawyers-6bead-3346b1210e45e77648e6cbc3599.
**44.** Rachel Muller-Heyndyk, "Pentagon Fires Intelligence Chief After Iran Attack Assessment," BBC News, August 23, 2025, bbc.com/news/articles/c2dj217z2w6o.
**45.** "National Security Leaders for America Warns Against the Politicization of U.S. Intelligence," National Security Leaders for America, November 6, 2025, nsl4a.org/nsl4a-announcements/nsl4a-warns-against-politicalization-intelligence.
**46.** Greg Jaffe, Eric Schmitt, and Helene Cooper, "Hegseth Is Purging Military Leaders with Little Explanation," *New York Times*, November 7, 2025, nytimes.com/2025/11/07/us/politics/hegseth-firing-military-leaders.html.
**47.** Seth Hettena, "SEAL Commander Fired After Clashes with Pentagon," *After-Action Report*, August 25, 2025, theiceman.substack.com/p/seal-commander-fired-after-clashes.
**48.** Ellen Mitchell, "Hegseth Ousted Navy Admiral Who Raised Concerns About Boat Strikes," *The Hill*, December 4, 2025, thehill.com/policy/defense/5634202-hegseth-holsey-boat-strikes/.
**49.** Colin Demarest, "Hegseth's Wartime Firing of Top Generals Stuns Officials: 'It's Insane,'" *Axios*, April 3, 2026, axios.com/2026/04/03/hegseth-george-hodne-army-fired-iran.
**50.** Jaffe, Schmitt, and Cooper, "Hegseth Is Purging Military Leaders with Little Explanation."
**51.** Ibid.
**52.** "President Trump Gives Remarks to Fort Bragg Military Families," C-SPAN, February 13, 2026, c-span.org/program/white-house-event/president-trump-gives-remarks-to-fort-bragg-military-families/673441.
**53.** Abigail Hauslohner, Liz Goodwin, and Meryl Kornfield, "Pete Hegseth Confirmed as Defense Secretary After Vance Breaks Tie," *Washington Post*, January 25, 2025, washingtonpost.com/national-security/2025/01/24/hegseth-senate-confirmation-vote/.
**54.** Chris Bocia, "Top Democrat Presses Hegseth on Supporting Accused War Criminals That Trump Pardoned," ABC News, January 14, 2025, abcnews.com/Politics/

top-democrat-presses-hegseth-supporting-accused-war-criminals/story?id=117669602.
**55.** "U.S. Military Strike on Alleged Drug Boat Kills 2 in Eastern Pacific," Associated Press, April 25, 2026, nbcnews.com/politics/politics-news/us-military-strike-alleged-drug-boat-kills-2-eastern-pacific-rcna342030.
**56.** "Chart Pack: Defense Spending," Peter G. Peterson Foundation, updated February 17, 2026, pgpf.org/article/chart-pack-defense-spending/.

## 3: AN UNAFFORDABLE ECONOMY

**1.** Lisa Lerer, Ruth Igielnik, and Camille Baker, "Voters See a Middle-Class Lifestyle as Drifting Out of Reach, Poll Finds," *New York Times*, January 26, 2026, nytimes.com/2026/01/26/us/politics/affordability-poll.html.
**2.** Ted Van Green, Andy Cerda, and Steven Shepard, "A Year into Trump's Second Term, Americans' Views of the Economy Remain Negative," Pew Research Center, February 4, 2026, pewresearch.org/politics/2026/02/04/a-year-into-trumps-second-term-americans-views-of-the-economy-remain-negative/.
**3.** Osmond Chia and Nick Marsh, "China Announces Record $1tn Trade Surplus Despite Trump Tariffs," BBC News, January 14, 2026, bbc.com/news/articles/c9wx1v84rzyo.
**4.** David Lynch and Rachel Siegel, "U.S. Runs Record Trade Deficit in Goods, Despite Trump's Tariffs Policy," *Washington Post*, February 19, 2026, washingtonpost.com/business/2026/02/19/tariffs-trade-deficit-2025/?utm_campaign=wp_main&utm_source=bluesky&utm_medium=social.
**5.** Sawdah Bhaimiya, "China's Tech Shock Threatens the U.S. Ai Monopoly and Is 'Just Getting Started,'" CNBC, February 16, 2026, cnbc.com/2026/02/16/chinas-tech-shock-ai-monopoly-us.html#:~:text=China%20is%20quickly%20catching%20up,and%20abundant%20low%2Dcost%20energy.
**6.** "Employment Situation Summary," U.S. Bureau of Labor Statistics, February 11, 2026, bls.gov/news.release/empsit.nr0.htm.
**7.** Steve Kopack, "U.S. Gained 130,000 Jobs Last Month, but Labor Market Growth Stalled in 2025," NBC News, February 11, 2026, nbcnews.com/business/economy/january-jobs-revisions-trump-rcna258398.
**8.** Chad P. Bown, "US-China Trade War Tariffs: An Up-to-Date Chart," Peterson Institute for International Economics, November 14, 2025, piie.com/research/piie-charts/2019/us-china-trade-war-tariffs-date-chart.
**9.** Robert McClelland and John Wong, "TPC Tariff Tracker," Tax Policy Center, April 6, 2026, taxpolicycenter.org/features/tracking-trump-tariffs.
**10.** Mary Amiti et al., "Who Is Paying for the 2025 U.S. Tariffs?," *Liberty Street Economics*, Federal Reserve Bank of New York, February 12, 2026, libertystreeteconomics.newyorkfed.org/2026/02/who-is-paying-for-the-2025-u-s-tariffs/.
**11.** Barath Harithas et al., "'Liberation Day' Tariffs Explained," Center for Strategic and International Studies, April 3, 2025, csis.org/analysis/liberation-day-tariffs-explained.

**12.** Marin Heusel, "Opinion: Liberation Day and the Impact on the American Stock Market," *Michigan Journal of Economics*, May 2, 2025, sites.lsa.umich.edu/mje/2025/05/02/opinion-liberation-day-and-the-impact-on-the-american-stock-market/.
**13.** Rob Wile, Colleen Long, and Shannon Pettypiece, "Trump Suddenly Backs Off Global Tariff Plan After Days of Economic and Market Turmoil," NBC News, April 9, 2025, nbcnews.com/business/economy/trump-tariffs-president-announces-90-day-pause-what-to-know-rcna200463.
**14.** "Survey: CEOS Start 2026 on Edge, Citing Uncertainty as Top Threat," Conference Board, January 15, 2026, conference-board.org/topics/c-suite-outlook/press/c-suite-outlook-2026.
**15.** Nich Tremper, "The State of Small Business 2025: Resilience Despite Rising Costs and Economic Uncertainty," Gusto, October 20, 2025, gusto.com/resources/gusto-insights/state-of-smb-2025.
**16.** Neil Bradley, "Latest Tariffs Spell $200 Billion Annual Tax for Small Businesses," U.S. Chamber of Commerce, August 1, 2025, uschamber.com/tariffs/latest-tariffs-spell-200-billion-annual-tax-for-small-businesses.
**17.** Scott Gerit, "Soybean Losses Continue Despite Assistance," American Soybean Association, January 27, 2026, soygrowers.com/news-releases/soybean-losses-continue-despite-assistance/.
**18.** Ken Roberts, "China Ends Longest Boycott of U.S. Soybeans, Still a 99% Decline," *Forbes*, February 5, 2026, forbes.com/sites/kenroberts/2026/02/05/china-ends-longest-boycott-of-us-soybeans-still-a-99-decline/.
**19.** Samantha Ayoub, "Farm Bankruptcies Continued to Climb in 2025," American Farm Bureau Federation, February 9, 2026, fb.org/market-intel/farm-bankruptcies-continued-to-climb-in-2025.
**20.** Daniel Munch and Faith Parum, "USDA Lowers 2025 Farm Income by $25 Billion," American Farm Bureau Federation, February 5, 2026, fb.org/market-intel/usda-cuts-2025-farm-income-as-weakness-persists-into-2026.
**21.** Eric Revell, "How Much Did Trade War Relief Cost During Trump's First Term?," Fox Business, April 2, 2025, foxbusiness.com/politics/how-much-did-trade-war-relief-cost-during-trumps-first-term.
**22.** Press release, "Trump Administration Announces $12 Billion Farmer Bridge Payments for American Farmers Impacted by Unfair Market Disruptions," U.S. Department of Agriculture, December 8, 2025, usda.gov/about-usda/news/press-releases/2025/12/08/trump-administration-announces-12-billion-farmer-bridge-payments-american-farmers-impacted-unfair.
**23.** Clark Packard and Alfredo Carrillo Obregon, "Manufacturing Employment Data Confirm the Concentrated Benefits—and Dispersed Costs—of Trump's Tariffs," Cato Institute, January 16, 2026, cato.org/blog/manufacturing-employment-data-confirms-concentrated-benefits-dispersed-costs-trumps-tariffs.
**24.** Lori Ann LaRocco, "Trump's Tariffs Trigger Rising Rate of Job Layoffs Inside

Supply Chain: ASCM/CNBC Survey," CNBC, January 12, 2026, cnbc.com/2026/01/12/trump-tariffs-jobs-layoffs-economy.html.
**25.** *Learning Resources, Inc. v. Trump*, 607 U.S. ____ (2026).
**26.** Edward Alden et al., "Geopolitics of Trump Tariffs: How U.S. Trade Policy Has Shaken Allies," Council on Foreign Relations, September 10, 2025, cfr.org/articles/geopolitics-trump-tariffs-how-us-trade-policy-has-shaken-allies.
**27.** Li Yuan, "Trump's Tariffs Set Off Day of Anger, Retaliation and Market Unease," *New York Times*, March 4, 2025, nytimes.com/live/2025/03/04/us/tariffs-us-canada-mexico-china.
**28.** DeLeon Thorton, Emily Park, and Shawn Baldwin, "How Boycotts on American Products and Travel Are Impacting the U.S.," CNBC, July 22, 2025, cnbc.com/video/2025/07/22/how-boycotts-on-american-products-and-travel-are-impacting-the-us.html.
**29.** Matinas Stevis-Gridneff and Ian Austen, "Betrayed: How Trump's Tariff Threats Tore the U.S.-Canada Bond," *New York Times*, February 11, 2025, nytimes.com/2025/02/08/world/canada/us-canada-relations-trump-tariffs.html.
**30.** Diego Marroquín Bitar, Ryan C. Berg, Christopher Hernandez-Roy, and Henry Ziemer, "From Monterrey to Michigan to Mississauga: The Engine Driving U.S. Competitiveness," Center for Strategic and International Studies, September 4, 2025, csis.org/analysis/monterrey-michigan-mississauga-engine-driving-us-competitiveness.
**31.** "Our Statement Regarding the U.S. Auto Tariffs," Canadian Chamber of Commerce, March 26, 2025, chamber.ca/news/our-statement-regarding-the-u-s-auto-tariffs/.
**32.** Curtis Heinzl, "U.S. Auto Market Share in Canada Hits Record Low on Tariff Turmoil," Bloomberg, January 16, 2026, bloomberg.com/news/articles/2026-01-16/us-auto-market-share-tumbles-in-canada-with-trade-war-raging?embedded-checkout=true.
**33.** Jack Ewing, "U.S. Automakers' Foreign Troubles Now Extend to Canada," *New York Times*, January 24, 2026, nytimes.com/2026/01/24/business/general-motors-ford-canada-china.html.
**34.** "Estimated Budgetary Effects of Public Law 119-21, to Provide for Reconciliation Pursuant to Title II of H. Con. Res. 14, Relative to CBO's January 2025 Baseline," Congressional Budget Office, July 21, 2025, cbo.gov/publication/61570.
**35.** "What Is the National Debt?," U.S. Treasury, March 11, 2026, fiscaldata.treasury.gov/americas-finance-guide/national-debt/#the-growing-national-debt.
**36.** "The Budget and Economic Outlook: 2018 to 2028," U.S. Congressional Budget Office, April 9, 2018, cbo.gov/publication/53651.
**37.** "T17-0314—Conference Agreement: The Tax Cuts and Jobs Act; Baseline: Current Law; Distribution of Federal Tax Change by Expanded Cash Income Percentile, 2025," Tax Policy Center, December 18, 2017, taxpolicycenter.org/model-estimates/conference-agreement-tax-cuts-and-jobs-act-dec-2017/t17-0314-conference-agreement.
**38.** Corey Husak, "7 Ways the Big Beautiful Bill Cuts Taxes for the Rich," Center for American Progress, November 20, 2025, americanprogress.org/article/7-ways-the-big-

beautiful-bill-cuts-taxes-for-the-rich/.
**39.** "Long-Term Impacts of the One Big Beautiful Bill Act, as Enacted on July 4, 2025," Yale Budget Lab, July 30, 2025, budgetlab.yale.edu/research/long-term-impacts-one-big-beautiful-bill-act-enacted-july-4-2025.
**40.** "Interest Costs on the National Debt Are Reaching All-Time Highs," Peter G. Peterson Foundation, updated February 12, 2026, pgpf.org/article/any-way-you-look-at-it-interest-costs-on-the-national-debt-will-soon-be-at-an-all-time-high/.
**41.** "Long-Term Impacts of the One Big Beautiful Bill Act."
**42.** Jim Edwards, "'Sell America': Investors Dump U.S. Assets in Fear of the End of Fed Independence," *Fortune*, January 12, 2026, fortune.com/2026/01/12/sell-america-stocks-fed-independence/.
**43.** "Board Members," Federal Reserve Board—Board Members, 2026, federalreserve.gov/aboutthefed/bios/board/default.htm.
**44.** Christopher Rugaber and Eric Tucker, "Justice Department Drops Criminal Probe of Fed Chair Powell, Likely Clearing the Way for Warsh," Associated Press, April 24, 2026, apnews.com/article/federal-reserve-investigation-powell-justice-department-28d04cc0d99cda25cea69931f65e25d3.
**45.** Steve Kopack, "Lisa Cook Bank Docs Appear to Contradict Mortgage Fraud Allegations," NBC News, September 13, 2025, nbcnews.com/politics/trump-administration/lisa-cook-federal-reserve-bank-documents-mortgage-fraud-allegations-rcna230964.
**46.** Luis I. Jácome and Samuel Pienknagura, "Central Bank Independence and Inflation Tail Risks—Evidence from Emerging Markets," *Journal of International Money and Finance* 153 (March 2025): 103285, doi.org/10.1016/j.jimonfin.2025.103285.
**47.** Nina Totenberg, "Supreme Court Doubtful of Trump Claim He Can Fire Fed Governors by Fiat," *All Things Considered*, NPR, January 21, 2026, npr.org/2026/01/21/nx-s1-5683968/supreme-court-federal-reserve-lisa-cook.
**48.** About 60 percent of the world's current reserves are held in dollars. Trevor Jackson, "The Struggle for the Fed," *New York Review of Books*, February 26, 2026, nybooks.com/articles/2026/02/26/the-struggle-for-the-fed-our-money-downey/.
**49.** Daniel Dale, "Fact Check: Trump's '$17 Trillion' Investment Figure Is Fiction," CNN, October 11, 2025, cnn.com/2025/10/11/politics/fact-check-trump-17-trillion-investment.
**50.** Josh Boak, "Trump Says the US Has Secured $17 Trillion in New Investments. The Real Number Is Likely Much Less," Associated Press, October 6, 2025, apnews.com/article/trump-tariffs-investment-trillions-economy-jobs-eb4ca4b9ed632bd12c559c1ec5fd5764.
**51.** River Akira Davis and Chloe Sang-Hun, "Murky Pledges of Investment Cast Shadow on Trump's Trade Deals," *New York Times*, July 31, 2025, nytimes.com/2025/07/31/business/trump-japan-south-korea-investment.html.
**52.** Eliot Brown, "A Multitrillion-Dollar Wave of Investment? Think Again, Says Goldman Sachs," *Wall Street Journal*, May 16, 2025, wsj.com/livecoverage/stock-market-

today-tariffs-trade-war-05-16-2025/card/a-multitrillion-dollar-wave-of-investment-think-again-says-goldman-sachs-VA1FFKzyk8ZTD9GGWxmk.

**53.** Spencer Kimball, "Trump Administration Equity Stakes Pose Risks to U.S. Companies and Markets," CNBC, February 7, 2026, cnbc.com/2026/02/07/trump-equity-stakes-pose-these-risks-to-us-companies-and-markets.html.

**54.** Ibid.

**55.** Louise Matsakis, "Nvidia's Campaign to Sell AI Chips to China Finally Pays Off," *Wired*, January 29, 2026, wired.com/story/made-in-china-china-nvidia-h200-beijing-approval/.

**56.** David E. Sanger, "Trump's Nvidia Chip Deal Reverses Decades of Technology Restrictions," *New York Times*, December 15, 2025, nytimes.com/2025/12/09/us/politics/trump-nvidia-ai-chips-china.html.

**57.** Annie Massa and Tom Maloney, "Trump Family's $6.8 Billion Fortune Is Increasingly Tied to Crypto," Bloomberg, January 20, 2026, bloomberg.com/news/features/2026-01-20/donald-trump-family-net-worth-increasingly-comes-from-crypto.

**58.** "Fact Sheet: President Donald J. Trump Establishes the Strategic Bitcoin Reserve and U.S. Digital Asset Stockpile," White House, March 6, 2025, whitehouse.gov/fact-sheets/2025/03/fact-sheet-president-donald-j-trump-establishes-the-strategic-bitcoin-reserve-and-u-s-digital-asset-stockpile/.

**59.** João da Silva, "Trump Crypto Soars as US President Offers Dinner to Top Holders," BBC News, April 24, 2025, bbc.com/news/articles/ce8g2kpzx0go.

**60.** Tonantzin Carmona, "Protecting the American Public from Crypto Risks and Harms," Brookings, June 2, 2025, brookings.edu/articles/protecting-the-american-public-from-crypto-risks-and-harms/.

**61.** "Speech: Donald Trump Holds a Campaign Rally in Savannah, Georgia—September 24, 2024," *Roll Call*, transcript, rollcall.com/factbase/trump/transcript/donald-trump-speech-campaign-rally-savannah-georgia-september-24-2024/.

**62.** Ibid.

**63.** "All Employees, Manufacturing," FRED, Federal Reserve Bank of St. Louis, March 6, 2026, fred.stlouisfed.org/series/MANEMP.

**64.** "All Employees, Coal Mining," FRED, Federal Reserve Bank of St. Louis, March 6, 2026, fred.stlouisfed.org/graph/?g=1SAmh.

**65.** "Table A-2. Employment Status of the Civilian Population by Race, Sex, and Age," U.S. Bureau of Labor Statistics, March 6, 2026, bls.gov/news.release/empsit.t02.htm.

**66.** "Progress: Jobs Report Shows Private Sector Gains, Wage Growth for American-Born Workers," White House, November 20, 2025, whitehouse.gov/articles/2025/11/progress-jobs-report-shows-private-sector-gains-wage-growth-for-american-born-workers/.

**67.** "Table A-7. Employment Status of the Civilian Population by Nativity and Sex, Not Seasonally Adjusted," U.S. Bureau of Labor Statistics, March 6, 2026, bls.gov/news.release/empsit.t07.htm.

**68.** Gina Plata-Nino, "SNAP's Critical Role in Rural Communities—and the Consequences of Cuts," Food Research & Action Center, August 25, 2025, frac.org/blog/snaps-critical-role-in-rural-communities-and-the-consequences-of-cuts.
**69.** "Preparing Americans for High-Paying Skilled Trade Jobs of the Future," White House, April 23, 2025, whitehouse.gov/presidential-actions/2025/04/preparing-americans-for-high-paying-skilled-trade-jobs-of-the-future/.
**70.** "Apprentices by State Dashboard," ApprenticeshipUSA, U.S. Department of Labor, apprenticeship.gov/data-and-statistics/apprentices-by-state-dashboard.
**71.** Anne Kim, "Trump's Broken Promise of 'One Million Apprentices,'" *Washington Monthly*, December 4, 2025, washingtonmonthly.com/2025/12/04/trump-one-million-apprenticeships-broken-promise/.
**72.** Paul Fain, "Widening DEI Purge," *Work Shift*, February 20, 2025, workshift.org/workforce-projects-eyed-as-part-of-widening-dei-purge/.

### 4: A SICKER, UNHEALTHIER AMERICA

**1.** "Fact Sheet: President Donald J. Trump Calls on Congress to Enact the Great Healthcare Plan," White House, January 15, 2026, whitehouse.gov/fact-sheets/2026/01/fact-sheet-president-donald-j-trump-calls-on-congress-to-enact-the-great-healthcare-plan/.
**2.** Kyle K. Moore, "Trump's Gutting of Public Health Institutions Is Setting the Stage for Our Next Crisis," Economic Policy Institute, April 21, 2025, epi.org/blog/trumps-gutting-of-public-health-institutions-is-setting-the-stage-for-our-next-crisis/.
**3.** "Measles Cases and Outbreaks," Centers for Disease Control and Prevention, April 24, 2026, cdc.gov/measles/data-research/index.html.
**4.** Teddy Rosenbluth, "Meeting on U.S. Measles Status Is Delayed Until November," *New York Times*, March 2, 2026, nytimes.com/2026/03/02/well/measles-elimination-status-us.html.
**5.** Jared Ortaliza et al., "How Will the One Big Beautiful Bill Act Affect the ACA, Medicaid, and the Uninsured Rate?," KFF, August 11, 2025, kff.org/affordable-care-act/how-will-the-2025-budget-reconciliation-affect-the-aca-medicaid-and-the-uninsured-rate/.
**6.** Max Kozlov, Jeff Tollefson, and Dan Garisto, "US Science After a Year of Trump," *Nature*, January 20, 2026, nature.com/immersive/d41586-026-00088-9/index.htmls.
**7.** "Before the ACA, 1 in 7 People Were Denied Coverage Because of Pre-Existing Conditions. Today: None," HealthNetwork, November 7, 2015, healthnetwork.com/blog/before-the-aca-1-in-7-people-were-denied-coverage-because-of-pre-existing-conditions-today-none/.
**8.** Teresa Coughlin, Haley Samuel-Jakobus, and Rachel Garfield, "Sources of Payment for Uncompensated Care for the Uninsured," KFF, April 6, 2021, kff.org/affordable-care-act/sources-of-payment-for-uncompensated-care-for-the-uninsured/.
**9.** Jared Ortaliza, Matt McGough, and Cynthia Cox, "The Affordable Care Act 101,"

KFF, October 8, 2025, kff.org/affordable-care-act/health-policy-101-the-affordable-care-act/?entry=table-of-contents-what-did-the-aca-change-about-health-coverage-in-the-u-s.

**10.** Jennifer Tolbert et al., "The Uninsured Population and Health Coverage," KFF, October 8, 2025, kff.org/uninsured/health-policy-101-the-uninsured-population-and-health-coverage/?entry=table-of-contents-introduction.

**11.** "Marketplace 2025 Open Enrollment Period Report: National Snapshot," CMS Newsroom, Centers for Medicare and Medicaid Services, January 17, 2025, cms.gov/newsroom/fact-sheets/marketplace-2025-open-enrollment-period-report-national-snapshot-2.

**12.** "Health Coverage Under the Affordable Care Act: Current Enrollment Trends and State Estimates," Office of Health Policy, Assistant Secretary for Planning and Evaluation, U.S. Department of Health and Human Services, March 22, 2024, aspe.hhs.gov/sites/default/files/documents/b07715d223280dc544cf26fcd19040fb/aspe-health-coverage-under-aca.pdf.

**13.** Gideon Lukens and Elizabeth Zhang, "Health Insurance Premium Spikes Imminent as Tax Credit Enhancements Set to Expire," Center on Budget and Policy Priorities, November 3, 2025, cbpp.org/research/health/health-insurance-premium-spikes-imminent-as-tax-credit-enhancements-set-to-expire.

**14.** Cynthia Cox, "ACA Insurers Are Raising Premiums by an Estimated 26%, but Most Enrollees Could See Sharper Increases in What They Pay," KFF, October 28, 2025, kff.org/quick-take/aca-insurers-are-raising-premiums-by-an-estimated-26-but-most-enrollees-could-see-sharper-increases-in-what-they-pay/.

**15.** Press release, "Wyden, Neal, Pallone Release Latest CBO Estimates Showing 16 Million People Will Become Uninsured from Republican Health Agenda," U.S. Senate Committee on Finance, June 4, 2025, finance.senate.gov/ranking-members-news/wyden-neal-pallone-release-latest-cbo-estimates-showing-16-million-people-will-become-uninsured-from-republican-health-agenda.

**16.** Noam Levey, "Republicans Push High Deductible Plans and Health Savings Accounts," NPR, December 8, 2025, npr.org/sections/shots-health-news/2025/12/08/nx-s1-5629249/hsa-high-deductible-health-plan.

**17.** Shameek Rakshit et al., "How Has U.S. Healthcare Spending Changed Over Time?," KFF, January 22, 2026, healthsystemtracker.org/chart-collection/u-s-spending-healthcare-changed-time.

**18.** "Why Health Insurance Is Important," HealthCare.gov, accessed April 26, 2026, healthcare.gov/why-coverage-is-important/protection-from-high-medical-costs/.

**19.** Raymond Kluender et al., "Medical Debt in the US, 2009–2020," *JAMA* 326, no. 3 (July 20, 2021): 250, doi.org/10.1001/jama.2021.8694.

**20.** Alice Burns, Elizabeth Hinton, Robin Rudowitz, and Maiss Mohamed, "10 Things to Know About Medicaid," KFF, February 18, 2025, kff.org/medicaid/10-things-to-know-about-medicaid/.

**21.** "Health Provisions in the 2025 Federal Budget Reconciliation Law," KFF, August 22, 2025, kff.org/medicaid/health-provisions-in-the-2025-federal-budget-reconciliation-law/#2ca666ac-5d15-4454-8973-241566e22bb5.
**22.** Edwin Park and Sabrina Corlette, "Medicaid, CHIP, and Affordable Care Act Marketplace Cuts and Other Health Provisions in the Budget Reconciliation Law, Explained," Center for Children and Families, July 22, 2025, ccf.georgetown.edu/2025/07/22/medicaid-chip-and-affordable-care-act-marketplace-cuts-and-other-health-provisions-in-the-budget-reconciliation-law-explained/.
**23.** "Supplemental Cost Estimate: Public Law 119-21, to Provide for Reconciliation Pursuant to Title II of H. Con. Res. 14 Title VII, Finance, Subtitle B, Health, Chapter 1, Medicaid," Congressional Budget Office, October 28, 2025, cbo.gov/system/files/2025-10/PL-119-21-Medicaid%20_0.pdf.
**24.** "Medicaid Cuts Likely to Affect Urban Safety-Net Hospitals," Healthcare Quality and Outcomes Lab, T. H. Chan School of Public Health, Harvard University, November 17, 2025, hsph.harvard.edu/health-quality/news/medicaid-cuts-likely-to-affect-urban-safety-net-hospitals/.
**25.** Center for Reproductive Rights, "Trump's (Second) First Year: New and Emerging Threats to Reproductive Rights," January 5, 2026, reproductiverights.org/wp-content/uploads/2026/01/12-01-2025_One-Year-Report_RRF.pdf.
**26.** Ibid.
**27.** Brittni Fredericksen, Ivette Gomez, and Alina Salganicoff, "Title X Grantees and Clinics Affected by the Trump Administration's Funding Freeze," KFF, April 15, 2025, kff.org/womens-health-policy/title-x-grantees-and-clinics-affected-by-the-trump-administrations-funding-freeze.
**28.** Irving Washington, Hagere Yilma, and Joel Luther, "Abortion Pill Safety Decisions by FDA Were Science-Based, New JAMA Study Finds," KFF, January 29, 2026, kff.org/health-information-trust/abortion-pill-safety-decisions-by-fda-were-science-based-new-jama-study-finds/.
**29.** "Healthcare Policy in Flux: The Impact of Trump Administration Changes to HHS," Debevoise & Plimpton, March 28, 2025, debevoise.com/insights/publications/2025/03/healthcare-policy-in-flux-the-impact-of-trump.
**30.** Aria Bendix, "National Institutes of Health Faces Leadership Vacuum as Director Positions Sit Open," NBC News, February 15, 2026, nbcnews.com/health/health-news/national-institutes-health-director-positions-unfilled-rcna257834.
**31.** Jan Hoffman, "Federal Agency Dedicated to Mental Illness and Addiction Faces Huge Cuts," *New York Times*, March 12, 2025, nytimes.com/2025/03/12/health/federal-cuts-substance-abuse-mental-health.html.
**32.** Dan Vergano, "Halted NIH Clinical Trials List Reveals Slashed Treatments for Cancer, Covid and Minority Health," ed. Claire Cameron, *Scientific American*, November 20, 2025, scientificamerican.com/article/halted-nih-clinical-trials-list-reveals-slashed-treatments-for-cancer-covid.

**33.** Bruce Y. Lee, "NIH Awarded 22% Fewer Grants in 2025, a 24% Drop in Cancer Research," *Forbes*, December 8, 2025, forbes.com/sites/brucelee/2025/12/08/nih-awarded-22-fewer-grants-in-2025-a-24-drop-in-cancer-research/.

**34.** Ekaterina Galkina Cleary et al., "Comparison of Research Spending on New Drug Approvals by the National Institutes of Health vs. the Pharmaceutical Industry, 2010–2019," *JAMA Health Forum* 4, no. 4 (April 28, 2023), doi.org/10.1001/jamahealthforum.2023.0511.

**35.** Leighton Ku et al., "Proposed Budget Cuts Not Only Hurt CDC and Public Health, They Also Harm State and Local Economies and Employment," Center for Health Policy Research, Milken Institute School of Public Health, George Washington University, September 10, 2025, publichealth.gwu.edu/new-research-proposed-cdc-budget-cuts-harm-public-health-and-state-and-local-economies.

**36.** Brandy Zadrozny, "CDC Is Pulling Back $11B in COVID Funding Sent to Health Departments Across the U.S.," NBC News, March 25, 2025, nbcnews.com/health/health-news/cdc-pulling-back-11b-covid-funding-sent-health-departments-us-rcna198006.

**37.** Sheryl Gay Stolberg, "Trump Administration Lays off Dozens of C.D.C. Officials," *New York Times*, October 11, 2025, nytimes.com/2025/10/11/us/politics/trump-administration-cdc-layoffs.html.

**38.** Press release, "CDC Acts on Presidential Memorandum to Update Childhood Immunization Schedule," Centers for Disease Control and Prevention, January 5, 2026, cdc.gov/media/releases/2026/2026-cdc-acts-on-presidential-memorandum-to-update-childhood-immunization-schedule.html.

**39.** Sophia Samantaroy, "US Shrinks Childhood Vaccine Schedule; Drops Six Common Vaccines from CDC Recommendations," *Health Policy Watch*, January 6, 2026, healthpolicy-watch.news/us-alters-childhood-vaccine-schedule-drops-six-common-vaccines/.

**40.** Press release, "Federal Changes to Childhood Vaccine Schedule Raise Alarm Among Physicians," California Medical Association, January 8, 2026, cmadocs.org/newsroom/news/view/ArticleId/51103/Federal-changes-to-childhood-vaccine-schedule-raise-alarm-among-physicians.

**41.** Adekunle F. Adeoye et al., "The 2025 United States Measles Crisis: When Vaccine Hesitancy Meets Reality," *Cureus Journal of Medical Science*, July 17, 2025, doi.org/10.7759/cureus.88196.

**42.** "Fact Checked: U.S. Vaccine Recommendations Are Appropriate for Children in the United States," American Academy of Pediatrics, December 4, 2025, aap.org/en/news-room/fact-checked/fact-checked-u.s.-vaccine-recommendations-are-appropriate-for-children-in-the-united-states.

**43.** Press release, "Kennedy, Rollins Unveil Historic Reset of U.S. Nutrition Policy, Put Real Food Back at Center of Health," U.S. Department of Agriculture, January 7, 2026, usda.gov/about-usda/news/press-releases/2026/01/07/kennedy-rollins-unveil-

historic-reset-us-nutrition-policy-put-real-food-back-center-health.
**44.** Richard Boxer, "Diminishing the National Cancer Institute Threatens Americans," *ASCO Post*, November 10, 2025, ascopost.com/issues/november-10-2025/diminishing-the-national-cancer-institute-threatens-americans.
**45.** Press release, "ACS Annual Report: Cancer Mortality Continues to Drop Despite Rising Incidence in Women; Rates of New Diagnoses Under 65 Higher in Women than Men," American Cancer Society, January 16, 2025, pressroom.cancer.org/2025Cancer-FactsandFigures.
**46.** F. André et al., "The Rising Tides of Cancers Among Young Adults," *ESMO Open* 10, no. 9 (September 2025): 105553, doi.org/10.1016/j.esmoop.2025.105553.
**47.** Bernie Sanders, "Minority Staff Report: Trump's War on Science," U.S. Senate, Health, Education, Labor, and Pensions Committee, May 13, 2025, sanders.senate.gov/wp-content/uploads/HELP-Committee-Minority-Report-Trumps-War-on-Science.pdf.
**48.** Allen Wilbanks, "2026 NCI Drops from $7.22B to $4.10B: Cancer Research Budget Cuts," *OncologyTube*, May 23, 2025, oncologytube.com/2026-cancer-research-budget-changes/.
**49.** Smita Bhatia et al., "Rural–Urban Disparities in Cancer Outcomes: Opportunities for Future Research," *Journal of the National Cancer Institute* 114, no. 7 (February 11, 2022): 940–52, doi.org/10.1093/jnci/djac030.
**50.** "What Recent Federal Law Changes Impact the Cancer Community?," Triage Cancer, February 24, 2026, triagecancer.org/what-recent-federal-law-changes-impact-the-cancer-community.
**51.** "Choose Europe for Science: EU Comes Together to Attract Top Research Talent," Directorate-General for Research and Innovation, European Union, May 23, 2025, research-and-innovation.ec.europa.eu/news/all-research-and-innovation-news/choose-europe-science-eu-comes-together-attract-top-research-talent-2025-05-23_en.

## 5: AN UNPRECEDENTED ATTACK ON EDUCATION

**1.** "Apr 23, 1635 CE: First Public School in America," *National Geographic*, accessed April 26, 2026, education.nationalgeographic.org/resource/first-public-school-america/.
**2.** "History," Boston Latin School, accessed April 26, 2026, bls.org/apps/pages/index.jsp?uREC_ID=206116&type=d.
**3.** Thomas Jefferson, "A Bill for the More General Diffusion of Knowledge," Thomas Jefferson Encyclopedia, Monticello, accessed April 26, 2026, monticello.org/encyclopedia/bill-more-general-diffusion-knowledge.
**4.** National Center for Education Statistics, "Public School Enrollment," Institute of Education Sciences, U.S. Department of Education, May 2024, nces.ed.gov/programs/coe/indicator/cga/public-school-enrollment.
**5.** "The U.S. Land-Grant University System: Overview and Role in Agricultural Research," Congressional Research Service, August 9, 2022, congress.gov/crs-product/R45897.

**6.** "History," National Science Foundation, accessed April 26, 2026, nsf.gov/about/history.
**7.** "2025–2026 Best Global Universities Rankings," *U.S. News & World Report*, accessed April 26, 2026, usnews.com/education/best-global-universities/rankings.
**8.** Sujai Shivakumar, Charles Wessner, Shruti Sharma, and Chris Borges, "U.S. Universities: Engines of Economic Growth," Center for Strategic and International Studies, October 29, 2025, csis.org/analysis/us-universities-engines-economic-growth.
**9.** Stephanie Marken, "Most Parents Prefer College Pathway for Their Child," Gallup, August 7, 2025, news.gallup.com/poll/693047/parents-prefer-college-pathway-child.aspx.
**10.** Zach Hrynowski and Stephanie Marken, "College Students, Grads See Strong Career Value in Degree," Gallup, February 24, 2026, news.gallup.com/poll/702284/college-students-grads-strong-career-value-degree.aspx.
**11.** Kent Phillippe, "Datapoints: Educational Attainment in the U.S.," *Community College Daily*, American Association of Community Colleges, September 9, 2025, ccdaily.com/2025/09/datapoints-educational-attainment-in-the-u-s/.
**12.** Jaison Abel and Richard Deitz, "Is College Still Worth It?," *Liberty Street Economics*, Federal Reserve Bank of New York, April 16, 2025, libertystreeteconomics.newyorkfed.org/2025/04/is-college-still-worth-it/.
**13.** "Education and Lifetime Earnings," U.S. Social Security Administration, November 2015, ssa.gov/policy/docs/research-summaries/education-earnings.html.
**14.** Katherine Knott, "J. D. Vance Called Universities 'The Enemy.' Now He's Trump's VP Pick," *Inside Higher Ed*, July 16, 2024, insidehighered.com/news/government/politics-elections/2024/07/16/trump-taps-jd-vance-sharp-critic-higher-ed-vp.
**15.** Emma Green, "Inside the Trump Administration's Assault on Higher Education," *New Yorker*, October 13, 2025, newyorker.com/magazine/2025/10/20/inside-the-trump-administrations-assault-on-higher-education.
**16.** "NAEP Report Card: Mathematics," *Nation's Report Card*, 2024, nationsreportcard.gov/reports/mathematics/2024/g4_8/?grade=8.
**17.** Press release, "Statement on President Trump's Executive Order to Return Power over Education to States and Local Communities," U.S. Department of Education, March 20, 2025, ed.gov/about/news/press-release/statement-president-trumps-executive-order-return-power-over-education-states-and-local-communities.
**18.** Ibid.
**19.** Mark Lieberman, "In Trump's First Year, at Least $12 Billion in School Funding Disruptions," *Education Week*, January 16, 2026, edweek.org/policy-politics/in-trumps-first-year-at-least-12-billion-in-school-funding-disruptions/2026/01.
**20.** Lily Klam, "Fact Sheet: How Eliminating the Department of Education Threatens Students with Disabilities," First Focus on Children, February 26, 2026, firstfocus.org/resource/fact-sheet-how-eliminating-the-department-of-education-threatens-students-with-disabilities/.
**21.** Jennifer Smith Richards and Jodi S. Cohen, "ProPublica Sues Education Department for Withholding Records About Discrimination in Schools," ProPublica, March 2, 2026,

propublica.org/article/education-department-civil-rights-office-foia-lawsuit.

**22.** Jennifer Smith Richards, Megan O'Matz, and Jodi S. Cohen, "Monkey Sounds, 'White Power' and the N-Word: Racial Harassment Against Black Students Ignored Under Trump," ProPublica, December 19, 2025, propublica.org/article/trump-education-department-civil-rights-racial-harassment.

**23.** Press release, "U.S. Department of Education's Office for Civil Rights Initiates Title VI Investigation into Portland Public Schools," U.S. Department of Education, February 17, 2026, ed.gov/about/news/press-release/us-department-of-educations-office-civil-rights-initiates-title-vi-investigation-portland-public-schools.

**24.** Drew Wilder, "Education Department to Withhold Grant Money for Fairfax County Magnet Schools," NBC4 Washington, September 25, 2025, nbcwashington.com/news/local/northern-virginia/education-department-to-withhold-grant-money-for-fairfax-county-magnet-schools/3993627/.

**25.** Juan Perez Jr., "Virginia Schools Sue Trump Administration over Transgender Student Funding Fight," *Politico*, August 29, 2025, politico.com/news/2025/08/29/virginia-school-districts-challenge-trump-administration-funding-threats-over-transgender-students-00536679.

**26.** "Fiscal Year 2026 Budget Summary," U.S. Department of Education, accessed April 26, 2026, ed.gov/media/document/fiscal-year-2026-budget-summary-110043.pdf.

**27.** "National Studies Find TRIO Programs Effective at Increasing College Enrollment and Graduation," Pell Institute, accessed April 26, 2026, pellinstitute.org/resources/national-studies-find-trio-programs-effective-at-increasing-college-enrollment-and-graduation.

**28.** Sequoia Carrillo, Cory Turner, and Elissa Nadworny, "What the 'One Big Beautiful Bill' Will Change for Students, Schools and Colleges," NPR, July 18, 2025, npr.org/2025/07/18/nx-s1-5459784/trump-school-college-student#loans.

**29.** Bruce A. Scott, "Federal Student-Loan Changes Would Worsen Physician Shortage," American Medical Association, June 3, 2025, ama-assn.org/about/leadership/federal-student-loan-changes-would-worsen-physician-shortage.

**30.** Press release, "American Nurses Association Submits Formal Comments to U.S. Department of Education on Graduate Student Loan Rulemaking," American Nurses Association, February 26, 2026, nursingworld.org/news/news-releases/2026-news-releases/american-nurses-association-submits-formal-comments-to-u.s-department-of-education-on-graduate-student-loan-rulemaking.

**31.** "Higher Education Research and Development (HERD) Survey 2023," National Science Foundation, November 25, 2024, ncses.nsf.gov/surveys/higher-education-research-development/2023.

**32.** Elissa Nadworny, "What Losing Billions in Federal Grants Means for Universities, and the Nation," NPR, May 16, 2025, npr.org/2025/04/25/nx-s1-5375033/trump-federal-grants-cuts-universities-could-mean.

**33.** Jeffrey Mervis, "NSF Slashes Graduate Fellowship Program," *Science*, April 8, 2025,

science.org/content/article/nsf-slashes-graduate-fellowship-program.
**34.** "United States Hosts 1.2 Million International Students at Colleges and Universities, Totaling 6% of U.S. Higher Education," Institute of International Education, November 17, 2025, iie.org/news/open-doors-2025-press-release/.
**35.** "Updates on Federal Actions and Budget Planning," Office of the President, Johns Hopkins University, June 2, 2025, president.jhu.edu/messages/2025/06/02/updates-on-federal-actions-and-budget-planning/.
**36.** Meredith Cohn, "HHS Cuts Millions in Grants to Hopkins and University of Maryland, Baltimore," *Baltimore Banner*, March 25, 2025, thebanner.com/community/public-health/johns-hopkins-maryland-nih-research-NLNPGM76LNBA5JTA3F4XRB3MM4/.
**37.** Public Health on Call, "How Cuts to mRNA Vaccine Development Will Set the U.S. Back," Bloomberg School of Public Health, Johns Hopkins University, August 13, 2025, publichealth.jhu.edu/2025/risks-of-cuts-to-mrna-vaccine-development.
**38.** "Mapping the Impacts of Science Funding Cuts," Science & Community Impacts Mapping Project, University of Maryland, College of Computer, Mathematical, and Natural Sciences, accessed April 26, 2026, scienceimpacts.org/.
**39.** "United States Hosts 1.2 Million International Students at Colleges and Universities."
**40.** "Most International Students: Regional Universities South," *U.S. News & World Report*, accessed April 26, 2026, usnews.com/best-colleges/rankings/regional-universities-south/most-international.
**41.** Robb King, "Michigan Public Universities Generate Nearly $45 Billion in Economic Impact According to Newly Published Study," University of Michigan–Flint, January 22, 2026, news.umflint.edu/2026/01/22/michigan-public-universities-generate-nearly-45-billion-in-economic-impact-according-to-newly-published-study.
**42.** Sujai Shivakumar, Charles Wessner, Shruti Sharma, and Chris Borges, "U.S. Universities: Engines of Economic Growth," Center for Strategic and International Studies, October 29, 2025, csis.org/analysis/us-universities-engines-economic-growth.
**43.** Chris Capot, "TEConomy Report: NC Life Sciences Growth Outpaces Nation, Passes 100,000 Job Milestone," North Carolina Biotechnology Center, February 4, 2025, ncbiotech.org/news/teconomy-report-nc-life-sciences-growth-outpaces-nation-passes-100000-job-milestone.
**44.** Press release, "Harvard University Loses Student and Exchange Visitor Program Certification for Pro-Terrorist Conduct," U.S. Department of Homeland Security, May 22, 2025, dhs.gov/news/2025/05/22/harvard-university-loses-student-and-exchange-visitor-program-certification-pro.
**45.** Juan Perez, "Trump Threatens Harvard Patents Worth Hundreds of Millions," *Politico*, August 8, 2025, politico.com/news/2025/08/08/trump-harvard-patents-00500814.
**46.** Sequoia Carrillo, Cory Turner, and Emily Piper-Vallillo, "Trump Administration Illegally Froze Billions in Harvard Funds, Judge Rules," NPR, September 3, 2025, npr.org/2025/09/03/nx-s1-5527314/trump-harvard-court-ruling-funding-boston.

**47.** "Agreement with Federal Government to Restore Brown Research Funding, Resolve Compliance Reviews," Brown University, accessed April 26, 2026, brown.edu/news/2025-07-30/brown-united-states-resolution-agreement.
**48.** "Our Resolution with the Federal Government," Columbia University, accessed April 26, 2026, columbia.edu/content/federal-resolution-agreement.
**49.** Aamer Madhani, "Trump Asks 9 Colleges to Commit to His Political Agenda for Better Access to Federal Money," PBS News, October 2, 2025, pbs.org/newshour/politics/trump-asks-9-colleges-to-commit-to-his-political-agenda-for-better-access-to-federal-money.
**50.** "White House Calls for Institutions to Sign Compact with Federal Government," American Council on Education, October 3, 2025, acenet.edu/News-Room/Pages/White-House-Calls-Institutions-Sign-Compact.aspx.
**51.** Lee C. Bollinger, "Universities Deserve Special Standing," *The Atlantic*, May 3, 2025, theatlantic.com/ideas/archive/2025/05/universities-special-standing/682670/.

## 6: A GUTTED AND WEAPONIZED GOVERNMENT

**1.** Ronald Reagan, "Inaugural Address 1981," Ronald Reagan Presidential Library and Museum, accessed April 26, 2026, reaganlibrary.gov/archives/speech/inaugural-address-1981.
**2.** "Reinventing Government," Clinton White House Archives, accessed April 26, 2026, clintonwhitehouse1.archives.gov/White_House/Publications/html/briefs/iv-1.html.
**3.** "President Truman with Hoover Commission Members," Harry S. Truman Library and Museum, accessed April 26, 2026, trumanlibrary.gov/photograph-records/58-337.
**4.** "Establishing and Implementing the President's 'Department of Government Efficiency,'" White House, January 20, 2025, whitehouse.gov/presidential-actions/2025/01/establishing-and-implementing-the-presidents-department-of-government-efficiency/.
**5.** "A Government in Chaos: Trump's First Year Back in Office," Partnership for Public Service, accessed April 26, 2026, ourpublicservice.org/publications/a-government-in-chaos-trumps-first-year-back-in-office/.
**6.** Jessie Blaeser, "Just How Much Has DOGE Exaggerated Its Numbers? Now We Have Receipts," *Politico*, August 12, 2025, politico.com/news/2025/08/12/trump-doge-contract-claims-savings-inflation-00498178.
**7.** Christa Marshall, "DOE Fires and Then Rehires Nuclear Staff," *E&E News*, February 18, 2025, eenews.net/articles/doe-fires-and-then-rehires-nuclear-staff/.
**8.** Drew Friedman, "Impacts of Federal Layoffs Will Be Felt for Years to Come, Good Government Group Warns," *Federal News Network*, February 21, 2025, federalnewsnetwork.com/workforce/2025/02/impacts-of-federal-layoffs-will-be-felt-for-years-to-come-good-government-group-warns/.
**9.** Gary Fields and Christine Fernando, "Young People Devoted to Government Service Dismayed By Trump Cutting the Federal Fellows Program," PBS News, March 10, 2025, pbs.org/newshour/politics/young-people-devoted-to-government-service-dismayed-by-trump-cutting-the-federal-fellows-program.

**10.** Chris Piper, "President Trump's Firing of Inspectors General Threatens Government Accountability and Efficiency," Partnership for Public Service, October 21, 2025, ourpublicservice.org/blog/president-trumps-firing-of-inspectors-general-threatens-government-accountability-and-efficiency/.
**11.** Press release, "Breaking: Trump Administration Fires, Suspends Whistleblowers After They Sound the Alarm on Civil Rights Violations in Housing," U.S. Senate, Committee on Banking, Housing and Urban Affairs, September 29, 2025, banking.senate.gov/newsroom/minority/breaking-trump-administration-fires-suspends-whistleblowers-after-they-sound-the-alarm-on-civil-rights-violations-in-housing.
**12.** "History of the Federal Civil Service," American Historical Association, April 7, 2025, historians.org/resource/history-of-the-federal-civil-service/.
**13.** Amna Nawaz and Azhar Merchant, "How the Latest Round of Federal Layoffs Could Impact Public Health," *PBS NewsHour*, October 14, 2025, pbs.org/newshour/show/how-the-latest-round-of-federal-layoffs-could-impact-public-health.
**14.** Richard G. Frank and Sherry Glied, "The Trump Administration's NIH and FDA Cuts Will Negatively Impact Patients," Brookings, May 14, 2025, brookings.edu/articles/the-trump-administrations-nih-and-fda-cuts-will-negatively-impact-patients/.
**15.** "IRS Prepares Layoffs in Middle of Tax Season as Democrats Try to Stop DOGE from Obtaining Sensitive Data," *FEDmanager*, February 18, 2025, fedmanager.com/news/irs-prepares-layoffs-in-middle-of-tax-season-as-democrats-try-to-stop-doge-from-obtaining-sensitive-data.
**16.** Spencer Woodman, "The IRS Unit That Audits Billionaires Has Lost 38% of Its Employees Since January, New Data Shows," International Consortium of Investigative Journalists, March 28, 2025, icij.org/news/2025/03/the-irs-unit-that-audits-billionaires-has-lost-38-percent-of-its-employees-since-january-new-data-shows/.
**17.** Vanessa Williamson and Ellis Chen, "A Hamstrung IRS Is a Gift to Rich Tax Cheats and a Headache for Honest Taxpayers," Brookings, March 6, 2025, brookings.edu/articles/a-hamstrung-irs-is-a-gift-to-rich-tax-cheats-and-a-headache-for-honest-taxpayers/.
**18.** Molly Weston Williamson, "The Social Security Administration Is Bleeding Staff," Center for American Progress, January 30, 2026, americanprogress.org/article/the-social-security-administration-is-bleeding-staff/.
**19.** Macy Byars, "USDA Lost 24,000 Workers Under Trump, Hurting Critical Resources for Farmers," *Harvest Public Media*, February 24, 2026, wglt.org/2026-02-24/federal-cuts-usda-staff-farmers-impact.
**20.** Shannon Hare, "Dairyland in Distress: Wisconsin Farmers Brace for USDA Job Cuts," *Badger Herald*, February 25, 2025, badgerherald.com/news/wisconsin/2025/02/25/dairyland-in-distress-wisconsin-farmers-brace-for-usda-job-cuts.
**21.** Democratic Staff, "Breaking the Pact: Impacts of Trump, DOGE, and Collins' Ongoing Assault on Veterans," U.S. Senate, Committee on Veterans Affairs, January 2026, veterans.senate.gov/services/files/A08A4C86-DB56-4A01-B98F-6ED1CF3F2B7A.

**22.** Nicholas Nehamas, Andrea Fuller, Danielle Ivory, and Ellen Barry, "Despite Promises, Veterans Affairs Department Cut Thousands of Roles for Doctors and Nurses," *New York Times*, March 3, 2026, nytimes.com/2026/03/03/us/politics/veterans-affairs-nurses-doctors-cut.html.
**23.** Democratic Staff, "Breaking the Pact."
**24.** Scott Dance, "NOAA Scrambles to Fill Forecasting Jobs as Hurricane Season Looms," *Washington Post*, May 14, 2025, washingtonpost.com/weather/2025/05/14/national-weather-service-vacancies-hurricane-season/.
**25.** Anna Clark, "Millions of People Depend on the Great Lakes' Water Supply. Trump Decimated the Lab Protecting It," ProPublica, May 6, 2025, propublica.org/article/noaa-michigan-lab-toxic-algae-blooms-great-lakes-drinking-water.
**26.** Mary Whitfill Roeloffs, "Why Kristi Noem Is Under Fire for Delayed FEMA Response to Texas Floods," *Forbes*, July 10, 2025, forbes.com/sites/maryroeloffs/2025/07/10/why-kristi-noem-is-under-fire-for-delayed-fema-response-to-texas-floods/.
**27.** Shannon Ogden, "National Parks Conservation Association Claims Trump Cuts Are Hurting Parks," Denver 7 News, August 27, 2025, denver7.com/news/politics/national-parks-conservation-association-claims-trump-cuts-are-hurting-parks.
**28.** Sam Sabin, "Top U.S. Cyber Agency Keeps Shrinking Under Trump 2.0," *Axios*, July 15, 2025, axios.com/2025/07/15/cisa-congress-budget-workforce-cuts.
**29.** Ken Dilanian, "Pam Bondi Ends FBI Effort to Combat Foreign Influence in U.S. Politics," NBC News, February 6, 2025, nbcnews.com/politics/national-security/bondi-ends-fbi-effort-combat-foreign-influence-us-politics-rcna191012.
**30.** Letter, "The Destruction of DOJ's Civil Rights Division: Why It Matters," December 9, 2025, thejusticeconnection.org/wp-content/uploads/2025/12/Civil-Rights-Division-Sign-On-Letter.pdf.
**31.** Eric Tucker, "FBI Forces Out More Leaders, Including Ex-Director Who Fought Trump Demand for Jan. 6 Agents' Names," Associated Press, August 7, 2025, apnews.com/article/fbi-jan-6-patel-driscoll-f4bd75766307f558dfdbdea736e026e8.
**32.** Joseph Ax, "They Quit Government to Protest Trump. Now They Are Running for Congress to Stop Him," Reuters, December 18, 2025, reuters.com/world/us/they-quit-government-protest-trump-now-they-are-running-congress-stop-him-2025-12-18/.
**33.** Evan Weinberger, "CFPB Shutdown Hearing Probes Courts' Sway over Trump-Era Firings," Bloomberg Law, February 24, 2026, news.bloomberglaw.com/banking-law/cfpb-shutdown-hearing-probes-courts-sway-over-trump-era-firings.
**34.** Eric Halperin and Allison Preiss, "Why Is the Trump Administration Holding Onto Your Money? More Than $360 Million Owed to Consumers from CFPB Enforcement Actions Is Already Gone or at Risk," Student Borrower Protection Center and Consumer Federation of America, July 29, 2025, consumerfed.org/wp-content/uploads/2025/07/Payments-to-Consumers-At-Risk-Memo.pdf.
**35.** David McCabe and Cecilia Kang, "Trump Fires Democrats on Federal Trade

Commission," *New York Times*, March 18, 2025, nytimes.com/2025/03/18/technology/trump-ftc-fires-democrats.html.

**36.** Tom Wheeler, "Not 'Deregulation' but Heavy-Handed Regulation at the Trump FCC," Brookings, February 25, 2025, brookings.edu/articles/not-deregulation-but-heavy-handed-regulation-at-the-trump-fcc/.

**37.** Ibid.

**38.** "Restoring Truth and Sanity to American History," White House, March 27, 2025, whitehouse.gov/presidential-actions/2025/03/restoring-truth-and-sanity-to-american-history.

**39.** Dorany Pineda, "From Slavery to Pollution, National Park Employees Flagged Material Deemed 'Disparaging' to US," Associated Press, September 10, 2025, apnews.com/article/trump-national-park-service-disparaging-d861b3c902ef68b0184c2bd776f707e4.

**40.** "Restoring Truth and Sanity to American History."

**41.** "Defending Women from Gender Ideology Extremism and Restoring Biological Truth to the Federal Government," White House, January 20, 2025, whitehouse.gov/presidential-actions/2025/01/defending-women-from-gender-ideology-extremism-and-restoring-biological-truth-to-the-federal-government/.

**42.** Jeffrey Brown and Simon Epstein, "Local Arts Groups Face Budget Gaps as NEA Pulls Grants," *PBS NewsHour*, June 4, 2025, pbs.org/newshour/show/local-arts-groups-face-budget-gaps-as-nea-pulls-grants.

**43.** Samantha Chery, "Trump Proposes Eliminating the NEA and NEH as Arts Grants Are Canceled," *Washington Post*, May 3, 2025, washingtonpost.com/style/2025/05/03/trump-budget-nea-neh-eliminate/.

**44.** Adria R. Walker, "Congress Restores Funding to Cultural Institutions Once on Trump's Chopping Block," *The Guardian*, February 20, 2026, theguardian.com/us-news/2026/feb/20/congress-funding-cultural-institutions.

**45.** Kanishka Singh, "Kennedy Center New Year's Eve Concerts Canceled After Addition of Trump's Name," Reuters, December 30, 2025, reuters.com/business/media-telecom/kennedy-center-new-years-eve-concerts-canceled-after-addition-trumps-name-2025-12-30/.

**46.** Gil Kaufman, "Amid Raft of Cancellations and Name Change Controversy, Donald Trump Announces Two-Year Kennedy Center Shut-Down," *Billboard*, February 2, 2026, billboard.com/culture/politics/trump-two-year-kennedy-center-shut-down-renovation-1236170523/.

**47.** "Trump Fires Head of Library of Congress in Part over Diversity, White House Says," Reuters, May 9, 2025, reuters.com/world/us/trump-fires-head-library-congress-new-york-times-reports-2025-05-09/.

**48.** Ted Anthony and Kevin Freking, "CPB Says It Is Shutting Down After Being Defunded by Congress, Targeted by Trump," PBS News, August 1, 2025, pbs.org/newshour/politics/cpb-says-it-is-shutting-down-after-being-defunded-by-congress-targeted-by-trump.

## 7: A COSTLY ATTACK ON CLIMATE

**1.** Simmone Shah, "Trump Is Following Project 2025's Anti-Climate Action Goals," *Time*, March 25, 2025, time.com/7271567/trump-project-2025-anti-climate-action/.
**2.** Rachel Jacobson and Mikaela Tajo, "Cuts to Climate, Energy Funding in House Bill Would Mean Higher Costs, Fewer Jobs, Poorer Health," Center on Budget and Policy Priorities, June 1, 2025, cbpp.org/research/climate-change/cuts-to-climate-energy-funding-in-house-bill-would-mean-higher-costs-fewer.
**3.** John Bistline et al., "Emissions and Energy Impacts of the Inflation Reduction Act," *Science* 380, no. 6652 (June 30, 2023): 1324–27, doi.org/10.1126/science.adg3781.
**4.** "Unleashing American Energy," White House, March 21, 2025, whitehouse.gov/presidential-actions/2025/01/unleashing-american-energy/.
**5.** Sarah Steffen, "Trump's EPA to Roll Back Cornerstone of Climate Action," *DW*, July 31, 2025, dw.com/en/lee-zeldin-to-end-endangerment-finding-vital-to-clean-air-act-and-us-environment-protection/a-73485787; Valerie Volcovici and Andrew Goudsward, "Judge Questions Trump Administration Claw Back of $20 Billion Climate Fund," Reuters, March 12, 2025, reuters.com/world/us/trump-administration-claws-back-20-billion-climate-funds-2025-03-12/.
**6.** "Unleashing American Energy."
**7.** Dennis Wamsted and Seth Feaster, "Nowhere to Go but Down for U.S. Coal Capacity, Generation," Institute for Energy Economics and Financial Analysis, October 24, 2024, ieefa.org/resources/nowhere-go-down-us-coal-capacity-generation.
**8.** Carrie Jenks, "Mercury and Air Toxics Standards," Environmental and Energy Law Program, Harvard Law School, March 30, 2025, eelp.law.harvard.edu/tracker/mercury-and-air-toxics-standards/.
**9.** Gavin Maguire, "US Coal Binge Helps Asia Pull Ahead of the West in Clean Power Push," Reuters, December 11, 2025, reuters.com/markets/commodities/us-coal-binge-helps-asia-pull-ahead-west-clean-power-push-2025-12-11/.
**10.** "Unleashing American Energy."
**11.** John P. Holdren, "The Science of Rapid Climate Change in Alaska and the Arctic: Sea Ice, Land Ice, and Sea Level," Belfer Center for Science and International Affairs, August 16, 2023, belfercenter.org/publication/science-rapid-climate-change-alaska-and-arctic-sea-ice-land-ice-and-sea-level.
**12.** "Unleashing American Energy."
**13.** Rebecca Lindsey, "Climate Change: Atmospheric Carbon Dioxide," Climate.gov, May 21, 2025, climate.gov/news-features/understanding-climate/climate-change-atmospheric-carbon-dioxide.
**14.** "WMO Confirms 2024 Warmest Year on Record at About 1.55°C Above Pre-Industrial Level," World Meteorological Organization, January 10, 2025, wmo.int/news/media-centre/wmo-confirms-2024-warmest-year-record-about-155degc-above-pre-industrial-level.
**15.** "Report: Clean Energy Jobs Grew 3x Faster than Rest of U.S. Workforce in 2024,

but Future Growth Now at Risk," Economy+Environment, September 19, 2025, e2.org/releases/report-clean-energy-jobs-grew-3x-faster-than-rest-of-u-s-workforce-in-2024-but-future-growth-now-at-risk/.

**16.** Mia Beams and Akkshath Subrahmanian, "Congress's 'One Big Beautiful Bill' Will Shrink Renewable Energy Investments—Yet Some Technologies Are Preserved," Council on Foreign Relations, August 4, 2025, cfr.org/articles/congresss-one-big-beautiful-bill-will-shrink-renewable-energy-investments-yet-some.

**17.** Press release, "EPA Launches Biggest Deregulatory Action in U.S. History," U.S. Environmental Protection Agency, March 12, 2025, epa.gov/newsreleases/epa-launches-biggest-deregulatory-action-us-history.

**18.** "Final Rule: Rescission of the Greenhouse Gas Endangerment Finding," U.S. Environmental Protection Agency, accessed April 24, 2026, epa.gov/regulations-emissions-vehicles-and-engines/final-rule-rescission-greenhouse-gas-endangerment.

**19.** *Massachusetts v. Environmental Protection Agency*, 549 U.S. 497 (2007).

**20.** Dennis Pillion, "Climate Scientists Look to Fight Back Against DOE's 'Antiscientific,' 'Deceptive' Climate Report," *Inside Climate News*, July 30, 2025, insideclimatenews.org/news/30072025/climate-scientists-fight-against-energy-department-report/.

**21.** "EPA Launches Biggest Deregulatory Action in U.S. History."

**22.** "Temporary Withdrawal of All Areas on the Outer Continental Shelf from Offshore Wind Leasing and Review of the Federal Government's Leasing and Permitting Practices for Wind Projects," White House, January 20, 2025, whitehouse.gov/presidential-actions/2025/01/temporary-withdrawal-of-all-areas-on-the-outer-continental-shelf-from-offshore-wind-leasing-and-review-of-the-federal-governments-leasing-and-permitting-practices-for-wind-projects/.

**23.** Adele Peters, "More than $32 Billion in U.S. Clean Energy Projects Were Canceled in 2025," *Fast Company*, December 29, 2025, finance.yahoo.com/news/more-32-billion-u-clean-100000825.html.

**24.** Ibid.

**25.** "Executive Summary—World Energy Investment 2025," International Energy Agency, accessed April 26, 2026, iea.org/reports/world-energy-investment-2025/executive-summary.

**26.** "Renewables Made Up More than 90 Percent of New Power Installed Globally Last Year," *Yale Environment 360*, March 26, 2025, e360.yale.edu/digest/renewable-capacity-irena-2024.

**27.** Hannah Ritchie, "Solar Panel Prices Have Fallen by Around 20% Every Time Global Capacity Doubled," Our World in Data, June 13, 2024, ourworldindata.org/data-insights/solar-panel-prices-have-fallen-by-around-20-every-time-global-capacity-doubled.

**28.** "Renewables Made Up More than 90 Percent of New Power Installed Globally Last Year."

**29.** U.S.-China Economic and Security Review Commission, "Chapter 10: Power Surge: China's Electrification Drive and Push for Global Energy Dominance," in *2025 Annual*

*Report to Congress* (Washington, DC: U.S.-China Economic and Security Review Commission, 2025), uscc.gov/sites/default/files/2025-11/Chapter_10--Power_Surge_Chinas_Electrification_Drive_and_Push_for_Global_Energy_Dominance.pdf.

**30.** Leslie Abrahams and Joseph Majkut, "U.S. Clean Tech Exports Are the Key to Long-Term U.S. Economic Growth," Center for Strategic and International Studies, August 11, 2025, csis.org/analysis/us-clean-tech-exports-are-key-long-term-us-economic-growth.

**31.** Lyuba Zarsky, "China Is Miles Ahead on Green Energy. Will It Also Lead on Climate Diplomacy?," *World Politics Review*, November 10, 2025, worldpoliticsreview.com/china-green-energy-climate-change/.

**32.** "National Climate Assessments Removed from Federal Websites," Sabin Center for Climate Change Law, Columbia Law School, accessed April 26, 2026, climate.law.columbia.edu/content/national-climate-assessments-removed-federal-websites.

**33.** Andrew Freedman, "Trump Wants to Slash Funding for Federal Climate and Weather Research. Congress Is About to Tell Him 'No,'" CNN, January 14, 2026, cnn.com/2026/01/14/climate/noaa-nasa-funding-congress-trump-climate.

**34.** Scott Neuman, "Scientists Push Back on Trump Plan to Break up a Critical Climate and Weather Center," *Weekend Edition Sunday*, NPR, December 19, 2025, npr.org/2025/12/19/nx-s1-5648270/trump-weather-climate-national-center-atmospheric-research-ncar.

**35.** Jean Chemnick, "EPA Erases References to Human-Caused Climate Change from Websites," *E&E News*, December 9, 2025, eenews.net/articles/epa-erases-references-to-human-caused-climate-change-from-websites/.

**36.** Sara Schonhardt, "So Long, Paris: US Officially Leaves Landmark Climate Pact," *Politico*, January 27, 2026, politico.com/news/2026/01/27/so-long-paris-u-s-officially-leaves-landmark-climate-pact-00746628.

**37.** Danny Aeberhard, Rachel Hagan, and Matt McGrath, "Trump Withdraws US from Key Climate Treaty and Dozens of Other Groups," BBC News, January 8, 2026, bbc.com/news/articles/cp80ln97py5o.

**38.** "Withdrawing the United States from International Organizations, Conventions, and Treaties That Are Contrary to the Interests of the United States," White House, January 7, 2026, whitehouse.gov/presidential-actions/2026/01/withdrawing-the-united-states-from-international-organizations-conventions-and-treaties-that-are-contrary-to-the-interests-of-the-united-states/.

**39.** Fiona Harvey, "Trump's USAID Cuts Will Have Huge Impact on Global Climate Finance, Data Shows," *The Guardian*, March 10, 2025, theguardian.com/environment/2025/mar/10/trumps-usaid-cuts-will-have-huge-impact-on-global-climate-finance-data-shows.

**40.** *National Security Strategy of the United States of America* (Washington, DC: White House, December 2025), whitehouse.gov/wp-content/uploads/2025/12/2025-National-Security-Strategy.pdf.

41. United Nations High Commissioner for Refugees, *UNHCR Focus Area Strategic Plan for Climate Action 2024–2030*, March 2024, unhcr.org/media/focus-area-strategic-plan-climate-action-2024-2030.

42. U.S. Committee for Refugees and Immigrants, International Refugee Assistance Project, and Human Security Initiative, *Climate of Coercion: Environmental and Other Drivers of Cross-Border Displacement in Central America and Mexico*, March 2023, refugees.org/wp-content/uploads/2023/03/Climate-of-Coercion-Report.pdf.

43. Press release, "Trump EPA Analysis: Proposed Rollback of Power Plant Pollution Standards Will Cause Thousands of Deaths, Cost Billions of Dollars," Environmental Defense Fund, June 17, 2025, edf.org/media/trump-epa-analysis-proposed-rollback-power-plant-pollution-standards-will-cause-thousands.

44. Maxine Joselow, "E.P.A. to Stop Considering Lives Saved When Setting Rules on Air Pollution," *New York Times*, January 12, 2026, nytimes.com/2026/01/12/climate/trump-epa-air-pollution.html.

45. Oliver Milman, "US Voters Linking Climate Crisis to Rising Bills Despite Trump's 'Green Scam' Claims," *The Guardian*, December 26, 2025, theguardian.com/us-news/2025/dec/26/us-voters-link-climate-crisis-affordability.

46. Lilith Fellowes-Granda, Marc Jarsulic, and Alexandra Thorton, "Managing the Climate Change–Fueled Property Insurance Crisis," Center for American Progress, April 2, 2025, americanprogress.org/article/managing-the-climate-change-fueled-property-insurance-crisis/.

47. Jasia Smith, Kalina Gibson, and Margaret Cooney, "How Fossil Fuels and Global Extreme Weather Increase Americans' Food Prices," Center for American Progress, December 22, 2025, americanprogress.org/article/how-fossil-fuels-and-global-extreme-weather-increase-americans-food-prices/.

48. Daniel Munch, "Hurricanes, Heat and Hardship: Counting 2024's Crop Losses," American Farm Bureau Federation, February 18, 2025, fb.org/market-intel/hurricanes-heat-and-hardship-counting-2024s-crop-losses.

49. Damien Gayle, "Extreme Weather Expected to Cause Food Price Volatility in 2025 After Cost of Cocoa and Coffee Doubles," *The Guardian*, February 15, 2025, theguardian.com/environment/2025/feb/15/extreme-weather-likely-to-cause-further-food-price-volatility-analysts-say.

50. Nicholas Stern, *The Growth Story of the 21st Century: The Economics and Opportunity of Climate Action* (London: LSE Press, 2025).

## 8: LAWLESS IMMIGRATION ENFORCEMENT

1. Press release, "Border Crossings Once Again at a Record Low in November 2025," Department of Homeland Security, December 4, 2025, dhs.gov/news/2025/12/04/border-crossings-once-again-record-low-november-2025.

2. Marina Dunbar, "US Immigration Agents Shot at People 16 Times Under Trump's Crackdown," *The Guardian*, January 9, 2026, theguardian.com/us-news/2026/jan/07/

trump-immigration-ice-shootings.
**3.** Pooja Salhotra and Edgar Sandoval, "A Fatal ICE Shooting Occurred in Texas Months Before Renee Good's Killing," *New York Times*, February 20, 2026, nytimes.com/2026/02/20/us/ruben-ray-martinez-ice-shooting-texas.html.
**4.** Maanvi Singh, Coral Murphy Marcos, and Charlotte Simmonds, "2025 Was ICE's Deadliest Year in Two Decades. Here Are the 32 People Who Died in Custody," *The Guardian*, January 4, 2026, theguardian.com/us-news/ng-interactive/2026/jan/04/ice-2025-deaths-timeline.
**5.** Brittany Gibson, "New Data: ICE Arrests Surge as Agency Chases Trump Quota," *Axios*, December 4, 2025, axios.com/2025/12/04/trump-ice-immigration-arrests-deportations.
**6.** Simon Rosenberg, "The Senate Advances 2 Week Funding Bill for DHS. Now to the House. We Are Now Having the Debate About DHS/ICE We Simply Must Have," *Hopium Chronicles*, January 31, 2026, hopiumchronicles.com/p/the-senate-advances-2-week-funding.
**7.** "Immigration Detention Quick Facts," TRAC Reports, February 7, 2026, tracreports.org/immigration/quickfacts/.
**8.** Shelby Bremer, "93% of People Detained by ICE Have No Violent Criminal Conviction, Data Shows," NBC 7 San Diego, June 25, 2025, nbcsandiego.com/news/local/ice-detentions-criminal-convictions-data/3856326/.
**9.** Press release, "ICE Announces Historic 120% Manpower Increase, Thanks to Recruitment Campaign That Brought in 12,000 Officers and Agents," Department of Homeland Security, January 3, 2026, dhs.gov/news/2026/01/03/ice-announces-historic-120-manpower-increase-thanks-recruitment-campaign-brought.
**10.** Michelle Hackman, Josh Dawsey, and Tarini Parti, "A Pilot Fired over Kristi Noem's Missing Blanket and the Constant Chaos Inside DHS," *Wall Street Journal*, February 12, 2026, wsj.com/politics/policy/chaos-kristi-noem-homeland-security-f095ac95.
**11.** Nicholas Nehamas and Hamed Aleaziz, "The Whistle-Blower's Account Comes Amid Scrutiny of ICE Agents' Use of Force," *New York Times*, February 23, 2026, nytimes.com/live/2026/02/23/us/trump-news?smid=nytcore-android-share#ice-training-whistle-blower.
**12.** Ibid.
**13.** Margy O'Herron, "Big Budget Act Creates a 'Deportation-Industrial Complex,'" Brennan Center for Justice, August 13, 2025, brennancenter.org/our-work/analysis-opinion/big-budget-act-creates-deportation-industrial-complex.
**14.** Kristian Jaime, "ICE Report Finds 60 Violations in 50 Days at Fort Bliss Migrant Facility in El Paso, Texas," *El Paso Times*, September 17, 2025, elpasotimes.com/story/news/immigration/2025/09/17/ice-finds-60-violations-at-fort-bliss-migrant-facility-in-texas/86199672007/.
**15.** Elisa Jacome, "The Effect of Immigration Enforcement on Crime Reporting: Evidence from Dallas," *Journal of Urban Economics* 128 (2022): 103395, elisajacome.

github.io/Jacome/Jacome_PEP_JUE.pdf.
**16.** Kristen Holmes and Priscilla Alvarez, "How Stephen Miller Micromanages Trump's Immigration Policies," CNN, January 29, 2026, cnn.com/2026/01/29/politics/stephen-miller-trump-immigration-minneapolis.
**17.** Rosa Barrientos-Ferrer, Ben Greenho, and Silva Mathema, "Congressional Republicans' One Big Beautiful Bill Act Creates an Unaccountable Slush Fund for the Trump Administration's Deportation Force," Center for American Progress, September 19, 2025, americanprogress.org/article/congressional-republicans-one-big-beautiful-bill-act-creates-an-unaccountable-slush-fund-for-the-trump-administrations-deportation-force/.
**18.** Kyle Cheney, "'ICE Will Comply': Top Minnesota Judge Threatens Criminal Contempt for Continued Defiance," *Politico*, February 26, 2026, politico.com/news/2026/02/26/ice-minnesota-judge-criminal-contempt-00803285.
**19.** Ibid.
**20.** Kyle Cheney, "Judges Across the Country Rebuke ICE for Defying Court Orders," *Politico*, January 30, 2026, politico.com/news/2026/01/30/ice-immigration-court-orders-00757894.
**21.** "New Funding Increases Immigration Enforcement," National Immigration Law Center, September 16, 2026, nilc.org/resources/new-funding-increases-immigration-enforcement/.
**22.** Rebecca Santana, "Immigration Officers Claim Sweeping Power to Enter Homes Without a Judge's Warrant, Memo Says," Associated Press, January 22, 2026, pbs.org/newshour/nation/immigration-officers-claim-sweeping-power-to-enter-homes-without-a-judges-warrant-memo-says.
**23.** "Immigration Detention Expansion in Trump's Second Term," American Immigration Council, January 2026, americanimmigrationcouncil.org/wp-content/uploads/2026/01/immigration-detention-report.pdf.
**24.** Kyle Cheney, "How ICE Defies Judges' Orders to Release Detainees, Step by Step," *Politico*, February 10, 2026, politico.com/news/2026/02/10/ice-immigration-detention-court-orders-00771727.
**25.** Joseph Nunn, "The Posse Comitatus Act, Explained," Brennan Center for Justice, September 29, 2025, brennancenter.org/our-work/research-reports/posse-comitatus-act-explained.
**26.** Hamed Aleaziz and Nicholas Nehamas, "Under Trump, a Shift Toward 'Absolute Immunity' for ICE," *New York Times*, January 15, 2026, nytimes.com/2026/01/15/us/politics/trump-ice-immunity.html.
**27.** Geoff Mulvihill, "Judge Orders 5-Year-Old Liam Conejo Ramos and His Dad Released from ICE Detention," Associated Press, January 31, 2026, apnews.com/article/immigration-minnesota-boy-detained-a1ef2144c03a0136ef123f5a3685ee44.
**28.** Muzaffar Chishti and Kathleen Bush-Joseph, "Trump Administration's Expansion of Fast-Track Deportation Powers Is Transforming Immigration Enforcement," Migration

Policy Institute, September 25, 2025, migrationpolicy.org/article/trump-expedited-removal.
**29.** "Weaponizing the System: One Year of Trump's Attacks on Due Process," Vera Institute, January 20, 2026, vera.org/explainers/weaponizing-the-system-one-year-of-trumps-attacks-on-due-process.
**30.** Kenichi Serino, "Trump Suspended the Refugee Program. Why Is He Inviting White South Africans to Find a New Home in the U.S.?," PBS News, May 12, 2025, pbs.org/newshour/politics/trump-suspended-the-refugee-program-why-is-he-inviting-white-south-africans-to-find-a-new-home-in-the-u-s.
**31.** "Temporary Protected Status," U.S. Citizenship and Immigration Services, Department of Homeland Security, accessed April 26, 2026, uscis.gov/humanitarian/temporary-protected-status.
**32.** "Temporary Protected Status (TPS): Fact Sheet," National Immigration Forum, April 9, 2026, forumtogether.org/article/temporary-protected-status-fact-sheet/.
**33.** Anusha Mathur and Ximena Bustillo, "U.S. Has a Quarter Fewer Immigration Judges Than It Did a Year Ago. Here's Why," NPR, February 23, 2026, npr.org/2026/02/23/g-s1-110911/trump-immigration-judges-dismissals-numbers.
**34.** Margy O'Herron, "Big Budget Act Creates a 'Deportation-Industrial Complex,'" Brennan Center for Justice, August 13, 2025, brennancenter.org/our-work/analysis-opinion/big-budget-act-creates-deportation-industrial-complex\.
**35.** Juan Carlos Chavez, "New Policy Will Make It Tougher for Immigrants to Appeal Deportation," *Tampa Bay Times*, February 13, 2026, yahoo.com/news/articles/policy-tougher-immigrants-appeal-deportation-144304296.html.
**36.** Sergio Marinez-Beltran and Ximena Bustillo, "How the Trump Administration Stripped Legal Status from 1.6 Million Immigrants," NPR, December 22, 2025, npr.org/2025/12/22/nx-s1-5652134/how-the-trump-administration-stripped-legal-status-from-1-6-million-immigrants.
**37.** "Prices for All Americans Are Set to Unnecessarily Rise Under Recent and Proposed Immigration Policies Impacting the U.S. Labor Force," FWD.us, June 25, 2025, fwd.us/protect-americas-workforce/#insights-analysis.
**38.** Abril Preciado, "Milwaukee ICE Raids, Small Businesses Feel Economic Strain," FOX6 News Milwaukee, April 17, 2025, fox6now.com/news/milwaukee-ice-raids-small-businesses.
**39.** Jason Rantala, "Meet Minneapolis Reports Deep Impact of ICE Surge on Economy," CBS News, February 3, 2026, cbsnews.com/minnesota/news/meet-minneapolis-impact-economy-operation-metro-surge/.
**40.** Nino Paoli, "Trump Immigration Policies Would Slash Workforce Estimate by 15.7 Million and Slow GDP Growth by a Third over the Next Decade, Study Says," *Fortune*, October 21, 2025, fortune.com/2025/10/21/trump-immigration-policy-jobs-work-force-american-workers-gdp-growth/.
**41.** "The Economic Impact of the Trump Administration's Immigration Polices," National Foundation for American Policy, October 2025, nfap.com/wp-content/

uploads/2025/10/Economic-Impact-of-The-Trump-Administration-Immigration-Policies.NFAP-Policy-Brief.2025-1.pdf.
**42.** Miriam Jordan, "Haitians Are Vital to U.S. Health Care. Many Are About to Lose Their Right to Work," *New York Times*, January 29, 2026, nytimes.com/2026/01/29/us/trump-tps-haitians-health-care-job-losses.html.
**43.** Press release, "AMA Urges DHS to Exempt Physicians from New $100,000 H-1B Visa Fee," American Medical Association, September 25, 2025, ama-assn.org/press-center/ama-press-releases/ama-urges-dhs-exempt-physicians-new-100000-h-1b-visa-fee.
**44.** Cameron J. Sabet et al., "Supporting International Medical Graduate Workforce Integration in the 2024 US Election," *Family Medicine* 56, no. 10 (October 31, 2024): 617–19, doi.org/10.22454/fammed.2024.706876.
**45.** Leslie Dellon, "USCIS Implements the H-1B Proclamation $100,000 Fee," American Immigration Council, October 31, 2025, americanimmigrationcouncil.org/blog/uscis-implements-h1b-100000-fee/.
**46.** Nicolas Morales, "Understanding the Potential Impact of H-1B Visa Program Changes," Federal Reserve Bank of Richmond, October 2025, richmondfed.org/publications/research/economic_brief/2025/eb_25-39.
**47.** Press release, "DHS Changes Process for Awarding H-1B Work Visas to Better Protect American Workers," Department of Homeland Security, December 23, 2025, uscis.gov/newsroom/news-releases/dhs-changes-process-for-awarding-h-1b-work-visas-to-better-protect-american-workers.
**48.** Samantha Walravens, "Trump's Student Visa Crackdown Threatens U.S. Innovation," *Forbes*, October 25, 2025, forbes.com/sites/geekgirlrising/2025/10/25/trumps-student-visa-crackdown-threatens-us-innovation/.
**49.** Press release, "DHS Ends Automatic Extension of Employment Authorization," U.S. Citizenship and Immigration Services, Department of Homeland Security, October 29, 2025, uscis.gov/newsroom/news-releases/dhs-ends-automatic-extension-of-employment-authorization.
**50.** "Ending Automatic Work Authorization Will Cost Billions," FWD.us, April 9, 2026, fwd.us/news/ending-automatic-work-authorization-will-cost-billions/.
**51.** Ben Greenho, Silva Mathema, and Rosa Barrientos-Ferrer, "The Trump Administration's Hostility to Legal Immigration Harms America's Global Leadership in Innovation," Center for American Progress, November 13, 2025, americanprogress.org/article/the-trump-administrations-hostility-to-legal-immigration-harms-americas-global-leadership-in-innovation.

## 9: THE SUPPRESSION OF FREE SPEECH

**1.** "Selected Quotations from the Thomas Jefferson Papers," Library of Congress, accessed April 26, 2026, loc.gov/collections/thomas-jefferson-papers/articles-and-essays/selected-quotations-from-the-thomas-jefferson-papers/.
**2.** Pamela Alma Weymouth, "My Grandmother Stood Up to Nixon—Jeff Bezos Should

Take Note," *The Nation*, June 26, 2025, thenation.com/article/society/trump-bezos-washington-post-press-freedom-amazon/.

**3.** Julie Hirschfeld Davis and Matthew Rosenberg, "With False Claims, Trump Attacks Media on Turnout and Intelligence Rift," *New York Times*, January 21, 2017, nytimes.com/2017/01/21/us/politics/trump-white-house-briefing-inauguration-crowd-size.html.

**4.** Peter Baker and Susan Glasser, *The Divider: Trump in the White House, 2017–2021* (New York, New York: Anchor Books, 2023).

**5.** Dan Mangan, "President Trump Told Lesley Stahl He Bashes Press 'to Demean You and Discredit You so … No One Will Believe' Negative Stories About Him," CNBC, May 22, 2018, cnbc.com/2018/05/22/trump-told-lesley-stahl-he-bashes-press-to-discredit-negative-stories.html.

**6.** David Folkenflik, "Judge Orders White House to Allow AP Access to News Events," NPR, April 9, 2025, npr.org/2025/04/08/nx-s1-5342369/ap-white-house-court-ruling-oval-office-gulf-of-mexico-america.

**7.** Ken Bensinger, "What's Going On with Trump Media's Streaming Service?," *New York Times*, July 14, 2025, nytimes.com/2025/07/14/business/media/trump-media-truth-plus-streaming.html.

**8.** Andrew Goudsward and Helen Coster, "US News Outlets Reject Pentagon Press Access Policy," Reuters, October 15, 2025, reuters.com/business/media-telecom/us-news-outlets-reject-pentagon-press-access-policy-2025-10-14/.

**9.** Bethany Irvine, "Playbook PM: The Speech Debate," *Politico*, September 16, 2025, politico.com/newsletters/playbook-pm/2025/09/16/the-speech-debate-00566627.

**10.** Michael M. Grynbaum, "Trump Scolds CNN's Kaitlan Collins for 'Not Smiling,'" *New York Times*, February 3, 2026, nytimes.com/2026/02/03/us/politics/kaitlan-collins-smile-trump.html.

**11.** Ashleigh Fields, "Trump Says *New York Times* a 'Serious Threat' to National Security After Epstein Piece," *The Hill*, December 23, 2025, aol.com/articles/trump-says-york-times-serious-150655608.html.

**12.** Jacob Wendler, "Trump Says He Hopes to See CNN Sold in Warner Bros. Merger," *Politico*, December 10, 2025, politico.com/news/2025/12/10/trump-cnn-warner-paramount-skydance-media-00685810.

**13.** Donald J. Trump, Truth Social post, accessed April 25, 2026, truthsocial.com/@realDonaldTrump/posts/116228130264134892.

**14.** Mike Wendling, "Trump Sues ABC News and Host Stephanopoulos over Rape Claim," BBC News, March 19, 2024, bbc.com/news/world-us-canada-68582953.

**15.** David Bauder, "Paramount Will Pay $16 Million in Settlement with Trump over '60 Minutes' Interview," Associated Press, July 2, 2025, ap.org/news-highlights/spotlights/2025/paramount-will-pay-16-million-in-settlement-with-trump-over-60-minutes-interview/.

**16.** Cheyanne M. Daniels, "CBS Names Bari Weiss as Editor in Chief," *Politico*, October 6, 2025, politico.com/news/2025/10/06/cbs-bari-weiss-editor-in-chief-00594957.

**17.** Jenna Amatulli and George Chidi, "Trump Files Amended $15bn Defamation Complaint Against *New York Times*," *The Guardian*, October 16, 2025, theguardian.com/us-news/2025/oct/16/trump-new-york-times-defamation-complaint.
**18.** Max Matza, "Trump Sues Murdoch and *Wall Street Journal* for $10bn over Epstein Article," BBC News, July 18, 2025, bbc.com/news/articles/c23g5xpggzmo.
**19.** Josh Gerstein, "Trump Is Still Going After the Press in Court. Here's Where His Lawsuits Stand," *Politico*, March 4, 2026, politico.com/news/2026/03/04/donald-trump-media-lawsuits-00812525.
**20.** "FCC Chair Threatens to Revoke Broadcasters' Licenses amid Trump Comments on Iran Coverage," Reuters, March 14, 2026, nbcnews.com/news/us-news/fcc-chair-threatens-revoke-broadcasters-licenses-trump-comments-iran-c-rcna263535.
**21.** Judy Kurtz, "FCC Got More Complaints About Jimmy Kimmel's Suspension than About His Charlie Kirk Remarks," *The Hill*, February 24, 2026, thehill.com/blogs/in-the-know/5752873-fcc-complaints-jimmy-kimmel-charlie-kirk-abc-carr/.
**22.** David McCabe, "Paramount Won Over Warner Bros. Now for the Regulators," *New York Times*, March 2, 2026, nytimes.com/2026/03/02/technology/paramount-deal-approval.html.
**23.** Brian Stelter, "Netflix Shockingly Bows out, Leaving Paramount as the Apparent Warner Bros. Winner," CNN, February 27, 2026, cnn.com/2026/02/26/media/netflix-paramount-wbd.
**24.** Dominick Mastrangelo, "Senators Reconsider FCC Broadcast Ownership Cap amid Nexstar-TEGNA Merger Push," *The Hill*, February 10, 2026, thehill.com/homenews/senate/5732004-fcc-broadcast-ownership-nexstar-tegna-hearing/.
**25.** Press release, "Neguse, Bennet Urge FCC Put Colorado Communities over Corporate Interest, Reject Nexstar Media–Tegna Merger," Office of Congressman Joe Neguse, October 24, 2025, neguse.house.gov/media/press-releases/neguse-bennet-urge-fcc-put-colorado-communities-over-corporate-interest-reject.
**26.** "FCC Chair Threatens to Revoke Broadcasters' Licenses."
**27.** Norman J. Ornstein, "Will Our Corporate Media Godzillas Have the Guts to Defend Democracy?," *New Republic*, September 30, 2025, newrepublic.com/article/201041/corporate-media-consolidation-defend-democracy-trump.
**28.** Alex Tekip, "Ask the Expert: Why Federal Funding for Public Media Is Critical for Communities," *MSU Today*, Michigan State University, May 13, 2025, msutoday.msu.edu/news/2025/05/ask-the-expert-why-federal-funding-for-public-media-is-critical-for-communities.
**29.** Bruce Wolpe, "Trump Is Aiming to Silence Public Media in the US—and If He Succeeds, His Supporters Here Will Take Note," *The Conversation*, July 9, 2025, theconversation.com/trump-is-aiming-to-silence-public-media-in-the-us-and-if-he-succeeds-his-supporters-here-will-take-note-260584.
**30.** Peter Charalambous et al., "Since Trump's Return to Office, Here's a List of Those Targeted by His Administration," ABC News, February 11, 2026, abcnews.com/US/

list-individuals-including-lisa-cook-targeted-trump-administration/story?id=124968309.
**31.** Alanna Durkin Richer and Eric Tucker, "Watch: Slotkin, Kelly Speak after Grand Jury Refuses to Charge Them over 'Illegal Orders' Video," PBS News, February 11, 2026, pbs.org/newshour/politics/watch-live-slotkin-kelly-speak-after-grand-jury-refuses-to-charge-them-over-illegal-orders-video.
**32.** Jon Schuppe and Erik Ortiz, "Trump's DHS Immigration Enforcement Officers Shot 14 People from September 2025 to February 2026. Here's What to Know," NBC News, March 4, 2026, nbcnews.com/news/us-news/ice-shootings-list-border-patrol-trump-immigration-operations-rcna254202.
**33.** Kat Lonsdorf, Jude Joffe-Block, and Meg Anderson, "ICE Has Spun a Massive Surveillance Web. We Talked to People Caught in It," *All Things Considered*, NPR, March 5, 2026, npr.org/2026/03/04/nx-s1-5717031/ice-dhs-immigrants-surveillance-confrontation-deportation-mobile-fortify.
**34.** *Olmstead v. United States*, 277 U.S. 438 (1928).

## 10: FREE AND FAIR ELECTIONS IN JEOPARDY

**1.** Voting Rights Act of 1965, Pub. L. 89–110, 79 Stat. 437.
**2.** "Joint Statement from Elections Infrastructure Government Coordinating Council & the Election Infrastructure Sector Coordinating Executive Committees," Cybersecurity and Infrastructure Security Agency, November 12, 2020, cisa.gov/news-events/news/joint-statement-elections-infrastructure-government-coordinating-council-election-infrastructure.
**3.** "Election Fraud Map," Heritage Foundation, updated December 12, 2025, electionfraud.heritage.org/.
**4.** Zoe Richards, "Georgia Republican Party Official Voted Illegally Nine Times, Judge Rules," NBC News, March 29, 2024, nbcnews.com/politics/politics-news/georgia-republican-party-official-voted-illegally-nine-judge-rules-rcna145563.
**5.** "Results of Lawsuits Regarding the 2020 Elections," Campaign Legal Center, 2021, accessed April 26, 2026, campaignlegal.org/results-lawsuits-regarding-2020-elections.
**6.** Karen Yourish and Charlie Smart, "Trump's Pattern of Sowing Election Doubt Intensifies in 2024," *New York Times*, May 24, 2024, nytimes.com/interactive/2024/05/24/us/politics/trump-election-results-doubt.html.
**7.** Stephen Richer, "Trump's Claims About Noncitizens Voting Are False. We Can Prove It," Cato Institute, February 5, 2026, cato.org/commentary/trumps-claims-about-noncitizens-voting-are-false-we-can-prove-it.
**8.** Inga Kiderra and Christine Clark, "Trust in Elections Declines Across Party Lines Ahead of 2026 Midterms, UC San Diego Survey Finds," *UC San Diego Today*, February 18, 2026, today.ucsd.edu/story/trust-in-elections-declines-across-party-lines-ahead-of-2026-midterms-uc-san-diego-survey-finds.
**9.** "Election Security, March 2026," Marist Poll, March 11, 2026, maristpoll.marist.edu/polls/election-security-march-2026/.

**10.** Sarah Bryner et al., "Understanding Evolving Republican Attitudes Towards Democracy," Public Agenda and SNF Agora Institute, November 2025, publicagenda.org/resource/pa-snf-2025/.
**11.** Martin Pengelly, "More than a Third of US Adults Say Biden's 2020 Victory Was not Legitimate," *The Guardian*, January 2, 2024, theguardian.com/us-news/2024/jan/02/poll-biden-2020-election-illegitimate.
**12.** U.S. Congress, House of Representatives, *Final Report of the Select Committee to Investigate the January 6th Attack on the United States Capitol*, 117th Cong., 2d Sess., 2022, Report 117-663, govinfo.gov/content/pkg/GPO-J6-REPORT/pdf/GPO-J6-REPORT.pdf.
**13.** Robert Hogan, "Pam Bondi's Recent History Is Troubling for the DOJ," Brennan Center for Justice, December 26, 2024, brennancenter.org/our-work/research-reports/pam-bondis-recent-history-troubling-doj.
**14.** Ryan Lucas, "New Attorney General Moves to Align Justice Department with Trump's Priorities," NPR, February 5, 2025, npr.org/2025/02/05/g-s1-46698/attorney-general-memos-weaponization-trump.
**15.** "Memorandum to All Employees: Restoring the Integrity and Credibility of the Department of Justice," U.S. Department of Justice, Office of the Attorney General, February 5, 2025, justice.gov/ag/media/1388506/dl?inline.
**16.** Sahil Kapur and Ryan Reilly, "RNC Hires a Prominent 'Stop the Steal' Advocate to Help Craft Its 2024 Platform," NBC News, June 7, 2024, nbcnews.com/politics/2024-election/rnc-hires-prominent-stop-steal-advocate-help-craft-2024-platform-rcna155298.
**17.** Daniel Barnes, "Trump's New Pardon Attorney Personally Reviewed Application for Jan. 6 Ringleader Stewart Rhodes," *Politico*, May 27, 2025, politico.com/news/2025/05/27/ed-martin-stewart-rhodes-jan-6-pardon-00371222.
**18.** Scott MacFarlane, "Senate Democrats to Investigate Firings of Justice Dept. Employees Who Worked for Special Counsel Jack Smith," CBS News, September 5, 2025, cbsnews.com/news/senate-democrats-investigate-firings-justice-dept-employees-jack-smith/.
**19.** Jacob Rosen, "Lawyers for Jack Smith Say Basis of Ethics Probe Against Him Is 'Imaginary and Unfounded,'" CBS News, August 26, 2025, cbsnews.com/news/lawyers-for-jack-smith-say-basis-of-ethics-probe-against-him-is-imaginary-and-unfounded/.
**20.** David Cohen, "Trump on Jan. 6 Insurrection: 'These Were Great People,'" *Politico*, July 11, 2021, politico.com/news/2021/07/11/trump-jan-6-insurrection-these-were-great-people-499165.
**21.** Soo Rin Kim, Lalee Ibssa, and Kelsey Walsh, "Trump Calls Jan. 6 Rioters 'Warriors' During Scorching Las Vegas Rally," ABC News, June 10, 2024, abcnews.com/Politics/scorching-heat-trump-rally-las-vegas-sends-6/story?id=110974299.
**22.** Max Matza, "Proud Boys and Oath Keepers Among over 1,500 Capitol Riot Defendants Pardoned by Trump," BBC News, January 20, 2025, bbc.com/news/articles/c5y7147xrpko.

**23.** Barnes, "Trump's New Pardon Attorney Personally Reviewed Application for Jan. 6 Ringleader Stewart Rhodes."
**24.** Carter Walker, "Trump Pardons Alleged 'Fake Electors' and Other Allies Who Tried to Undo His 2020 Election Loss," *Votebeat*, November 10, 2025, votebeat.org/2025/11/10/trump-pardon-fake-elector-2020-election/.
**25.** Jane C. Timm, "Trump Says Republicans Should 'Nationalize' Elections," NBC News, February 2, 2026, nbcnews.com/politics/elections/trump-republicans-nationalize-elections-rcna257098.
**26.** Executive Order of March 25, 2025, "Preserving and Protecting the Integrity of American Elections," White House, whitehouse.gov/presidential-actions/2025/03/preserving-and-protecting-the-integrity-of-american-elections/.
**27.** Jude Joffe-Block, "19 States Sue over Trump's Voting Executive Order, Arguing It's Unconstitutional," NPR, April 3, 2025, npr.org/2025/04/03/nx-s1-5351751/voting-executive-order-lawsuit.
**28.** "Ensuring Citizenship Verification and Integrity in Federal Elections," White House, March 31, 2026, whitehouse.gov/presidential-actions/2026/03/ensuring-citizenship-verification-and-integrity-in-federal-elections/.
**29.** Nicholas Riccardi, "Democrats Sue to Block Trump's Executive Order Targeting Mail Ballots," PBS News, April 2, 2026, pbs.org/newshour/politics/democrats-sue-to-block-trumps-executive-order-targeting-mail-ballots.
**30.** Press release, "Justice Department Sues Five Additional States for Failure to Produce Voter Rolls," Office of Public Affairs, U.S. Department of Justice, February 26, 2026, justice.gov/opa/pr/justice-department-sues-five-additional-states-failure-produce-voter-rolls.
**31.** Devlin Barrett, "The FBI's Extraordinary Seizure of Voting Records," interview by Michael Barbaro, *The Daily*, *New York Times*, February 3, 2026, audio, nytimes.com/2026/02/03/podcasts/the-daily/fbi-trump-voting-records-georgia-gabbard.html.
**32.** Alan Feuer and Ashley Ahn, "Trump Regrets not Seizing Voting Machines After 2020 Election," *New York Times*, January 11, 2026, nytimes.com/2026/01/11/us/trump-voting-machines-2020-election.html.
**33.** David Bauder, Randall Chase, and Geoff Mulvihill, "Fox, Dominion Reach $787M Settlement Over Election Claims," Associated Press, April 18, 2023, apnews.com/article/fox-news-dominion-lawsuit-trial-trump-2020-0ac71f75acfacc52ea80b3e747fb0afe.
**34.** "United States: Freedom in the World 2026 Country Report," Freedom House, 2026, freedomhouse.org/country/united-states/freedom-world/2026.
**35.** "A History of Voting by Mail," Smithsonian Institution, September 19, 2024, si.edu/collections/snapshot/history-voting-mail.
**36.** *Election Administration and Voting Survey 2024 Comprehensive Report: A Report from the U.S. Election Assistance Commission to the 119th Congress*, U.S. Election Assistance Commission, June 2025, eac.gov/sites/default/files/2025-06/2024_EAVS_Report_508c.pdf.
**37.** Wendy R. Weiser and Harold Ekeh, "The False Narrative of Vote-by-Mail Fraud,"

Brennan Center for Justice, April 10, 2020, brennancenter.org/our-work/analysis-opinion/false-narrative-vote-mail-fraud.
**38.** Thad Kousser and Megan Mullin, "Will Vote-by-Mail Elections Increase Participation? Evidence from California Counties," Election Assistance Commission, 2017, eac.gov/sites/default/files/document_library/files/Will-Vote-by-Mail-Elections-Increase-Turnout.pdf.
**39.** Kathleen Bush-Joseph, "Explainer: Noncitizen Voting in U.S. Elections," Migration Policy Institute, September 2024, migrationpolicy.org/content/noncitizen-voting-us-elections.
**40.** Eliza Sweren-Becker and Owen Bacskai, "New SAVE Act Bills Would Still Block Millions of Americans from Voting," Brennan Center for Justice, updated April 19, 2026, brennancenter.org/our-work/analysis-opinion/new-save-act-bills-would-still-block-millions-americans-voting.
**41.** Luona Lin, "About 8 in 10 Women in Opposite-Sex Marriages Say They Took Their Husband's Last Name," Pew Research Center, September 7, 2023, pewresearch.org/short-reads/2023/09/07/about-eight-in-ten-women-in-opposite-sex-marriages-say-they-took-their-husbands-last-name/.
**42.** Amy B. Wang, Scott Clement, and Lydia Sidhom, "The Voting Bill Trump Says Will Secure Victory Could Backfire," *Washington Post*, March 18, 2026, washingtonpost.com/politics/2026/03/18/save-america-act-trump-voting-republicans/.
**43.** Gary Fineout, "DeSantis Signs Florida's Version of SAVE America Act, Draws Immediate Lawsuit," *Politico*, April 1, 2026, politico.com/news/2026/04/01/desantis-signs-floridas-version-of-save-america-act-draws-immediate-lawsuit-00854039.
**44.** Nicole Marcus, "Trump Wants 5-Seat Pickup from Redraw of Texas Congressional Map," *Politico*, July 15, 2025, politico.com/news/2025/07/15/trump-five-seat-pickup-redraw-texas-congressional-map-00454301.
**45.** Drew DeSilver, "Redistricting Between Censuses Has Been Rare in the Modern Era," Pew Research Center, August 28, 2025, pewresearch.org/short-reads/2025/08/28/redistricting-between-censuses-has-been-rare-in-the-modern-era/.
**46.** "Changing the Maps: Tracking Mid-Decade Redistricting," National Conference of State Legislatures, updated April 22, 2026, ncsl.org/redistricting-and-census/changing-the-maps-tracking-mid-decade-redistricting.
**47.** "2026 CPR House Race Ratings," *Cook Political Report*, April 22, 2026, cookpolitical.com/ratings/house-race-ratings.
**48.** "Research Brief: Primary Voters Elect Most of Congress. They're Not Like Most Americans," Unite America Institute, January 2026, uniteamericainstitute.org/research/research-brief-primary-voters-elect-most-of-congress-theyre-not-like-most-americans.
**49.** Steven Levitsky and Lucan A. Way, "The New Competitive Authoritarianism," *Journal of Democracy* 31, no. 1 (January 2020): 51–65, journalofdemocracy.org/articles/the-new-competitive-authoritarianism/.

## 11: RAMPANT CORRUPTION AND SELF-DEALING

**1.** David D. Kirkpatrick, "Trump's Profiteering Hits $4 Billion," *New Yorker*, January 31, 2026, newyorker.com/news/a-reporter-at-large/trumps-profiteering-hits-four-billion-dollars.
**2.** Richard Luscombe, "Trump Hikes Mar-a-Lago Membership to $1m, Raising Concerns of Selling Access," *The Guardian*, August 5, 2024, theguardian.com/us-news/article/2024/aug/05/trump-mar-a-lago-membership-price-hike.
**3.** Brad Heath, "Trump Picks Golf Club, Mar-a-Lago Members as Ambassadors," *USA Today*, February 10, 2019, usatoday.com/story/news/investigations/2019/02/08/donald-trump-picks-ambassadors-golf-club-mar-lago-members/2748260002.
**4.** Maria Aspan, "How Trump's Latest Crypto Launch Enriches His Family," NPR, September 3, 2025, npr.org/2025/09/03/nx-s1-5527047/trump-crypto-family-world-liberty-financial.
**5.** "Fact Sheet: President Donald J. Trump Signs GENIUS Act into Law," White House, July 18, 2025, whitehouse.gov/fact-sheets/2025/07/fact-sheet-president-donald-j-trump-signs-genius-act-into-law/.
**6.** Angus Berwick, "Trump Family Amasses $6 Billion Fortune After Crypto Launch," *Wall Street Journal*, September 1, 2025, wsj.com/finance/currencies/trump-family-amasses-6-billion-fortune-after-crypto-launch-567faec5.
**7.** Sharon LaFraniere, "Trump Says He Has No Issue with His Family's Foreign Business Deals," *New York Times*, January 8, 2026, nytimes.com/2026/01/08/us/politics/trump-family-foreign-business-deals.html.
**8.** Alexander Bolton, "Cruz: Gift of Qatari Jet to Trump 'Poses Significant Espionage' Concerns," *The Hill*, May 13, 2025, thehill.com/homenews/senate/5297715-cruz-trump-qatar-air-force-one/.
**9.** Klaus Gründler and Niklas Potrafke, "Corruption and Economic Growth: New Empirical Evidence," *European Journal of Political Economy* 60 (December 2019): 101810, doi.org/10.1016/j.ejpoleco.2019.08.001.
**10.** "Historical Background on the Foreign Emoluments Clause," Legal Information Institute, Cornell University, accessed April 27, 2026, law.cornell.edu/constitution-conan/article-1/section-9/clause-8/historical-background-on-the-foreign-emoluments-clause.
**11.** "Foreign Emoluments Clause Generally," Constitution Annotated, Congress.gov, accessed April 27, 2026, constitution.congress.gov/browse/essay/artI-S9-C8-3/ALDE_00013206/.
**12.** Zephyr Teachout and Seth Barrett Tillman, "The Foreign Emoluments Clause: Article I, Section 9, Clause 8," National Constitution Center, accessed April 27, 2026, constitutioncenter.org/the-constitution/articles/article-i/clauses/759.
**13.** Kat Lonsdorf, "Trump Administration Officially Accepts Jet from Qatar for Use as Air Force One," *Morning Edition*, NPR, May 21, 2025, npr.org/2025/05/21/nx-s1-5406420/trump-accepts-qatar-plane-air-force-one.

**14.** Walker Davis, "Switzerland's Publicly-Owned Central Bank Bought $1.8 Million in Trump Media Shares," Citizens for Responsibility and Ethics in Washington, January 31, 2025, citizensforethics.org/reports-investigations/crew-investigations/swiss-national-bank-bought-trump-media-shares/.
**15.** Kevin Liptak et al., "Gold Crown, Golf Clubs and a Jet: Tracking Trump's Gifts from Foreign Leaders This Year," CNN, October 30, 2025, cnn.com/politics/gift-tracker-trump-foreign-leaders-vis.
**16.** Max Matza, "Venezuelan Nobel Peace Prize Winner Presents Her Medal to Trump," BBC News, January 16, 2026, bbc.com/news/articles/cx2w94wp4p1o.
**17.** Press release, "Oversight Democrats Release Evidence Showing Trump First Family Failed to Disclose and Account for More than $250,000 Worth of Foreign Government Gifts," U.S. House of Representatives, Committee on Oversight, March 17, 2023, oversightdemocrats.house.gov/news/press-releases/oversight-democrats-release-evidence-showing-trump-first-family-failed-to.
**18.** Garrett Downs, "United Arab Emirates' 'Spy Sheikh' Bought Secret Stake in Trump Crypto Company: WSJ," CNBC, February 1, 2026, cnbc.com/2026/02/01/spy-sheikh-stake-trump-crypto.html.
**19.** Press release, "Murphy on Trump's Secret Deal with the UAE: The White House Is a Non-Stop Corruption Machine," Office of Senator Chris Murphy, February 3, 2026, murphy.senate.gov/newsroom/press-releases/murphy-on-trumps-secret-deal-with-the-uae-the-white-house-is-a-non-stop-corruption-machine.
**20.** Andrew R. Chow, "Trump Is Rewriting How the U.S. Treats AI Chip Exports—and the Stakes Are Enormous," *Time*, May 14, 2025, time.com/7285232/trump-ai-middle-east-chip-export/.
**21.** Garrett Downs, "Warren to Call for Reversal of Trump's UAE Chip Sales After 'Spy Sheikh' Revelations," CNBC, February 5, 2026, cnbc.com/2026/02/05/warren-trump-chip-sales-spy-sheikh.html.
**22.** "Emoluments Clause and Presidential Compensation," Constitution Annotated, Congress.gov, accessed April 27, 2026, constitution.congress.gov/browse/essay/artII-S1-C7-1/ALDE_00000233/.
**23.** "Trump Administrations: 2025 Inauguration Donors," OpenSecrets, accessed April 27, 2026, opensecrets.org/trump/2025-inauguration-donors.
**24.** Ali Swenson, "Trump, a Populist President, Is Flanked by Tech Billionaires at His Inauguration," Associated Press, January 20, 2025, apnews.com/article/trump-inauguration-tech-billionaires-zuckerberg-musk-wealth-0896bfc3f50d941d62cebc3074267ecd.
**25.** Desmond Butler et al., "Elon Musk's Business Empire Is Built on $38 Billion in Government Funding," *Washington Post*, February 26, 2025, washingtonpost.com/technology/interactive/2025/elon-musk-business-government-contracts-funding/.
**26.** Skyler Bernards, "Top Government Contracts Won by Amazon Web Services," *ExecutiveGov*, August 11, 2023, executivegov.com/articles/top-government-contracts-

won-by-amazon-web-services.
**27.** Casey Newton, "Everything Mark Zuckerberg Has Gotten from Donald Trump so Far," *Platformer*, August 28, 2025, platformer.news/trump-zuckerberg-meta-partnership-eu-dsa-ai-dma.
**28.** Jake Johnson, "Trump Drops or Pauses Cases Against 17 Corporations That Funded His Inauguration," *Truthout*, April 22, 2025, truthout.org/articles/trump-drops-or-pauses-cases-against-17-corporations-that-funded-his-inauguration/.
**29.** Kathryn Watson, "Trumps Host White House Easter Egg Roll with Corporate Sponsorships," CBS News, April 21, 2025, cbsnews.com/news/trumps-host-white-house-easter-egg-roll-corporate-sponorships/.
**30.** Kenneth P. Vogel, Lisa Friedman, and David A. Fahrenthold, "For $1 Million, Donors to U.S.A. Birthday Group Offered Access to Trump," *New York Times*, February 8, 2026, nytimes.com/2026/02/08/us/politics/freedom-250-trump-donors.html.
**31.** Rebecca Jacobs, "Trump's Properties Remain an Epicenter of His Conflicts and Corruption in Second Term," Citizens for Responsibility and Ethics in Washington, February 24, 2026, citizensforethics.org/reports-investigations/crew-reports/trumps-properties-remain-an-epicenter-of-his-conflicts-and-corruption-in-second-term/.
**32.** Dan Diamond, Aaron Schaffer, and Jonathan Edwards, "Legality of Trump's $400M in Private Funding for White House Ballroom at Issue," *Washington Post*, February 9, 2026, washingtonpost.com/politics/2026/02/09/trump-ballroom-judge-ruling/.
**33.** Diana Nerozzi and Jacob Wendler, "Tech, Crypto, Tobacco, Other Companies Fund Trump's White House Ballroom," *Politico*, October 23, 2025, politico.com/news/2025/10/23/trump-ballroom-donors-list-00620230.
**34.** David A. Fahrenthold et al., "Who Won a Seat at Trump's Crypto Dinner?," *New York Times*, May 28, 2025, nytimes.com/2025/05/23/us/politics/trump-crypto-dinner-attendees.html.
**35.** Ana Faguy, "Trump Launches Cryptocurrency with Price Rocketing," BBC News, January 18, 2025, bbc.com/news/articles/c9vmym2jvy9o.
**36.** Sharon LaFraniere and David Yaffe-Bellany, "S.E.C. Settles Its Case Against Justin Sun, an Investor in the Trumps' Crypto Coins," *New York Times*, March 5, 2026, nytimes.com/2026/03/05/us/politics/sec-justin-sun.html.
**37.** Fahrenthold et al., "Who Won a Seat at Trump's Crypto Dinner?"
**38.** LaFraniere and Yaffe-Bellany, "S.E.C. Settles Its Case against Justin Sun."
**39.** "Justice Manual—Title 9: Criminal—9-140,000—Pardon Attorney," U.S. **Department** of Justice, accessed April 27, 2026, justice.gov/jm/jm-9-140000-pardon-attorney#9-140.112.
**40.** Jeremy Kohler, "How Trump Has Exploited Pardons and Clemency to Reward Allies and Supporters," ProPublica, November 12, 2025, propublica.org/article/trump-pardons-clemency-george-santos-ed-martin.
**41.** Memorandum, "President Trump's Pardons Cheat Victims out of an Astounding $1.3 Billion in Restitution and Fines, Allowing Fraudsters, Tax Evaders, Drug

Traffickers to Keep Ill-Gotten Gains," House Judiciary Committee Democratic Staff, June 17, 2025, democrats-judiciary.house.gov/sites/evo-subsites/democrats-judiciary.house.gov/files/evo-media-document/2025-06-17.dem-memo-re-$1.3b-cost-of-trump-pardons.pdf.

**42.** Alan Jaffe, "Addressing Trump's Claims About the Pardon of Binance Founder," FactCheck.org, November 12, 2025, factcheck.org/2025/11/addressing-trumps-claims-about-the-pardon-of-binance-founder/.

**43.** David Yaffe-Bellany, "Binance Gives Trump Family's Crypto Firm a Leg Up," *New York Times*, February 9, 2026, nytimes.com/2026/02/07/business/binance-trump-crypto.html.

**44.** "Political Donors Should Not Be Above the Law," Brennan Center for Justice, September 12, 2025, brennancenter.org/our-work/analysis-opinion/political-donors-should-not-be-above-law.

**45.** Saurav Ghosh and Maha Quadri, "Seeking Pardon, Foreign Billionaire Allegedly Funneled Millions to Trump Super PAC," Campaign Legal Center, February 17, 2026, campaignlegal.org/update/seeking-pardon-foreign-billionaire-allegedly-funneled-millions-trump-super-pac.

**46.** Katherine Faulders, Rachel Scott, and Hannah Demissie, "Trump's Flurry of Pardons Include Some to Campaign Contributors," ABC News, May 29, 2025, abcnews.com/US/trumps-flurry-pardons-include-campaign-contributors/story?id=122313284.

**47.** Kenneth P. Vogel, "Trump Pardoned Tax Cheat After Mother Attended $1 Million Dinner," *New York Times*, May 27, 2025, nytimes.com/2025/05/27/us/politics/trump-pardon-paul-walczak-tax-crimes.html.

**48.** Lisa O'Carroll, "Swiss Gold and Rolex Gifts to Trump Arouse 'Disgust' in Europe," *The Guardian*, November 21, 2025, theguardian.com/us-news/2025/nov/21/swiss-gold-and-rolex-gifts-to-trump-raise-questions-over-personalisation-of-us-presidential-power.

**49.** Chris Megerian, "Trump Scores Golden Gifts as United States and Seoul Advance Trade Talks," Associated Press, October 29, 2025, pbs.org/newshour/politics/trump-scores-golden-gifts-as-united-states-and-seoul-advance-trade-talks.

**50.** "Addressing Risks from Perkins Coie LLP," White House, March 6, 2025, whitehouse.gov/presidential-actions/2025/03/addressing-risks-from-perkins-coie-llp/.

**51.** Gary Grumbach, Raquel Coronell Uribe, Daniel Arkin, and Ryan J. Reilly, "Trump Administration Drops Effort Against Law Firms After Judges Find President's Orders Unconstitutional," NBC News, March 2, 2026, nbcnews.com/politics/trump-administration/doj-drops-suits-law-firms-judges-find-executive-orders-unconstitutiona-rcna261434.

**52.** Ryan J. Reilly and Lawrence Hurley, "Legal Community Shaken by a Powerful Law Firm's Decision to Give In to Trump's Demands," NBC News, March 21, 2025, nbcnews.com/politics/trump-administration/legal-community-shaken-powerful-law-firm-paul-weiss-trump-rcna197490.

**53.** Michael Schmidt, Matthew Goldstein, and Maggie Haberman, "Two Big Law Firms

Said to Be Doing Free Work for Trump Administration," *New York Times*, August 20, 2025, nytimes.com/2025/08/20/us/politics/law-firms-free-work-trump-administration.html.

**54.** David Folkenflik, "ABC Settles with Trump for $15 Million. Now, He Wants to Sue Other News Outlets," *All Things Considered*, NPR, December 16, 2024, npr.org/2024/12/16/nx-s1-5230274/abc-settles-with-trump-for-15-million-now-he-wants-to-sue-other-news-outlets.

**55.** Alice Masquelier-Page, "Paramount Will Pay $16 Million in Settlement with Trump over '60 Minutes' Interview," Associated Press, July 7, 2025, ap.org/news-highlights/spotlights/2025/paramount-will-pay-16-million-in-settlement-with-trump-over-60-minutes-interview/.

**56.** Jamie Burch, "Trump Files $10B Lawsuit in Amarillo Against CBS over '60 Minutes' Interview with Harris," ABC 7 News, October 31, 2024, abc7amarillo.com/news/local/former-president-donald-trump-files-lawsuit-against-cbs-in-amarillo-federal-court.

**57.** Barbara Ortutay and Michael Liedtke, "YouTube to Pay $24.5 Million to Settle Lawsuit over Trump's Account Suspension After Jan. 6 Attack," Associated Press, September 30, 2025, pbs.org/newshour/nation/youtube-to-pay-24-5-million-to-settle-lawsuit-over-trumps-account-suspension-after-jan-6-attack.

**58.** Bobby Allyn, "Meta Agrees to Pay Trump $25 Million to Settle Lawsuit over Facebook and Instagram Suspensions," NPR, January 29, 2025, npr.org/2025/01/29/nx-s1-5279570/meta-trump-settlement-facebook-instagram-suspensions.

**59.** Josh Gerstein, "Trump Is Still Going After the Press in Court. Here's Where His Lawsuits Stand," *Politico*, March 4, 2026, politico.com/news/2026/03/04/donald-trump-media-lawsuits-00812525.

**60.** Laura Wagner and Scott Nover, "Trump Has Ramped Up Lawsuits Against the Media. Here's Where They Stand," *Washington Post*, January 25, 2026, washingtonpost.com/business/2026/01/25/trump-media-lawsuits/.

**61.** Devlin Barrett and Tyler Pager, "Trump Said to Demand Justice Dept. Pay Him $230 Million for Past Cases," *New York Times*, October 21, 2025, nytimes.com/2025/10/21/us/politics/trump-justice-department-compensation.html.

**62.** Mary Katherine Browne, "Attorneys Sound Alarm over Trump's $10 Billion IRS Lawsuit," *Tax Notes*, February 9, 2026, taxnotes.com/featured-news/attorneys-sound-alarm-over-trumps-10-billion-irs-lawsuit/2026/02/07/7tymp.

**63.** Giacomo Tognini, "How Peace Envoy Steve Witkoff Got Richer Thanks to Trump and Elon Musk," *Forbes*, April 4, 2026, forbes.com/sites/giacomotognini/2026/04/04/how-peace-envoy-steve-witkoff-got-richer-thanks-to-trump-and-elon-musk.

**64.** Rob Copeland and Maureen Farrell, "Jared Kushner Solicits Funds for His Firm While Working as Mideast Envoy," *New York Times*, March 13, 2026, nytimes.com/2026/03/13/business/jared-kushner-affinity-mideast-funds.html.

**65.** David D. Kirkpatrick and Kate Kelly, "Before Giving Billions to Jared Kushner, Saudi Investment Fund Had Big Doubts," *New York Times*, April 10, 2022, nytimes.

com/2022/04/10/us/jared-kushner-saudi-investment-fund.html.
**66.** Monica Hunter-Hart and Giacomo Tognini, "How Jared Kushner's Bold Bets in the Middle East Made Him a Billionaire," *Forbes*, September 17, 2025, forbes.com/sites/monicahunter-hart/2025/09/16/how-jared-kushners-bold-bets-in-the-middle-east-made-him-a-billionaire/.
**67.** Nora Redmond, "Trump's Media Company Gave a Roughly $800,000 Stock Award to His Pick for FBI Director," *Business Insider*, February 7, 2025, businessinsider.com/donald-trump-fbi-pick-share-award-trump-media-group-2025-2.
**68.** Louise Matsakis, "Trump's FBI Pick Kash Patel Took up to $5M in Stock from Chinese Ecommerce Giant Shein," *Wired*, February 7, 2025, wired.com/story/kash-patel-elite-depot-shein/.
**69.** Justin Elliott, Joshua Kaplan, and Alex Mierjeski, "Firm Tied to Kristi Noem Secretly Got Money from $220 Million DHS Ad Contracts," ProPublica, November 14, 2025, propublica.org/article/kristi-noem-dhs-ad-campaign-strategy-group.
**70.** Amelia Benavides-Colon and Taylor Giorno, "Rep. Jamie Raskin Opens Investigation into Howard Lutnick and His Former Firm's Tariff Dealings," *NOTUS*, February 27, 2026, notus.org/congress/jamie-raskin-howard-lutnick-congress-house-investigation-tariffs.
**71.** Sophia Cai and Daniel Lippman, "Tensions Simmer over Howard Lutnick, Trump's Favorite Dealmaker," *Politico*, February 26, 2026, politico.com/news/2026/02/26/howard-lutnick-trumps-dealmaker-tensions-00798716.
**72.** Press release, "Ranking Member Robert Garcia and Rep. Suhas Subramanyam Demand Answers After Secretary Hegseth Attempted to Make Multimillion-Dollar Investment in Defense Companies Before Iran Strikes," U.S. House of Representatives, House Committee on Oversight, March 31, 2026, oversightdemocrats.house.gov/news/press-releases/ranking-member-robert-garcia-and-rep-suhas-subramanyam-demand-answers-after-secretary-hegseth-attempted-to-make-multimillion-dollar-investment-in-defense-companies-before-iran-strikes.
**73.** Paul Murphy et al., "Pete Hegseth's Broker Looked to Buy Defence Fund Before Iran Attack," *Financial Times*, March 31, 2026, ft.com/content/744ea8dc-6d93-4fe9-a5e3-36de4f5d06db?syn-25a6b1a6=1.
**74.** Jordan Pandy, "Guess Who Bought JD Vance's House Outside DC for over Asking Price? A Former Trump Official," *Business Insider*, March 31, 2025, businessinsider.com/jd-vance-quickly-sold-alexandria-virginia-house-sales-price-2025-3.
**75.** Chris Piper, "President Trump's Firing of Inspectors General Threatens Government Accountability and Efficiency," Partnership for Public Service, October 21, 2025, ourpublicservice.org/blog/president-trumps-firing-of-inspectors-general-threatens-government-accountability-and-efficiency/.
**76.** Ken Dilanian, "Firings, Pardons and Policy Changes Have Gutted DOJ Anti-Corruption Efforts, Experts Say," NBC News, June 3, 2025, nbcnews.com/politics/justice-department/firings-pardons-policy-changes-gutted-doj-anti-corruption-

efforts-expe-rcna200571.
**77.** *Trump v. United States*, 603 U.S. 593 (2024).
**78.** Hanna Ziady, "The US Slips to Its Lowest-Ever Rank in a Global Corruption Index," CNN, February 10, 2026, cnn.com/2026/02/10/business/corruption-index-transparency-international-united-states-intl.

## 12: A COLLAPSE IN CIVIL DISCOURSE

**1.** David Brody, "Donald Trump: 'We Must Make America Great Again,'" Christian Broadcasting Network, May 31, 2015, cbn.com/news/politics/donald-trump-we-must-make-america-great-again.
**2.** Lazaro Gamio and Scott Clement, "South Carolina Republican Exit Poll Results," *Washington Post*, February 20, 2016, washingtonpost.com/graphics/politics/2016-election/primaries/south-carolina-exit-poll/?itid=lk_inline_manual_2.
**3.** Caroline Tanner, "Study Finds Trump Voters Believe Trump Is Authentic, Even If He Appears to Lie," *USA Today*, May 2, 2018, usatoday.com/story/news/politics/onpolitics/2018/05/02/trump-supporters-were-more-enthusiastic-their-support-him-candidate-extent-they-justified-trumps-lie/573371002/.
**4.** "Transcript: Donald Trump's Taped Comments About Women," *New York Times*, October 8, 2016, nytimes.com/2016/10/08/us/donald-trump-tape-transcript.html.
**5.** Daniella Diaz, "3 Times Trump Defended His 'Locker Room' Talk," CNN, October 9, 2016, cnn.com/2016/10/09/politics/donald-trump-locker-room-talk-presidential-debate-2016-election.
**6.** James FitzGerald, "Trump Calls 6 January 'Day of Love' When Asked About Capitol Riot," BBC News, October 17, 2024, bbc.com/news/articles/ckgnxej1dn0o.
**7.** Maggie Astor, "Trump Doubles Down on Migrants 'Poisoning' the Country," *New York Times*, March 17, 2024, nytimes.com/2024/03/17/us/politics/trump-fox-interview-migrants.html.
**8.** Ben Schreckinger, "Trump on Protester: 'I'd Like to Punch Him in the Face,'" *Politico*, February 23, 2016, politico.com/story/2016/02/donald-trump-punch-protester-219655.
**9.** Rachel Levinson-Waldman, "Labeling Renee Good a 'Domestic Terrorist' Distorts the Law," Brennan Center for Justice, January 16, 2026, brennancenter.org/our-work/analysis-opinion/labeling-renee-good-domestic-terrorist-distorts-law.
**10.** Zachary Basu, "Trump Campaign Defends 'Vermin' Speech amid Comparisons to Fascist Leaders," *Axios*, November 13, 2023, axios.com/2023/11/13/trump-vermin-fascist-language-speech.
**11.** Daniel Dale, "Almost Eight Years Later, Trump Confirms He Used the Phrase 'Shithole Countries,'" CNN, December 10, 2025, cnn.com/2025/12/10/politics/donald-trump-shithole-countries-phrase.
**12.** Josh Campbell, "Trump's Celebration of Robert Mueller's Death Sparks Scorn—and Echoes of History," CNN, March 29, 2026, cnn.com/2026/03/29/us/mueller-trump-fbi-presidents-standoff.

**13.** Will Weissert, Josh Boak, and Nicole Winfield, "Trump Says He Won't Apologize to Pope Leo and Explains His Reason for Posting Much-Criticized Meme," Associated Press, April 13, 2026, apnews.com/article/trump-pope-leo-xiv-02f6b4554ea4b83af02af15987ae1f2d.
**14.** Glenn Kessler, "Trump Made 30,573 False or Misleading Claims as President. Nearly Half Came in His Final Year," *Washington Post,* January 23, 2021, washingtonpost.com/politics/how-fact-checker-tracked-trump-claims/2021/01/23/ad04b69a-5c1d-11eb-a976-bad6431e03e2_story.html.
**15.** Glenn Kessler and Joe Fox, "The False Claims That Trump Keeps Repeating," *Washington Post,* January 20, 2021, washingtonpost.com/graphics/politics/fact-checker-most-repeated-disinformation/.
**16.** Jackie Flynn Mogensen, "The Unexpected History Behind Donald Trump's Favorite Debate Strategy," *Mother Jones*, September 10, 2024, motherjones.com/politics/2024/09/donald-trump-debate-strategy-kamala-harris-gish-gallop/.
**17.** Daniel Dale, "Fact Check: Trump's Mathematically Impossible Promise to Cut Drug Prices by '1,000%,'" CNN, September 23, 2025, cnn.com/2025/09/23/politics/fact-check-drug-prices-trump.
**18.** Jeremy Venook, "20 Conspiracy Theories Trump Has Pushed Before and During His Presidency," Center for American Progress Action Fund, May 19, 2020, americanprogressaction.org/article/20-conspiracy-theories-trump-pushed-presidency/.
**19.** Emily Bell, "At White House Press Conferences, No Questions Allowed," *The Atlantic*, January 13, 2019, theatlantic.com/politics/archive/2019/01/donald-trump-continues-to-call-the-media-fake-news/579670/.
**20.** "Media Offenders," White House, accessed April 26, 2026, whitehouse.gov/mediabias/.
**21.** "Americans Reject Political Violence, but See It as an Imminent Threat," Polarization Research Lab, September 22, 2025, polarizationresearchlab.org/report/report-americans-reject-political-violence-but-see-it-as-an-imminent-threat.
**22.** "Trump Calls Democrats 'Crazy' in Combative State of the Union Address," CBS News, youtube.com/watch?v=uX_5wOWVSGs.
**23.** Jonathan Allen and Amanda Terkel, "Trump Blames the 'Radical Left' for Charlie Kirk's Killing," NBC News, September 10, 2025, nbcnews.com/politics/politics-news/charlie-kirks-death-prompts-outpouring-shock-grief-condemnations-polit-rcna230472.
**24.** Alexandra Marquez, "'The Enemy from Within': Trump Calls Democrats More Dangerous than U.S. Foreign Adversaries," NBC News, October 13, 2024, nbcnews.com/politics/2024-election/-enemy-trump-claims-democrats-are-dangerous-us-foreign-adversaries-rcna175198.
**25.** Sarah Bryner et al., "Understanding Evolving Republican Attitudes Towards Democracy," Public Agenda and SNF Agora Institute, November 2025, publicagenda.org/resource/pa-snf-2025/.
**26.** Megan Brenan, "U.S. Political Parties Historically Polarized Ideologically," Gallup, January 16, 2025, news.gallup.com/poll/655190/political-parties-historically-

polarized-ideologically.aspx.
**27.** Elliott Ash et al., "From Viewers to Voters: Tracing Fox News' Impact on American Democracy," *Journal of Public Economics* 240 (December 2024): 105256, doi.org/10.1016/j.jpubeco.2024.105256.
**28.** Bill Bishop and Robert G. Cushing, *The Big Sort: Why the Clustering of Like-Minded America Is Tearing Us Apart* (Boston, MA: Mariner Books, 2009).
**29.** "As Partisan Hostility Grows, Signs of Frustration with the Two-Party System," Pew Research Center, August 9, 2022, pewresearch.org/politics/2022/08/09/republicans-and-democrats-increasingly-critical-of-people-in-the-opposing-party/.
**30.** Jeffrey M. Jones, "Americans Agree Nation Is Divided on Key Values," Gallup, September 23, 2024, news.gallup.com/poll/650828/americans-agree-nation-divided-key-values.aspx.
**31.** Seth Borenstein, "Trump Calls Climate Change Threat to Public Health 'a Scam' but Scientific Findings Show Otherwise," Associated Press, February 13, 2026, pbs.org/newshour/science/trump-calls-climate-change-threat-to-public-health-a-scam-but-scientific-findings-show-otherwise.
**32.** Jess Bidgood, "Trump's Anti-Vaccine Problem," *New York Times*, June 14, 2024, nytimes.com/2024/06/14/us/politics/trump-anti-vax.html.
**33.** Eric Tucker, "Trump Repeats False Claims over 2020 Election Loss, Deflects Responsibility for Jan. 6," Associated Press, September 11, 2024, apnews.com/article/jan-6-trump-capitol-riot-debate-harris-trump-election-walz-vance-144e136901013ddc9c8fab6a1d2bdf07.
**34.** Elisa Shearer, "Most Americans Say Republican and Democratic Voters Cannot Agree on Basic Facts," Pew Research Center, July 30, 2025, pewresearch.org/short-reads/2025/07/30/most-americans-say-republican-and-democratic-voters-cannot-agree-on-basic-facts/.
**35.** Kirsten Eddy and Elisa Shearer, "How Americans' Trust in Information from News Organizations and Social Media Sites Has Changed over Time," Pew Research Center, October 29, 2025, pewresearch.org/short-reads/2025/10/29/how-americans-trust-in-information-from-news-organizations-and-social-media-sites-has-changed-over-time/.
**36.** "Public Trust in Government: 1958–2025," Pew Research Center, December 4, 2025, pewresearch.org/politics/2025/12/04/public-trust-in-government-1958-2025/.
**37.** Audrey Kearney et al., "KFF Tracking Poll on Health Information and Trust: Trust in the CDC and Views of Federal Childhood Vaccine Schedule Changes," KFF, February 6, 2026, kff.org/health-information-trust/trust-in-cdc-and-views-of-federal-childhood-vaccine-schedule-changes/.
**38.** "Stark Divide: Americans More Confident in Career Scientists at U.S. Health Agencies than Leaders," Annenberg Public Policy Center, University of Pennsylvania, March 5, 2026, annenbergpublicpolicycenter.org/stark-divide-americans-more-confident-in-career-scientists-at-u-s-health-agencies-than-leaders/.
**39.** Erika Edwards, "RFK Jr. Vowed to Restore Public Trust in Health. It's Not Working,

a New Survey Suggests," NBC News, March 5, 2026, nbcnews.com/health/health-news/rfk-jr-vowed-restore-public-trust-health-not-working-new-survey-sugges-rcna261943.

**40.** Barbara Sprunt, Tamara Keith, Franco Ordoñez, and Alana Wise, "Trump Again Casts Doubt on Fauci as Covid-19 Cases Surge," NPR, July 13, 2020, npr.org/2020/07/13/890384330/trump-again-casts-doubt-on-fauci-as-covid-19-cases-surge.

**41.** "Unemployment Concerns, Gaza, Epstein, Trust and Medicine, Guns, and Team Names: August 1–4, 2025 Economist/YouGov Poll," YouGov, August 5, 2025, yougov.com/en-us/articles/52716-unemployment-concerns-gaza-israelis-palestinians-jeffrey-epstein-investigation-trust-medicine-health-vaccines-guns-team-names-nfl-mlb-commanders-guardians-august-1-4-2025-economist-yougov-poll.

**42.** Steve Kopack, Monica Alba, and Laura Strickler, "Trump Fires Labor Statistics Boss Hours After the Release of Weak Jobs Report," NBC News, August 1, 2025, nbcnews.com/business/economy/trump-orders-firing-bls-commissioner-weak-jobs-report-rcna222531.

**43.** Ben Johansen, "Trump Says 'We Have to Beat the Hell' Out of 'Radical Left Lunatics' After Kirk Killing," *Politico*, September 11, 2025, politico.com/news/2025/09/11/trump-says-we-have-to-beat-the-hell-out-of-radical-left-lunatics-after-kirk-killing-00559170.

**44.** "Data Snapshot: Threats Against Local Officials Spike After Charlie Kirk Shooting," Bridging Divides Initiative, Princeton University, December 18, 2025, bridgingdivides.princeton.edu/updates/2025/data-snapshot-threats-against-local-officials-spike-after-charlie-kirk-shooting.

**45.** Jonathan Friedman and Elly Brinkley, "Charlie Kirk's Murder Spurs McCarthy-Esque Crackdown on Free Expression," PEN America, September 15, 2025, pen.org/charlie-kirks-murder-spurs-mccarthy-esque-crackdown-on-free-expression/.

**46.** Press release, "USCP Threat Assessment Cases for 2025," United States Capitol Police, January 27, 2026, uscp.gov/media-center/press-releases/uscp-threat-assessment-cases-2025.

**47.** Al Weaver, "Sen. Kelly Says Death Threats Have Increased Since Trump Called for His Execution," *The Hill*, December 1, 2025, thehill.com/homenews/senate/5628706-sen-mark-kelly-threats-increase/.

**48.** "Protective Investigations—Threat Statistics," U.S. Marshals Service, April 15, 2026, usmarshals.gov/what-we-do/judicial-security/protective-investigations-threat-statistics.

**49.** Lawrence Hurley, "Chief Justice John Roberts Warns Personal Attacks on Judges Have 'Got to Stop,'" NBC News, March 17, 2026, nbcnews.com/politics/supreme-court/chief-justice-john-roberts-warns-personal-attacks-judges-got-stop-rcna263927.

**50.** Alana Wise, "Trump Condemns Capitol Hill Violence, Ignores His Role in Inciting the Mob," NPR, January 7, 2021, npr.org/sections/insurrection-at-the-capitol/2021/01/07/954587997/white-house-condemns-violence-on-capitol-hill-without-addressing-trumps-role.

**51.** Piper McDaniel and A. J. Vicens, "More than a Dozen Accused Capitol Rioters

Say Trump Incited Them," *Mother Jones*, February 8, 2021, motherjones.com/politics/2021/02/capitol-insurrection-siege-trump-incitement-fbi-charges-rioters/.

**52.** Jeremy Diamond, "Trump on Protester: 'Maybe He Should Have Been Roughed Up,'" CNN, November 23, 2015, cnn.com/2015/11/22/politics/donald-trump-black-lives-matter-protester-confrontation.

**53.** Kathleen Ronayne and Michael Kunzelman, "Trump to Far-Right Extremists: 'Stand Back and Stand By,'" Associated Press, September 30, 2020, apnews.com/article/election-2020-joe-biden-race-and-ethnicity-donald-trump-chris-wallace-0b32339da25fbc9e8b7c7c7066a1db0f.

**54.** Press release, "Proud Boys Leader Sentenced to 22 Years in Prison for Seditious Conspiracy and Other Charges Related to U.S. Capitol Breach," Office of Public Affairs, United States Department of Justice, September 5, 2023, justice.gov/archives/opa/pr/proud-boys-leader-sentenced-22-years-prison-seditious-conspiracy-and-other-charges-related.

**55.** Chris Cameron, "Trump Calls for Law Cracking Down on Crime and 'Rogue Judges,'" *New York Times*, March 25, 2026, nytimes.com/2026/03/25/us/politics/trump-judges-rogue-law.html.

**56.** "Reagan on America," Ronald Reagan Presidential Foundation & Institute, accessed April 27, 2026, reaganfoundation.org/ronald-reagan/quotes/its-the-american-vision-of-creating-a-new-nation-of.

**57.** "Address During the Cuban Missile Crisis," John F. Kennedy Presidential Library and Museum, accessed April 27, 2026, jfklibrary.org/learn/about-jfk/historic-speeches/address-during-the-cuban-missile-crisis.